JOYCE WETHERED

THE GREAT LADY OF GOLF

JOYCE WETHERED

THE GREAT LADY OF GOLF

BASIL ASHTON TINKLER

The History Press

TO DAVE AND MIKE, TWO GREAT SONS

First published 2004
Reprinted 2018

The History Press
The Mill, Brimscombe Port,
Stroud, Gloucestershire, GL5 2QG
www.thehistorypress.co.uk

British Library Cataloguing in Publication Data.
A catalogue record for this book is available from the British Library.

ISBN 978 0 7524 2927 4

Typesetting and origination by Tempus Publishing Limited
Printed in Great Britain by TJ International Ltd, Padstow, Cornwall

CONTENTS

ACKNOWLEDGEMENTS

I am indebted to a whole host of people and organisations for permitting interviews, or sending me information, or assisting my researches in one way or another. I am sure those mentioned will not be comprehensive and I apologise to anyone who feels left out.

Much of my information was gleaned by a comprehensive study of the memorabilia in the Golf Room at Knightshayes Court. I am grateful to Sir Ian Amory, Lady Amory's next-of-kin, and the National Trust for allowing me access to those items.

Other organisations which have been helpful to me include the Ladies' Golf Union (LGU), the British Golf Museum (St Andrews), St Andrews University Library, East Devon College, Worplesden Golf Club, West Surrey Golf Club, Surrey History Centre at Woking, Goldaming Museum, Tiverton Golf Club, Bristol Central Library, Corpus Christi College at Oxford, the Newspaper Library at Colindale, Christ Church College at Oxford, Clifton College, the Royal and Ancient Golf Club of St Andrews (R&A), The Honourable Company of Edinburgh Golfers, Fortnum & Mason, Eton College, United States Golf Association Museum, Bridgwater Library, Taunton Library.

Chatto & Windus Ltd are thanked for allowing me to include as an appendix the extract from *The Englishwoman's Garden*.

Acknowledgement is given to IPC Country and Leisure Media Ltd for permission to use the cover picture from *The Field* magazine of May 1935.

Several of the photographs have been taken with the permission of the National Trust and some are copies from their library. Grateful acknowledgement is given.

Individual people who have assisted me, some representatives of the organisations listed above, include Sir John and Lady Palmer, Penny Woollams, Laura Beresford, Norman James, June Carter, Michael Hickson, Mr and Mrs Llewellyn, Fiona Lockhart, R.T. Crabb, Elinor Clark, F.R. Furber, Kathryn Baker, Malcolm Harvey, Harry Britton, Hilary Cossham, Lady S. Vernon, Mrs M.M. Wethered, Susan Dean, Dr M.M.N. Stansfield, Judith Curthoys, Tom Gover, Angela Morrison, Gp. Capt. John Prideaux, Lewine Mair, Liz Pook, Andrea Duncan, Penelope Hatfield, Janet Seagle, Rand Jerris, Catherine Lacoste, Mr Tew (Dornoch), and Marjorie Hopson.

Finally, I thank James Howarth and Tempus Publishing. Without a publisher, a book is an unread bundle of words. Tempus is the instrument which has allowed my story to be told.

1
INTRODUCTION

It was Whitsuntide 1929 and the Great Western Railway had provided no less than 124 express trains at Paddington on the Friday and Saturday, to cope with the exodus from the metropolis to the seaside. Whoever said they couldn't run railways in those days! In South Wales, the respective candidates in the parliamentary elections were addressing themselves to the new incalculable factor – the woman's vote. Women outnumbered men by several thousand in their constituencies. Up in Glasgow, the Communists were contesting three of the seats. Whilst further east, at 'the old grey toone', history was also in the making. St Andrews, the home of golf, was hosting the Ladies' British Open Championship.

The United States, still very much in its infancy in the golfing world, had recently started winning everything. The British Men's Open had been the first to succumb, when Jock Hutchison had beaten Roger Wethered in 1921, and ever since 'the claret jug' had remained American property. There were some pretty fearsome American ladies on the scene also, and the worst was feared for the outcome of the Ladies' Championship. But then there were rumours and eventually confirmation, that a lady on a white charger was entering the lists on behalf of the beleaguered British. Joyce Wethered was coming back!

In just six years, and before reaching the age of twenty-four, Joyce Wethered had become a golfing heroine and a legend. Starting in 1920, she had won five consecutive English championships, and had won three out of five British championships, finishing as a finalist and a semi-finalist on the two rogue occasions. She was a golfer without equal. The great Bobby Jones later said that she was the best golfer he had ever seen, man or woman.

But Joyce Wethered had retired from championship golf in 1925; could she really come back four years later and take up where she had left off? Why was she entering at all? Did she have a desire to see off the American challenge? Well, I think she did. Not that Joyce would ever have publicly admitted to it, but behind that quiet, charming exterior there was a pretty tough cookie, and I suspect she was a touch more patriotic than some would think. I am not suggesting that her challenge would be anything other than ladylike to the extreme, and should she fail in her quest nobody would be more generous in defeat, but this was an opportunity which she was tickled pink to be taking. Besides, there was her brother's 1921 defeat to avenge. Yes, Roger Wethered, who had lost to Jock Hutchison, was Joyce's brother.

Maybe some of what I have written is conjecture; however, what is pure fact is that Joyce loved St Andrews, and to have missed the championship over her beloved course would have been heartbreaking.

The British public had no doubt whatsoever that Joyce would put her foes to the sword. If she could have read that she would have chastised me for being melodramatic, but that is how many of her supporters viewed the event.

The championship in those days was a knockout match-play format. Over the rounds preceding the final, Joyce had done nothing to worry those who were expecting her to bring home the bacon. Indeed, she had fairly waltzed through the earlier rounds. *The Times* correspondent, reporting on the Friday quarter-final, wrote:

> *It was this morning Miss Molly Gourlay's turn to be led out and shot at dawn. She had a fine day for her execution, if that was any satisfaction, and she was dealt with most mercifully and swiftly. She is a very good golfer and seemed to play well, but she had to get a two at the eighth to win her only hole.*

Miss Wethered went 4, 5, 3, 4, 4, 4, 4, 3, 4 = 35 and 4, 3, 4, 4. She dropped one shot only and had two birdies and at the Long Hole, measuring 480 yards, was on the green in two. (This was 1929, with hickory shafts etc.) By the end of the afternoon semi-final, she had beaten Miss Guedella by five and four.

By contrast, Glenna Collett had not been at her best, but she had survived. Glenna was America's answer to Joyce Wethered; she had a string of victories to her name, including six US Amateur titles, and was known as 'the Queen of American Golf'. Thus the final was, as had been predicted, Wethered *v.* Collett.

Joyce had entered the championship in a light-hearted manner. Yes, she would like to win, and if she didn't, it would certainly not be for the want of trying. But she had been away from the international scene for four years, and therefore expected to be allowed to enjoy the championship without too much being expected of her. This proved a somewhat naïve expectation – the Brits wanted a winner and were depending on her. On the Thursday evening before the quarter- and semi-finals, the two ladies had dined together, and Joyce had said:

> I remember that she dined with us at Russak's that evening, and I watched her as she walked over from the Grand Hotel, a charming and striking picture in blue and gold against the background of the grey buildings. She was not particularly happy that evening, a little dispirited with the course, and rather depressed and dispirited with her golf.

But the next day, Glenna had disposed of two doughty opponents, Mrs J.B. Watson and Doris Park. Joyce again – 'Glenna showed such convincing form in those two matches, that I ruefully and truthfully prophesied that there was trouble brewing for me on the morrow.'

The final was played over thirty-six holes. Three thousand spectators were there to watch the tee-off on the Saturday morning, a number which would double for the afternoon round. The two combatants were dressed in the uniform of the time, long woollen cardigans or jumpers, tweed skirts, mid-calf length, and small cloche hats. Joyce's prediction immediately came true, with Glenna coming out of the starting blocks like the thoroughbred which she was, notching seven consecutive fours, a two, and another four to be out in thirty-four. Phew!

JW could only hang on. In view of the large gallery, the players had each been allotted an attendant and Joyce's aide walked close by her side with a stiff, rather noisy, raincoat over her arm. Joyce was famous for her concentration and all of her willpower had to be called into play in those first holes to eliminate from her mind the squeaky rainwear. She was not putting well either. By the turn she was five holes down, and it is part of the legend of St Andrews that a mournful postman proceeded on his round through the town that morning, announcing to all and sundry, 'She's fife doone.'

She had been five down before and had come back from the almost dead to win a major championship. Indeed, in her first championship win ever, at Sheringham in the English Open in 1920, she had been six down to Cecil Leitch and fought back to win, but it is an awfully big start to give to your opponent. Could she pull this one out of the fire?

For four holes after the turn, the two matched one another, stroke for stroke – 4, 3, 5, 4. The tide had not turned yet, but Miss Collett was now studying her putts with increasing care and not always with success. On the long twelfth she had a four-footer to go six up, but it stayed out. The long, flowing upright strokes of the English girl were now beginning to dominate the match as her American challenger's flatter swing became quicker and more abbreviated.

By the end of the morning round, JW had reduced the deficit to just two holes, and by the turn in the afternoon she had a four-hole lead. In fourteen holes, Miss Wethered won ten and lost only one. She had played the first nine of the afternoon round in thirty-five, virtually equalling Miss Collett's morning achievement.

It seemed to be all over bar the shouting, but no!! Back came Glenna, come on the United States! She took the tenth and the eleventh with beautiful birdie threes. Back to two down with seven to play. At the fourteenth, the gallery were even treated to a short period of farce when both players hacked their way to the green like twenty-four handicappers (or should that be thirty-six handicappers), and the hole was won by a seven.

Time was running out for the girl from across the water, and it all came to an end at that hole which has witnessed so much grief and suffering, the seventeenth – the infamous Roadhole. In modern times, the most recent tragedy in a major tournament was the torment of David Duval, who, when still in the hunt to win the 2000 Open from Tiger Woods, and while being watched by millions across forty different countries, had put his second into the green-side bunker and taken four more before he emerged. Miss Collett avoided the bunker but, unfortun-ately, took four to get onto the green, and it was all over. Joyce Wethered had returned and taken the title by three holes with one to play.

As the thousands of spectators roared their appreciation, the old town nodded its approval. Miss Wethered made a short polite speech, thanking the Royal and Ancient and the match referee, before bestowing generous acclaim on her opponent. The Captain Elect of the R&A presented the prizes. He referred to Miss Wethered as the best lady golfer there had ever been, and then, would you believe, had the consummate bad manners to tell all the lady competitors that they should practise their putting!

JW had accomplished what she set out to achieve. She simply wanted to win at St Andrews. Having come out of a four-year retirement, and still only twenty-seven, she withdrew from the championship scene once more. You see, she still regarded golf as a game – a delightful game, a challenging game, but only a game. It was a recreation to her and she was happiest in that knowledge. She didn't want it to become a chore. She didn't want it to take over her life. She wanted to be in control of the situation, and in her quiet, charming way she was, for the whole of her life.

She had been fortunate to be born into a family of independent means and had enjoyed that advantage throughout her life. At Whitsuntide 1929, although she did not know it for some months to come, that privilege was soon to be withdrawn. The Wall Street Crash in October of 1929 would eliminate, almost at a stroke, the fortunes of many, and Joyce's father would be one of the victims. It would mean some drastic changes in her lifestyle and the need for the first time in her life to fend for herself.

This is the story, with due respect to the many excellent female golfers of today and yesterday, of the greatest British lady golfer ever. You doubt that statement? Well, reserve your judgement until the end of the book.

2
BEFORE THE COMING

It was the coal industry which bequeathed an early life of comfort and modest affluence on Joyce Wethered. Her grandfather, Henry Wethered, was one of a family of five sons and three daughters, of William Wethered of Little Marlow in Buckinghamshire. In 1848, his sister Elizabeth married Handel Cossham of Bristol, who later became MP for Bath. Her grandfather and his brothers soon became partners with Handel in opening coal mines north of Bristol.

In their heyday, the Cossham/Wethered partnerships owned 3,000 acres of freehold mineral property, and provided work for 1,500 people. When the mines were sold after Handel's death, they realised £61,000. That was a great deal of money in the nineteenth century, and is a guide to the source of Henry Wethered's wealth.

Henry had benefited greatly from his alliances with his brothers and the industrious Handel, but he had other irons in the fire, and co-owned the Bristol Marine Insurance Company. For thirty-five years he was a director of the London and South Western Bank. He lived at Tyndall's Park, Bristol, in one of the more affluent areas of the city, and had a great love of trees and flowers. He was an accomplished artist and exhibited his paintings. At the late age of seventy-three, he started to give public expression to his poetic feelings with readings given at the Victoria Rooms. He lived to the ripe old age of eighty-eight.

Henry, who had married a Mary Llewellin, had three sons and a daughter, and the youngest son was Herbert Newton Wethered, the father of our heroine Joyce and her brother Roger. Herbert was educated at Clifton College and Corpus Christi College, Oxford, where he read modern history, obtaining his degree in 1892. In 1890, whilst still up at Oxford, he married Marion Emmeline Lund, the sister of a contemporary and presumably a friend. Her father was described as a worsted spinner and manufacturer in Leeds. He was a JP and the Deputy Lieutenant of the West Riding of Yorkshire. The son and friend of Herbert was described as a landowner and the Lord of the Manor of Lund Forest and Ellerton Hall; so it seems in marrying Marion, Herbert made what is sometimes termed 'a good match'. Thus, the industry of her grandfather and marriage of her father had ensured that Joyce would be born into a comfortable life.

It is worth dwelling on Herbert Newton Wethered a while longer, for he was an extraordinary man. At university, he combined sport with learning. He captained the college cricket eleven and was regarded as a very good bowler. Indeed, the college records bear testament to that fact. He was also an athlete, and presumably played golf. He was a member of the college essay club. As such, he must have been a frequent user of the college library. It was amusing to read that, in 1881, there had been complaints that the library in the winter was much too cold and that the authorities were considering a scheme to warm it. The college magazine, *The Pelican*, reports, 'It would, however, be out of the question to make it into a comfortable sitting room. It is probable, by the way, that the bedroom attached to the library will sooner or later be abolished to make room for new bookshelves.' The mind boggles at the implications behind those statements. Perhaps the bedroom was provided for students at their studies burning the midnight oil. The report ends with a notice, 'A list of books missing from the library will be posted up shortly, and it is hoped that everyone, especially those who are going down, will make certain that none of them are among their own books.' Ah, was it ever thus! Surely there is a grammatical error in the sentence also – and from the library of one of the nation's principal seats of learning! Oh dear, Homer has nodded.

Shortly after leaving university, Herbert Newton Wethered must have moved home to Surrey, where his address was Coombefield, Malden Road, Malden, Surrey. Unencumbered of the need to earn a living by dint of the inheritances of his wife and himself, he was still an extremely industrious author, producing books on a range of subjects, including appreciations of well-known nineteenth-century authors, the devel-opment of painting, gardening, natural history, medieval craftsmanship and the art of autobiography. He also combined with T. Simpson to produce a book on golf-course architecture, and later, in 1933, produced a book, *The Perfect Golfer*. I have also discovered that he produced a publication in 1929, *The Architectural Side of Golf*. This appears to be a different book from that written in conjunction with Simpson. A 1982 publication relating to the values of golfing memorabilia, entitled *Golf Collectors' Price Guide*, by John Taylor, put the value of this book at £150–£200! I have reason to think that it was a limited edition, and rather nicely produced, and so scarcity value would enhance its price. Newton, as his daughter said when referring to him, was a man of many talents.

He was a very artistic man, like his father, and was a painter; indeed, his description of occupation on Joyce's birth certificate stated 'Artist Painter'. An excellent example of his talent in this direction hangs in 'the golf room' at Knightshayes Court (now National Trust) near Tiverton, Devon. This was Joyce's home after she married Sir John Heathcoat-Amory. The painting is some 4in by 20in, and is a portrait of Joyce. He also produced marvellous tapestries and embroideries, his daughter inheriting many of these talents.

As has been previously indicated, he had two brothers and a sister. All three boys attended Clifton College. Henry Llewellin Wethered was the senior brother, eight years older than Herbert, and his occupation was described in the 1881 census as 'leather factor'. Clifton College registers record him as a partner in the firm of Llewellin and James, Bell Founders. He obviously joined his maternal grandfather in business. The second son was Vernon, four years Herbert's senior, and possibly an influence upon Herbert. He obviously inherited his father's love of painting and, after obtaining a degree in the humanities at Oriel College, Oxford, he attended the Slade School of Art in London. His record in the Clifton College registers denotes him as a former company director and chairman, now 'painting'!

I always think that Herbert must have been a very lucky man to have been able to live off his inheritance and spend his life as he wished, but I have an even greater respect for him in that he did not waste that opportunity. He could have opted for a life of indolent luxury, but that was not in the Wethered nature.

We shall later see that Joyce's great love after golf was gardening, and this is not surprising when we discover that early in Joyce's life the family moved to the striking Lutyens house, Tigbourne Court, near Goldaming, Surrey. The house was built in 1899 for Edgar House, MP for Guildford. The famous Edwin Lutyens/Gertrude Jekyll combination had produced a property which was very futuristic in house design, complemented by flower gardens, the plans for which are unfortunately no longer available. Rhododendrons and azaleas replaced the sweeps of perennials and cottage garden appearance of the past.

Tigbourne Court is within a mile or so of West Surrey Golf Course, and the Wethered family took their Sunday walks through the intervening woods and heath land and over the fields which would become the golf course, in the years before the ceremonial opening of the course on 9 June 1910. J.H. Taylor and James Braid were both present on that auspicious occasion, the famous pair having no less than eight British Open victories between them at that time.

An excellent book has been produced by a member, Derek Sumpter, to record the first sixty years of the club's history. I was delighted to find that the secretary of the club at the time of the inauguration was R.C.N. Palairet, the Somerset cricketer, whose brother Lionel together with one Bert Hewett created a world record when they scored 346 runs for the first wicket for Somerset in a match against Yorkshire in 1892. The book is graced with a frontispiece comprising a photograph of Lady Heathcoat-Amory, stating that, as Joyce Wethered, she was the club's most famous member. The frontispiece also includes a print of the letter which the club had received from Lady Amory, sending her message of best wishes to the club. It reads, 'I have great pleasure in sending you my best wishes for your future success. I shall always have happy memories of my playing days at West Surrey with my brother Roger; and the family walks we used to take across your beautiful course.'

She did state on another occasion that she had never worried too much about bad lies throughout her golfing career because she had started her golf at West Surrey on fairways, which only a short time previously had been agricultural land, and could become very wet and uneven!

Joyce actually joined the West Surrey club when she was twelve, but she used to watch the club's first professional, Fred Robson, playing and giving lessons when she was nine. It is common knowledge that she asserts that she had only one lesson throughout her life...

Her means of learning was through watching and imitation. At a tournament, watching a professional she admired, she would follow him and carefully note all the characteristics of his swing and then could be found at the back of the crowd practising the stroke in the manner she had just observed.

Derek Sumpter's book gives us some idea of golf finance at the time of the opening of the West Surrey club in 1910. The first professional was paid a retainer of £85 per year, though he also received 5s a week for acting as caddie master. Male members paid five guineas joining fee and 5 guineas annual subscription; ladies paid 2 guineas in each category. A green fee for visitors was 2s 6d. You could have your boots cleaned for 2d. Incidentally, the total cost of setting up the club, including purchase of 189 acres, building the clubhouse and constructing the course was £11,250.

The late and much-loved golfer and commentator, Henry Longhurst, used to play at West Surrey when he was at school at Charterhouse. He used to cycle the few miles from Charterhouse with his golf bag round his neck, and used the celebrated trick of every young boy of catching hold of the tailboard of a passing lorry to obtain a tow. He remembered the wonderful day when he picked up a coal lorry at Godalming, which actually delivered its coal to the clubhouse!

Joyce's brother Roger was a little older than his sister, having been born on 8 January 1899, as opposed to Joyce, who was born on 17 November 1901. He had joined West Surrey before Joyce, which means he must have almost been a founder member, albeit as a boy. For some time I could not understand why their parents did not play at the same course, particularly as it was so close to their home. The answer was simple; they were there before the course. They had been members at the Puttenham club, north of Goldaming, and no doubt decided to remain with old friends when the new course at West Surrey opened. Joyce referred to her father in a letter as Newton Wethered, so we will use that name henceforth.

Puttenham Golf Club had come into being in 1894 (a boom time for new golf clubs), and thus celebrated its centenary in 1994. The club historian, researching information for the centennial book, discovered that an unknown H.N. Wethered, together with W.C. Butterworth, had won the annual foursomes by seven and six. The same person had won the Charterhouse Cup in 1913.

A letter, printed in the centennial book, is from Lady Heathcoat-Amory at Knightshayes and reads as follows:

Dear Mr...
It is very easy for me to identify the unknown Wethereds – they were my mother and father. They lived at Tigbourne until the early thirties and then moved to another house at Brook – I was with them until I married. Actually, they were Mr and Mrs Newton Wethered and both died in the 1950s. My father had a handicap in single figures, but alas my mother, who struggled hard, never got under eighteen.
Best wishes for your memoirs.
Joyce, Lady Amory.

The reference to moving from Tigbourne to a house at Brook was probably as a result of the Wall Street Crash, when Newton Wethered's investments suffered the fate of so many others. Tigbourne Court would have been a valuable property, and a decision may have been made to realise some of that value to keep the ship afloat. It was at the same time that Joyce took her first paid employment.

In 1934 Joyce wrote a book, entitled *Golfing Memories and Methods*. It was probably written as much out of her desire to earn some money and assist her parents in their hour of need, as to indulge herself in a combination of autobiography and instruction. She was certainly not going to put her inner secrets in print. There is nothing more certain than that – she was a much too private person. I would encourage any would-be golfer to read it. It is certainly one of the clearest and most informative golfing manuals that I have seen.

I refer to the book now as it gives insight into Joyce's introduction to the world of golf and her thoughts as she moved from childhood through adolescence to the championship scene. More importantly, it gives a number of clues on why she became, arguably, the greatest lady golfer of the century.

She recalls that she more or less drifted into golf, for the simple reason that others around her were playing the game. She started slowly, without exhibiting any great propensity to stardom, but she had characteristics which would later develop to project her to the front line of championship golf. She writes of one player who, in his waning years, was pleased to be described as a shadow of his former self, because it left him with the warming thought of how good he must have been considered at one time. Joyce comments, 'I think we should all agree that it is better to possess a shadow than never to have been somebody.' To me, that reveals ambition.

In considering the reasons for the popularity of golf, she enumerates the social aspect, the desire to take exercise, the gambling instinct to relieve an opponent of half-a-crown, or hitting the ball out of sight, but states, 'Where, however, it seems to gain a firmer grip is with the player to whom the technical side of the game makes an irresistible appeal.' She confesses that she was such an addict not simply because she wanted to know all the nuances of a perfect swing, but because, 'there is nothing I hate so much as to be in an undecided state of mind, of not knowing what to do or what to think for the best. I long to get out of the wood and resume the straight path once more.' This suggests technical understanding, coupled with clarity of thought and determination.

Then there was her spirit of enquiry:

> Each week has in store the possibility of further developments and new discoveries, and there is never any end to tracking down the greater secrets. In this particular direction I have had many adventurous experiences myself, so I can speak with some conviction, perhaps not altogether unmixed with occasional doubts. As I grew up the discoveries I made spurred me on to further efforts.

This surely demonstrates in Joyce a desire for perfection.

> If I had to cut down trees, I should begin to wonder how the real woodcutter would set about swinging his axe. In playing billiards, even if my skill rarely allowed me to make a minute series of cannons, I should still want to know how Lindrum held his cue.

Here we see her attention to detail.

She apologises in her book for devoting so many pages to competitive golf, but writes:

> Competitive golf should have a place, I feel (for a short time at least) in every golfer's progress, if a real interest is to be shown. It must be good for us to be roused sometimes to serious action and made to experience feelings strange and different from anything we have felt before. Where the greatest value of competitions lies is in their forming landmarks to show

us how good, bad or indifferent our golf may be in comparison with that of everyone else. As adventures in discovering to what lengths our game is good enough to carry us, they may be thrilling beyond anything we may have anticipated.

Here is another illustration of a competitive nature.

Joyce Wethered in early life was a quiet, affable, retiring young lady and I doubt whether she had an enemy in the world, but don't let that fool you into thinking she did not have the qualities that make a champion. She was a determined young lady, with the ability to understand the technical side of the game, the determination to conquer it by careful study and experiment, and the ambition to get to the top of the tree. She had other qualities, of course, and concentration, so important in the sporting arena, was one of them. Like all the best competitors she rarely showed her emotions on the field of play, whether things were going well or badly (not that they often went badly), and any worries were kept within, away from prying eyes. Indeed, in spite of all her talents, it was often this latter attribute which caused her to outlast her opponents and cause them to buckle.

Joyce's earliest memory of golf was when the family were holidaying in north Cornwall, and she played on a course laid out for children and ladies of high handicap. Indeed, it was at Bude that she had her only full golfing lesson. Most of her memories in her adolescent years relate to Dornoch in Scotland, described in *The World Atlas of Golf Courses* thus: 'Royal Dornoch is the least known and least played of all the great links courses. It may well be the finest natural golf course in the world.' Dornoch is about sixty miles north of Inverness and recently hit the headlines as the venue for the marriage of Madonna at Skibo Castle, although I imagine that the locals can think of more worthy reasons why it should become the focus of the world's media.

Royal Dornoch is first mentioned as a golf course in 1616, which would place it third in age behind St Andrews and Leith. It was not until 1906 that Edward VII, with the influence of Millicent the Duchess of Sutherland, granted the course the royal title. The course has drawn praise from a number of international golfers, Tom Watson being one who has played there a number of times because he so enjoyed the experience. The great American writer and coach, Herbert Warren Wind, wrote in 1964, 'I found Dornoch all I had hoped it would be – a thoroughly modern old links with that rare equipoise of charm and character that only great courses possess.' What he would have written if he had visited with the wind blowing we can only surmise. Unfortunately, the course is rather too far north to make it a contender for many events of international stature, though the Home Internationals were played there in 1980 and the British Amateur in 1985. It seems unbelievable that it is on the same latitude as Hudson's Bay in Canada, and actually lies north of Moscow!

The Wethereds certainly liked Dornoch, to the extent that Newton bought a house which bordered the course. Joyce recalled that they had only to cross the road and drop over a low wall to find themselves in front of the big bunker which for many years defeated their best drives from the second tee. From her bedroom window she witnessed many an irregularity when the offenders thought that they were hidden from view. All visitors, of course! She was sometimes tempted to shout to them that they should not tee their ball in a bunker. The nearness of the house to the course was occasionally only too evident, when an outrageous hook crashed through a window.

Perhaps West Surrey does not receive enough of the credit, but it is Dornoch that Joyce remembered with great affection. I suppose it was their holiday home and holidays are usually recalled as the highlights of a year, whilst home life is... well, home life. At first she was confined to the second course laid out on the flats which bordered the Firth. She thought them rather lonely and desolate, and was frightened by the frisky black bullocks which shared them with the golfers.

As there were few visitors to the course, she was soon allowed to progress to the main links and made up a family four ball. We now discover another reason why JW became a champion. We have already seen that her father was a handy golfer with a single-figure handicap, and although Joyce decried her mother's handicap of eighteen, it wasn't a bad handicap, especially for a lady. So there was golf in the blood. But more importantly, her brother Roger, three years older than Joyce, was already smitten with the bug, and he was to play a huge part in her development; not by taking her under his wing and sweetly coaching her in the finer points, but by the more usual brotherly traits of cajoling, daring, and challenging. Roger was destined to become one of the leading amateur golfers in the country, and his example spurred Joyce to greater things. She describes him as an autocrat where the seriousness of golf was concerned. It was Roger who devised a system of charts to monitor their golfing progress, and Joyce had little option but to toe the line. They had to keep a record of every round and Joyce remembered that, with her head full of the wildest hopes; she chose a figure of eighty-four as her zenith. Her nadir was 120, illustrating that she knew her limitations at that stage. No sudden child prodigy this, she was going to have to work for her later glory. We do not know the figures which Roger chose for the limits of his chart, but I am surprised that he allowed Joyce to choose her own. She adored and respected him, but a little self-determination was already showing.

She remembered the need to keep a score and the fact that it would be registered on the chart for all to see (well, the family anyway), always hung like a millstone around her neck as she stood on the first tee. This was good preparation for important, stomach-wrenching occasions later in her career, I should think. At first the scores were calculated a little leniently. Ah, don't we all remember awarding ourselves that little two-footer! Later they kept their exact scores, scrupulously accurately. During the last year that she kept a record, which must have been in about 1916, when she was fourteen, her chart had a top limit of ninety-nine, which demonstrates her progress, steady rather than exceptional.

In early 1917 Roger matriculated to Christ Church College, Oxford, to read English. Both he and Joyce had been privately educated at home. We do not know a great deal about that education, other than that it was sometimes slightly bizarre. For example, a prestigious golf tournament might find them in the crowd with their tutors, and an important art exhibition in London would certainly see them there with their father. Why do I call that bizarre? It was a full, far-reaching education. Their father knew what he valued in life, and no doubt decided that the syllabus followed in most schools at the time did not encompass all of those subjects. He was sufficiently wealthy that he could give his children a tailor-made education. It certainly included the three R's, but a number of other subjects also. I have no evidence for this assertion, but I would be surprised if they did not include substantial dollops of art, poetry, botany and natural history.

Roger had been at Oxford for only eight months when he was called up to help the fight against the Kaiser, and he served as a Second. Lieutenant in France and Belgium. On his return to Oxford, he took one of the short courses designed for servicemen and passed his examinations in English in 1921. Strangely, he did not receive his BA until 1963. The Christ Church College archivist was kind enough to explain to me that it is the tradition at Oxford that, unless special arrangements are made, a graduate must attend a degree ceremony at the Sheldon Theatre in order to be awarded his degree. There was obviously some delay in Roger's case.

Roger's years at Oxford were probably as influential on Joyce's golfing career as any period in her life. There was a group of very good young amateur golfers at Oxford, and Roger had become a leading player. Consequently, Joyce often attended matches and had the opportunity to watch the leading players. As a seventeen-year-old, she was probably captivated by some of these handsome young men; she certainly enjoyed their golf. She recalled a highlight when she was having tea with Roger one afternoon in the clubhouse, and the famous Cyril Tolley graciously enquired after her golf, a complimentary notice which had her blushing delightedly.

Watching the men spurred her to greater ambitions, and she benefited greatly from the frequent invitations which she received to play with Roger and his friends. These golfers were the cream of the country at that particular time. She said that there was no surer and quicker way to improvement than playing with men, both stronger and better than herself. It meant that when she played in ladies' matches, she had much greater confidence.

Joyce, still only seventeen, was now on the threshold of greatness. In 1919 she made her debut for the Surrey Ladies' Team, getting the first taste of public events. In the following year, the *Surrey Advertiser* reported that the Surrey Ladies' Championship was played at Worplesden in May and Miss J. Wethered, playing off a handicap of five, had an eighty-five and took second prize in the handicap competition.

In the Surrey Championship she proceeded as far as the semi-finals, where she was beaten by Mrs Deane of Stoke Poges. That championship was won by Molly Griffiths, who had become Joyce's great friend.

In her first year in the limelight, JW was making her presence felt. Watch out everybody, a star is about to be born.

In case I give the impression that Miss Wethered was bowling along to glory without any hiccups, we should hear a word from the good lady herself.

At this time I was having a good deal of trouble with my game. The first thing I attempted to do was to change a naturally flat swing into an upright one — a change that I had been led to believe was the sounder method of the two. I found it an extremely difficult thing to do, and there is no doubt that in making the change I formed it much too stiffly. Everything, however, takes time and trouble and it was not for several years that I improved my rhythm by altering the pivot and transferring my weight more freely. I used in those early days to pin my left side very firmly by keeping the left heel on the ground during the backswing. This was an unduly severe restriction; what it gained in keeping the body steady it undoubtedly lost in freedom and elasticity and, in consequence, distance.

Roger often had golfing friends to stay at the house, and they liked to discuss the intricacies of the game, different techniques, etc. Joyce was a keen listener on such occasions, and, importantly, had the capacity to separate what was worthwhile from the dross.

A particular annoyance to her was her inability to put backspin on her approach shots, and she recalled seeing the ball through a mist of tears when practising the shot. What could better illustrate her determination to succeed? Of course, she continued with her practice until she mastered the problem, unlike some of us.

In June 1920, Molly Griffiths persuaded Joyce to go with her to Sheringham for the English Championship. Her parents agreed, and she set forth mainly as a companion for Molly, rather than expecting to do anything in the competition. At that time there was no handicap limit which prevented, shall we say, moderate golfers from entering for the championship. Don't forget this was still a time when many of those playing ladies' golf were there for the country-house après-golf bonhomie and entertainment as much as for the golf itself. Consequently, there was a vast gulf between the best and worst competitors. In 1920, for the first and only time, there was a qualifying round for the event, to reduce the numbers to an acceptable total for the championship proper.

Before we consider Joyce's first taste of championship golf, it may be as well to remind ourselves of the state of golf at that time, to what extent it had developed, who were the principal players of the time, and what sort of equipment they were using. It is only too easy to forget that, back then, much was different from golf in the twenty-first century. It would also be sensible to take a look at the country and society outside of golf, because, again, situations were very different, particularly for ladies, compared to the way things are today.

The reign of 'The Great Triumvirate' – Vardon, Braid and Taylor – had come to an end. For twenty years before the outbreak of the First World War, they had reigned supreme and taken the British Open title no fewer than sixteen times between them, six to Vardon and five apiece to the other two. Taylor, distinctively known throughout his career as J.H. Taylor, was the first Englishman to take the title, wresting it from a long line of Scots, going all the way back to Old Tom Morris. Harry Vardon was a Channel Islander, and is probably the best known of all British golfers, not least because he left to posterity the 'Vardon' grip, used by most golfers, professional and amateur, good and bad. His tremendous skills are put into perspective when it is taken into account that he suffered ill-health throughout his career, and was often a victim of the putting malady, the 'yips'. James Braid was a tall gangling Scot, who also had to overcome troubles on the greens. His eyesight was not good, after having lime thrown in his face when he was an apprentice joiner, and he often putted with a driving cleek, equivalent to a modern three-iron, as did many professionals at the turn of the century. We forget that the greens were much rougher than today, and the putting method comprised crouching over the ball and popping it forward. Persuasion by a club-maker for him to use one of his new aluminium-headed putters was a godsend to Braid, who never looked back.

Unfortunately for Britain, the places of the triumvirate were increasingly being filled by Americans, who had not taken up golf in earnest until the late nineteenth century, and even then their early stars had mostly been imported Scottish professionals. But now they were on the scene with a vengeance, and Walter Hagen and his successors were here to stay.

The standing of a golf professional was still that of servant class. They were not allowed into the clubhouse, and the story is told of Hagen being refused entry to the clubhouse on the occasion of his first British Open appearance at Deal in 1920. Told to change in the professionals' shop with all the other professionals, the next day he turned up in a chauffeur-driven limousine, changed his shoes in full view of the club-house, and then had his chauffeur pour him champagne from a hamper. I wish I had been there to see that! Trust the Yanks to snuff out the snobbery. But, as with other sports, notably cricket, it would be a number of years before the rules were relaxed. Remember, in county cricket, the professionals were not allowed in the same dressing room as the amateurs. They even entered the field of play through a separate gate!

It was 1925 before the professionals were allowed to change in the clubhouse at the British Open, and that was only after fierce opposition from certain quarters, notably the older members. Nothing changes! In 1920, Ted Ray won the US Open, and in honour of the achievement his home club, Oxhey, accorded him honorary membership. Can you imagine the discussions in the clubhouses around the country, as they downed their whisky and sodas! However, it was an idea that became quite popular, and not only Vardon and other celebrities benefited by similar treatment, but club professionals generally started to be accorded the honour. In 1903, the PGA (Professional Golfers' Association) had been formed to try to improve the lot of the professional, but it was many years later, in the 1930s, before it really began to improve their status.

It has to be remembered that golf was still mainly an upper-class sport. It would be some time before even artisan sections were generally accepted. So, how did the ladies fare in all of this? Golf in the nineteenth century had not been considered suitable for the wives of gentlemen, though a few high-spirited ladies had raised two fingers to that. It was not thought that the actual muscular effort involved in striking the ball was 'quite nice', at a time when physical exertion was considered something to be restricted to the working classes. In 1868 a ladies' club had been formed at Westward Ho!, but it was run by the men. The ladies had their own course and were not allowed to play on the main course. They were allowed to play only on every other Saturday from May to October, and under no circumstances were they to use any club other than a wooden putter!

The ladies were persistent and in 1893 formed the Ladies' Golf Union, and in the same year held the first British Ladies' Championship at Royal Lytham and St Annes. Whether it was played on the main course, I know not. It would be surprising if it was, because the ladies still played mainly on small, par-three type courses. However, they had their composite foot in the door and gradually they forced more concessions out of the men, even being allowed in their own quarters in the clubhouse – though not the bar, of course.

Into the twentieth century, and Emily Pankhurst and the Suffragettes made themselves felt by destroying golf greens, and even removing the pants of the Prime Minister, David Lloyd George, whilst he was playing at Walton Heath. A bigger impact in golfing circles was caused by Cecil Leitch, about whom we shall hear a great deal more later, in her epic battles with Joyce Wethered. The men's amateur champion in 1910, Harold Hilton, had the misfortune to play a challenge match against the formidable Miss Leitch. They played from the same tees, but Miss Leitch was allowed an extra shot on alternate holes. The event attracted a large audience, and the result when Miss Leitch won caused a major impact across the country and the golfing scene. By 1920, ladies had discarded their stiff-starched collars, hacking jackets and ankle-length voluminous skirts, which must have inhibited their golf swings greatly. They had, of course, adopted other clothing, but of a less restrictive nature. Ladies' golf had established itself, and the standard of play had improved enormously.

Golf courses in general were not the manicured areas of beauty we see today. Although the industrial revolution had spawned steam engines, fairways received nothing like the attention which is devoted to them weekly in the modern age. Indeed, in the earliest years, golf was a spring, autumn and winter pastime, the grass being too long in the summer months. Horses and mowers or sheep and cattle were the most likely means of keeping the grass under some kind of control. This is doubtless why the links courses were the best. That type of turf required much less attention and fairways often looked after themselves. Today's professionals would have been appalled by the state of the greens, which were often little more than mown pasture. Hazards were more likely to be natural, than conceived by the course architect. As technological advances were made and more equipment became available, so golf courses progressed towards the paradises we see today.

The personal equipment of the golfer went through a similar evolution. The first real golf ball was 'the feathery'. It comprised three sections of untreated bull's hide, soaked in alum. It was stitched together with waxed twine, leaving a gap through which to insert boiled chicken or goose feathers. Before the feathers were inserted, the leather was turned inside out so that the smoother surface was on the outside. It was quite a task to ram the leather sufficiently full, (a top-hat full of feathers was used) to complete the ball and apply the final stitches. Left out to dry, the hide contracted and the feathers expanded, making a hard ball, which was usually painted with a lead-based paint to protect it against the wet. The balls were very expensive, as a man could produce only four to six in a day. It was a dangerous trade, as the maker was continually exposed to the paint and dust, causing chest problems not unlike those hat-makers experienced when continually working with glue.

The feathery remained supreme for a long period, until 'the gutty' made its appearance, a latex solution called gutta-percha. When softened by heat it could readily be moulded. It retailed at about a quarter of the cost of the feathery and therefore there was no match. The feathery was consigned to the museums and collectors' cabinets. The gutty travelled further than the feathery when struck, and all we golfers know what that means. Golfers would play with a banana if it went a few yards further than the alternative. However, as a smooth ball, it tended to duck in flight. And now we know why we play with dimpled balls. It was discovered that indenting the smooth surface improved the flight characteristics of the gutty. Apparently there was a rule at that time that when a ball disintegrated, as it sometimes did, the player was allowed to play his new ball from the position where the largest piece of the old ball landed.

The gutty had a much shorter life than the feathery – considered 'in' by the middle of the nineteenth century, it was out soon after that century ended. Coburn Haskell, an American from Cleveland, experimented with rubber strips wound around a rubber core. Again, it went further than the gutty, although some said that it was more difficult to control. In the same way that anything adopted by Tiger Woods today must be good, the 'Haskell', as it was known, became the ball to be used when Alec Herd played with it in the 1902 Open and won the day. By 1920 there had been variations on the Haskell, but, in essence, that was the ball in play. It was a three-piece ball with an inner core, elastic windings and a plastic cover.

Having looked at the balls being used, it is logical to consider the clubs with which the ball was struck. If there is one thing that the old golfers can teach the modern generation, it is in the naming of their clubs. Everything goes by numbers today, but in the old days every club had its own magical name. I make no apology for naming them here. I would like to hear them again, and I can't believe that you wouldn't.

From the top, we have the driver (No.1 wood), brassie (No.2 wood), spoon (No.3 wood), and baffy (No.4 wood). Then, there is the cleek (No.2 iron), jigger (No.4 iron), mashie (No.5 iron), mashie-niblick (No. 7 iron), and niblick (No.9 iron). The weapon for extricating oneself from sand was called a blaster – now could you think of anything more apt than that? Although I have known these names for years, they still have a magic to me. I'm sure I would get much closer to the hole with a mashie-niblick than I ever would with a seven-iron. Don't ask me where the name came from, I don't want to know. Mashie-niblick – with clubs like that you could break sixty! In 1920, when Joyce played her first championship, many of those names were still in use – I am sure they inspired her on her way.

The Haskell ball damaged the old traditional woods used for the club-heads, and a change was made to the North American wood, 'persimmon', with ivory or bone inserts. The shafts at that time were hickory, but mass manufacture was just around the corner and steel would soon be challenging. JW played with hickory shafts throughout her career at the top level.

Before we finish with painting the picture of golf in 1920, we should not forget those most important of people, the caddies. The stories told about caddies would fill an encyclopedia. Here are three from the great Scottish golfer and raconteur, Andra Kirkaldy, and you will notice that they are all Scotsmen and have the last word!

'Come along', a golfer shouted impatiently to his caddie, who had a heavy load of wood and iron. 'I'm comin, but ye dinna expect a sheet o' lightning for eichteen pense d'ye?'.

A dry old stick was Bobbie Greig. An Aussie visitor gave him a card to mark the strokes. 'Well, did you keep my score?' 'Nae, but I kept count o' the pieces o' turf yer cut, an I've put back 165.'

A golfer who played in spectacles suspected his caddie of carelessness in the matter of searching for balls. 'Are you short-sighted,' he asked. 'Nae,' replied the caddie, 'I'd ha bin wearin specs if I was.'

They all seem to show a degree of contempt for the golfer, don't they? I'm sure that was not true in all master/caddy relationships, but it has to be remembered that many of these caddies were good golfers in their own right, and it must have been galling to spend three or four hours in the company of an incompetent hacker, who was pompous and overbearing to boot. The gulf in their social standings would also cause some grief, with many caddies existing just above the breadline. There they would stand, in the caddie shed, to be fetched out by the caddie master to carry a stranger's clubs, like a horse fetched out of its stable to pull a cart.

Caddies had their moments, though. The Prime Minister, Lord Balfour, was a keen golfer and became the Royal and Ancient Captain in 1904. A caddie at North Berwick told Andra Kirkaldy that he had a very close relationship with Mr Balfour. Intrigued, Andra pleaded to be told more. 'What d'ye mean?', he asked. 'Just this,' said the caddie, pointing to his legs, 'I'm wearing a pair of Mr Balfour's trousers.' It's the way you tells them that matters!

Incidentally, in 1920, none other than Field Marshall Earl Haig was captain of the R&A. Apparently he was an old boy of St Andrews school. He was described as 'ordinary' on the course! Oh dear, if ever there was a word which hides another, it is 'ordinary'.

An article appeared in the January 1920 edition of *Golf Illustrated and Outdoor Life*, entitled 'Solving the Caddie Problem'. Apparently, the main problem was that certain members would tip the caddies excessively as a sort of retaining fee. This made life difficult for those members of a more conservative disposition and allegedly led to dissatisfaction and unrest amongst the caddies. The St George's Hill Club at Weybridge tackled the problem by having notices printed asking the members not to tip in excess of 6d a round. In addition, the club introduced a training scheme, which gives a valuable insight into the life of a caddie at that period.

Each permanent caddie was guaranteed a minimum wage of 18s per week. They received 2s for a morning round, including 6d for lunch, and 1s 6d for other rounds. If they caddied for sufficient rounds in the week to earn in excess of the minimum wage, so be it, they benefited accordingly. Moreover, to be fair to all the caddies, they were allotted to the members in strict rotation – the work was evenly shared. Those who were not required for carrying were put at the disposal of the head green-keeper for the morning, learning the skills of that particular profession. In the afternoon they were taught the skills of boot repair by the caddie master.

The scheme must have applied to young men and boys rather than old dyed-in-the-wool caddies, because after two years those who had behaved themselves were awarded a £5 bonus and the club secretary used his influence to find them permanent employment in gardening or boot repair. These were obviously caddies for carrying the clubs rather than giving advice to the members on the playing of shots, but it seems a very commendable scheme. The caddie master would issue the boys with a 6d voucher for their lunch and they could obtain a substantial lunch of bread and cold meat. There were forfeits for those who were not of good behaviour, and it was possible to lose all or part of their bonus. More repressive, perhaps, was the knowledge that other adjacent clubs had an agreement that they would not employ a lad who had been dismissed.

One other point about this period: in Scotland, at least, there were still clubs which did not allow play on the Sabbath. The 500 members of the Turnhouse Club near Edinburgh held a vote on the subject with a convincing 248 against Sunday play, 160 for and ninety-two abstentions. How could so many of them abstain on a vote of that kind? It clearly wasn't a hidden vote. I suspect a good many of the abstentions would have liked to vote for Sunday play but didn't like to be observed doing so. Perhaps I am totally wrong.

I think we have done sufficient to set the scene for golf in 1920, but perhaps the state of the country, more importantly, should be considered, and women's position within the country. Dealing with the latter first, the emancipation of women was gaining momentum. In 1918, the first women became entitled to vote in political elections, and the following year Nancy Astor became the first female MP. Mrs Ada Summer became the first woman JP. In 1920, Oxford University gave women professors equal status with their male colleagues, and later that year the first hundred women were admitted to study for full degrees. The following year, the university granted an honorary degree to Queen Mary, the first full degree awarded to a woman by that university.

On the medical front and following work and publications by Dr Marie Stopes, the first family-planning clinic was opened in London. On the legal side, on 25 January 1921, six women were sworn in as jurors in the divorce court – the first of their sex to serve in a case concerning marital breakdown. Some feared that the details of the case might shock the ladies, but none chose to stand down. But they were still 'protected' to some extent, as when what were described as 'abominable and beastly letters' were produced in evidence. It was agreed (I don't know by whom) that the content of the letters would offend and even terrify the lady jurors, and therefore only the men were permitted to read them. Can you believe that! Nevertheless, the women had been included in the jury, and progress was being made. A year later Dr Ivy Williams was called to the bar, the first woman barrister in the country. The first advertisements appeared in newspapers for lingerie and underwear, and the new freedom allowed a girl to go to the cinema, unchaperoned, with her boyfriend. Whatever next! Unfortunately, the divorce rates started to go into overdrive, but it can be argued that this was also progress, particularly for the ladies.

The main topic of concern in the country was – as is still the case today, but perhaps less so – the Irish problem. The rebellion in Ireland had led to the formation of the 'black and tans', many of them jobless war veterans from the First World War. They were attached to the Royal Irish Constabulary, but were an elitist group who seemed to be operating under a policy of 'shoot to kill'. In 1921, after much bloodshed, a peace treaty resulted in the formation of the Irish Free State in the south and 'the six counties' in the north. There were many opposed to the treaty and the division of the country, and the same grievance is still with us nearly a century later.

On a lighter note, the Austin Seven motor car was introduced. White lines were painted on the roads to help reduce accidents. Charlie Chaplin returned to his native London and was mobbed by thousands of ecstatic fans. The BBC came into being, and crystal sets were selling at £2. *Woman's Hour* was broadcast for the first time.

3
A STAR IS BORN

This was the country in 1920, as Joyce Wethered, at eighteen years of age, arrived at Sheringham for her first taste of championship golf. The format was one round of medal play to sort out the wheat from the chaff, and the best sixty-four then entered a knockout match play, playing two rounds of the tournament each day, each over eighteen holes, and a thirty-six-hole final.

JW started with an uninspiring ninety-four, but still qualified. She wasn't depressed by the round because her expectations were not high. The format thereafter was knockout match play, and she had hoped perhaps for one good day but expected to be an early casualty. Her friend Molly Griffiths had the lowest qualifying score of eighty-three.

To give some idea of Joyce's standing (or lack of standing) at that time, she was constantly referred to as 'Roger Wethered's sister.' Cecil Leitch, who had been the dominant lady player since well before the war, (you remember, she was the lady who had challenged and beaten Harold Hilton, the Open champion) was the title-holder. Everyone expected her to retain the trophy.

After her indifferent qualifying round, Joyce sailed along quite happily, even though she had the beginnings of some malady not yet diagnosed. Without dwelling on the intermediate rounds, suffice it to say that she found herself through to the final, and in so doing defeated some doughty opponents on the way, including Dolly Fowler, a one-time champion, and Gladys Bastin. In each round she had played in a calm, concentrated manner, assisted by the fact that in the later rounds at least she was not expected to win. I don't think being the underdog quite gives one the advantage that is often stated, but without doubt there is more to gain and less to lose than there is for one's opponent. We will let Joyce talk us through the final, but the pieces in brackets are mine.

On the morning of the final I soon became three down, and at this point my father joined the gallery. He had heard the news on the previous evening and had arrived from London on the milk train in a somewhat surprised and I think resigned state of mind. Cecil had begun with a birdie three at the first hole – an ominous opening to the match – and had secured a lead of four holes by the time we reached the turn. The fact that she failed to collect any more holes in the second nine was a matter of considerable consolation to me. I was even conscious of feeling quite satisfied with the position of affairs at the end of the round, not because I had any thoughts of winning but because I thought that I was putting up quite a good show. The fact that the championship was played in June and on a course that was baked hard as a board had, I am sure, a great deal to do with the final result. The course, though by no means a short one, was in this way very much reduced in length, and a great many of the holes became merely drives and pitches [if that isn't the talk of a champion, I don't know what is], *whereas in ordinary times a full-iron shot or even more would have been needed. The length of our drives often seemed really enormous owing to the dry ground* [modesty!]. *At the downhill holes they went frequently over the 300-yard mark.* [Yes, 300 yards – ladies – in 1920]. *There was one instance in the afternoon, at the twelfth hole of 296 yards, where I remember I found the green from the tee, very luckily* [modesty again] *by running between guarding bunkers, while Cecil's ball lay hole high to the right. Had it not been for the conditions, I should never have produced the string of threes in the afternoon which reduced a deficit of three down to all square in three consecutive holes beginning at the eleventh. This sequence definitely caused the tide to turn in my favour and made all the difference in the result. This only goes to show that a magical effect can come about in a tight game, or even a very doubtful one, with a series of exceptionally good figures. These runs of good fortune come as a pleasant surprise* [they're nothing short of miraculous when they happen to me – which isn't very often] *and what is more important still in match play, have an unwelcome effect* [I love the understatement] *on an opponent in a crisis.*

Joyce wrote the above about fourteen years after the event, so I can't claim that they are the words of an eighteen-year-old, but the modesty shines through all the time. Note to her final paragraph:

Though I finally won by two and one, and it cannot be denied that the result was the biggest surprise that ladies' golf had ever had sprung upon it, I feel that if it had been a question of playing long iron shots against Cecil in those days it would have been a very different story. She stood in a class by herself in that department of the game, and it was due to her example that the prevailing belief amongst the opposite sex that ladies were incapable of hitting an iron shot effectively was at last dissipated.

There was never any boasting in Joyce's triumphs; a quick celebration of her success and then she would divert attention away from herself and applaud the efforts of others. Yes, she was a lady even before she was a Lady.

Joyce had suffered a rising temperature through the week and when all was over she was diagnosed with a very virulent form of whooping cough, which was bad enough to keep her side-lined for three months. She was suspected of passing it on to other competitors, and received an irate letter from the mother of one such asking whether she was aware of what she had given to her daughter. 'I certainly was not; nor do I see how very well I could have avoided it,' was Joyce's tetchy response. She may have been charming, but there are limits.

It was at Sheringham that the famous phrase, 'What train?' originates. Anyone who knows anything about Joyce Wethered whatsoever knows the story, even if they know nothing else about her. In fact, I am tempted to title this book, 'What train?' You will know by now whe-ther I did.

As she was putting for the match on the seventeenth green, a train passed by, hissing and puffing. The spectators were worried that it might disturb her concentration at this most crucial point, but the putt went sweetly into the hole. Asked afterwards if the train hadn't been a nuisance, Joyce replied, 'What train?' Her concentration had been such that she never even noticed it. That concentration was to become one of her hallmarks. With the passage of time, the story has become associated with other courses, but Joyce thought that Sheringham was probably the right venue. Rather than acknowledge that her concentration had been supreme, Joyce offered another explanation. 'Possibly I was so bewildered at the thought of what I was doing that if the very heavens had fallen, I should not have noticed.'

The French Ladies' Open championship took place the following week. JW was not present, as she was in bed with the whooping cough. The degree of interest in golf in France at the time can be judged from the fact that there were only sixteen starters, and just one of them was French! Miss Helme, a golfer of renown, was at the time writing a column for the magazine *Golf Illustrated*. She wrote, 'After all the paraphernalia inevitable in such big affairs as the Open and English Championships, it was extraordinary to go across to France and play with the lightest heart in the world.' The visit was not all light-hearted, however, and she recalled the struggles with French railway porters who manhandled the precious clubs without any idea of their importance or their worth, making her a nervous wreck. She also deplored having to handle the greasy French banknotes. 'They were the one thing we were pleased to leave behind,' she wrote with feeling.

In the following month, at the meeting of the LGU, it was recommended that no lady with a handicap higher than twelve should be allowed to enter national championships. Cecil Leitch, no doubt aware that one bad round could put her out of a championship based on the knockout format, proposed that the early rounds should be based on medal play, with those with the lower totals going forward into a knockout phase. There is little doubt that medal play over a number of rounds produces the most deserving winner, with much less depending upon one brilliant or one terrible round. However, she did not win her way, and the knockout format stayed for several more years. The fact that it did has allowed us to realise the brilliance of Joyce Wethered.

Although in asking this I am getting ahead of myself, just imagine winning five consecutive national championships of the knockout variety, which is what JW achieved in the English championship in the years from 1920 and 1924. It means you can't afford to have one bad round for all of that period; or, put another way, if only sixty-four starters were permitted each year (and I believe in some years it was more), you had to play five matches each year plus two rounds in the final, making seven rounds each year. Over five years that is thirty-five rounds, without losing one of them!

But wait a minute, there was the other major championship each year, the Ladies' British Open. Lo and behold, our heroine landed four of these; and in the other two she played in, she reached the final on one occasion and the semi-final on the other. My calculations show that she lost only twice, therefore, in about seventy rounds.

For the sake of completeness, I should also state that she played in one other national championship – the French – in 1921, and again reached the final.

Joyce Wethered had well and truly arrived on the golfing scene in 1920, but she did not have it all her own way just yet. Cecil Leitch had been queen of British golf and she enjoyed the position. She wasn't going to relinquish the title without a fight. She was an overpowering sort of lady, who could dominate her opponents with her personality as well as her golf. JW was the very antithesis of Cecil, and imposed herself on nobody. She used to wrap herself in her own cocoon of concentration and thus avoided Cecil's presence. Indeed, she claimed to have seldom watched when Cecil played her shots, partly because their styles were so different. Cecil was very strong and gave the ball a good thump with a fast hard swing. Joyce had enormous respect for Cecil's golfing abilities, but she didn't particularly like playing against her. Cecil had an entourage of supporters who were used to seeing her win and Joyce felt there was always an uncomfortable edge to proceedings.

In 1921, their paths soon crossed as they played each other in county matches. Joyce had become the Surrey No. 1 and Cecil already held that position for her county. They played two singles and shared the honours, winning a match each. The Ladies' British Open was held at Turnberry that year, and JW was still not yet twenty. In the first round she was taken to the nineteenth hole by Gladys Bastin, after being one down as she stood on the eighteenth tee. A squeaky start! She had succumbed to a sudden tendency to slice her shots. She still proceeded through the week to the final, but the slice stayed with her and, if anything, had come more into evidence. The other finalist was none other than Cecil Leitch. Cecil played with confidence throughout the match and Joyce had to concede that she was outplayed by a stronger player. By lunchtime Cecil was seven up and although Joyce retrieved three of the holes she was well beaten by four and three.

Bernard Darwin, reporting for *The Times*, attended that championship. He was a good friend of Roger Wethered and, in time, of Joyce, but he had no hesitation in writing that Cecil Leitch was the outstanding figure of the championship. In the very first round she was drawn to play Alexa Stirling, the American champion. It was unfortunate that two prospective finalists should meet so soon. Bernard, a Classics scholar, quoted:

> *One of us two, Herminius,*
> *Shall never more go home.*
> *I will lay on for Tusculum,*
> *And lay thou on for Rome.*

It was a grossly unpleasant day, with strong winds and driving rain. The two ladies were soaked to the skin. They did not have the almost impenetrable golfing wear of today. The grips on their clubs had become impossible, and the greens were crossed by small rivulets, but they produced scores which would have more than done them justice in ideal conditions. Miss Stirling played like a champion, but it was Cecil's day and she was unstoppable.

I have included this short report of the match as a prelude to what I think is the best description of Cecil Leitch that I have seen. A little later we shall hear what JW thought of her arch rival, but for the moment savour this:

> *Miss Leitch was in an irresistible mood. I have a vision of her with her familiar bandeau on her head and some sort of handkerchief knotted round her neck, affronting the tempest, revelling in her defiance of it. The wide stance, the little duck of the right knee, the follow-through that sends the club through low as if boring its way through the wind – all the characteristic movements stand out in memory against the grey and lowering background. Think of Madame Defarge leading the women of St Antoine against the Bastille, think of anything frightfully grand, and you have a picture of Miss Leitch in that match.*

In the French Open at Fontainebleau in June, JW fared even worse against Cecil. It was the first time that Joyce had ventured abroad and she and Molly Griffiths stayed with friends in Paris. There were obviously more competitors than in the previous year, and more French ladies too, because Joyce had the pleasure of playing against one or two of them. Alexa Stirling, the American star who had been knocked out of the British Open by Miss Leitch, was one of the competitors and Joyce played her in the semi-final, winning on the fourteenth green. She thought that Alexa was perhaps more interested in the attractions of Paris than in devoting herself wholeheartedly to the golf, added to which Americans were unused to playing two rounds in a day. Yet another final was Leitch *v.* Wethered and Cecil again went seven up by the end of the first round. This time Joyce could make no impression in the afternoon and lost by seven and six.

It was a thumping and Joyce knew it, and she did not hesitate to acknowledge that Cecil was much the better player in every department of the game. Joyce considered that she had still to prove that Sheringham was no flash in the pan. The fact that she consistently went through to the finals of each tournament beating many good players en route, and was being beaten by only one person, did not appear to occur to her. However pleasant a girl she was, she (possibly unconsciously) had the burning ambition to be number one and did not consider her goal achieved until she was. Cecil went off to America at the time that the English Championship was being played, and so the opportunity to take her on again that year did not materialise. Little did Cecil know at the time, but she would never beat Joyce Wethered again!

The English Open took place at Royal Lytham and St Annes, and JW certainly made hay in Cecil's absence. In the first round, she signalled her intentions by winning by eight and six. This was followed in the second round with a six and five victory. The third was a little less dramatic, being three and two. The fourth round she won comparatively easily by four and three, cruised through the fifth round six and five, and took the semi-final five and four. Her opponent in the final was Mrs Mudford, over thirty-six holes, of course; it was a non-event, with Joyce winning by thirteen and eleven. Poor Mrs Mudford; I will not go into the details, it would be too depressing for her progeny.

1921 was so very nearly brother Roger's year. The British Open (a medal-play event) had returned to the headquarters of golf, St Andrews, and Roger had proceeded very nicely through the first three rounds, with the exception that he had unfortunately trodden on his own ball in the third round and incurred a penalty. One of the American challengers was a Scot, if that makes sense. Jock Hutchison had been born near St Andrews and had caddied there for wealthy American visitors. W.C. Carnegie had been so impressed with him (I told you that not all player/caddie relationships were bad), that he had persuaded him to go back with him in 1904 to Fernandino in Florida, where he became a naturalised American. W.C. Carnegie was the nephew of Andrew Carnegie, and therefore he was not short of a bob or two, and Hutchison became his personal coach and professional. Hutchison won the American PGA Championship and in 1920 just missed taking the American Open by one stroke. He was on a roll when he arrived at St Andrews and of course he knew the terrain like the back of his hand.

There are two stories about Roger Wethered and this championship, and for all I know they could both be true, but I suspect that they are variations of the same story. In the fourth and final round he was drawn to play late in the day. We have to assume that the leaders were not accorded the honour of playing in the last grouping as occurs today. Roger requested that he be given an early start as he was due to play in a cricket match in the London area on the following day! In the event, Roger the amateur and Jock Hutchison the professional tied for first place, and the rules of the time required a replay over thirty-six holes. They liked to milk an event in those days. So we proceed to the second story. Roger was extremely upset at the thought of letting down his cricketing chums and indicated that he would not be able to stay for a play-off the following day. Common sense prevailed, but not before he was persuaded of his priorities and that he should remain for the play-off. Whichever story is correct, it illustrates the lifestyle of well-to-do amateurs in those days. They lived a merry whirl and lived life to the full. The play-off resulted in a win for Hutchison by nine shots, the scores for the two rounds being seventy-four and seventy-six to the winner and seventy-seven and eighty-two to the loser. Those scores are not as bad as they sound for the final of an Open, because the SS (Standard Scratch) scores of most courses in those days was between seventy-five and eighty. During that tournament, Hutchison created a record which I believe still stands to this day. In the first round, he had a hole-in-one at the eighth hole and followed it with a two at the ninth – two consecutive holes in three strokes! He also caused a mighty hoo-ha in the corridors of golfing power, from the fact that he had his clubs deeply grooved for the championship. He knew the course well and the grooves allowed him to stop the ball very quickly on the hard greens. That type of club was later outlawed by the R&A and the

American authorities. People used to get up to all sorts of tricks (many quite legitimate) to give them an advantage over their opponents. A favourite was to allow the face of an iron to become rusty, thereby increasing its holding power on the ball and increasing the backspin. Jock Hutchison was in the news again on 14 June 1922, when he played Joe Kirkwood of Australia over the Old Course. They played the round in one hour and twenty minutes! Hutchison went out in thirty-seven and won by four and three, but of course they played the eighteen holes.

It is always difficult to compare the achievements of players of different eras in a particular sport. So many things change. This is particularly true of golf. A pure comparison of scores alone means nothing. The equipment has changed, the courses have changed, the rules have changed. *The Royal and Ancient Golfers' Handbook* for 1998 includes the average winning scores in the Open, decade by decade (excluding the war years):

1905–14	302	1956–65	280
1920–29	295	1966–75	280
1930–39	289	1976–85	277
1946–55	284	1986–95	273

The falling totals in themselves mean little, but they do give an indication of what was considered a good score in a particular decade. It will be noted that between 1920–29, when Joyce Wethered and her contemporaries were playing, and 1986–95, the most recent period available, there is a fall of twenty-two shots, i.e. 5.5 shots per round. Crudely, therefore, one might say that a seventy played in the 1920s is equivalent to a sixty-four played in the 1980/1990s. That is for men's golf. When looking at scores in the Wethered era, this might be helpful.

Before we leave the 1921 Open, I think you may like to know that Bobby Jones was a competitor in the event. Bobby had many glorious days in tournaments and became a great friend of the Wethereds. Indeed, he was Joyce's hero, and we shall dwell more on this later, but things went sadly astray in 1921 and I'm sorry to report that he tore up his card in the third round after a string of bad holes. He was only nineteen at the time, being a few months younger than JW, and it distressed him for the rest of his life that he had acted in such a boorish manner. He had come over to Britain as the youngest member of the American Walker Cup side and helped them to win, but his performance in the British Amateur at Hoylake was less than inspiring as he tumbled out in the fourth round. His first visit to Britain gave little indication that he would become the golfing idol of not only the Americans but the British also.

Roger Wethered had many successful days on the golf course, not least in the Walker Cup matches against the United States. In the very first of these matches in America, at Long Island in 1922, he and Aylmer were the only winners in the foursomes, winning by five and four. In 1923 he again was a winner in the foursomes, this time by six and five with Cyril Tolley. He also halved his singles match against Ouimet, though that must have been a great disappointment as he needed to win the game to give the home side a tie in the overall match result. He was two up with three to play but his opponent finished 3, 4, 3 against 4, 4, 4, and United States won by one point.

In 1926 he played in his third Walker Cup and again won in the foursomes, playing with E. Holderness. That year he also won his singles match. In 1930 he played in his fourth Walker Cup, this time as captain, and once more won his foursomes match, with Cyril Tolley once again. He had a most impressive record against the US. He had other notable achievements, but we will leave those for later.

1921 was also notable in the golfing world for the introduction of the first limitations on the size and weight of the ball. The R&A and the USPGA agreed that, after 1 May, the weight of the ball should not be greater than 1.62 ounces (45.88g) and the diameter not less than 1.62in (41.55mm).

1920 had seen Joyce Wethered opening the door on an illustrious career, 1921 was a year of hovering on the threshold, but 1922 saw her firmly established as the first lady of golf, and she was still only twenty. The Prince of Wales was captain of the Royal and Ancient that year and he was by no means the first 'royal' to have that honour. Indeed, the previous Prince of Wales, later to become Edward VII, had also been a captain. Edward's brother, George VI, as Duke of York kept up what had almost become a tradition. Other royal personalities to enjoy the honour were the Duke of Kent and Prince Leopold. If they could play golf, or rather, if they played golf, they were almost bound to get the call. I haven't researched the handicaps of any of them, but you can't help wondering how they achieved their handicaps. It must have been somewhat embarrassing. If a high handicap was accorded a royal person, it would appear an insult to someone who was used to being appointed to the top of the tree – head of state, head of the armed forces, etc. How could you say, 'Well, you aren't very good, so we will give you a twenty-four handicap'. On the other hand, you could not give a low handicap if it was not deserved, because he would not be able to play to it, and he would be beaten every time. It would cost him a small fortune. I expect that problem could partly be overcome by always playing in four balls and ensuring that the royal person had a damned good partner. Of course, I am writing of yesteryear. Today, I am pretty sure that even the Duke of York (2003 captain of the R&A) would have to earn his handicap – yet another disadvantage of royalty getting closer to the people. They can't win, can they....

A joke from 1922:

> *The Major: 'Now caddie, I've never played this course so I want you to point out the bunkers to me.' He proceeds to hit a long ball slightly off line. The caddie: 'That's one of them ye're in now, sir.'*

Another 1922 joke:

> *Sandy, the taciturn Scots professional, had partnered a city gent of limited ability and pulled him through to a win. On being congratulated on his faultless round, he responded, 'I'm sae busy correctin ither fowk I've nae time for makin' faults myself'.*

The Ladies' British Open was played at Prince's, Sandwich, on the Kent coast, an old club with a long tradition, though most of the early championships were played on the St George's course, rather than Prince's, which had now come into its own. It is a links course and the golfer needs to be on her game to play it. The narrow fairways require accuracy off the tee and straightness thereafter, and the course is long and heavily bunkered. If the wind gets up, a difficult course becomes very difficult. In the magazine, *Golfing*, a week or two before the event, there was a letter which reveals that the par for the course for the ladies was eighty-two, and that off the everyday tees. They had elected to play off the back tees at the same par total. The correspondent thought this iniquitous and did not think that there would be more than three who would score less than eighty-eight. The letter is signed 'Anon', so we do not know the gender of the correspondent, and whether it was a lady paling at the thought of what was to be required of her, or whether it was a chivalrous man with a Sir Walter Raleigh disposition. I don't suppose the letter had a jot of effect on those administering the tournament, but a decision was made not to play off the back tees, which was just as well as the weather was pretty awful.

Prior to the championship proper, the home internationals were played as had become the tradition. England was dominant and dropped only one game out of nine in each match. Their dominance was confirmed in the championship, as the last eight surviving competitors were all English. In the championship, JW had little trouble in progressing through to the final, though Mrs Bond of Ashdown Forest took her to the seventeenth before going down by two and one. JW also had the benefit of three stymies in this match and an in–off when her shot hit the opponent's ball.

Stymies were still played at that time. The balls on the green were not marked as they are today; they were left where they had come to rest. If the player furthest from the hole and therefore the next to play found that her opponent's ball lay on her line to the hole, that was a stymie. In such circumstances the player could either play as close to the hole as she was able, avoiding the other ball, or she could attempt to jump her ball over the other ball. This, of course, originated from the fact that the greens in former times were quite uneven and players often putted with a club with an inclined face rather than a straight face. Players were quite within their rights 'to lay a stymie' by positioning their ball on the line of their opponent's putt.

There was one American and one Canadian playing in the championship, both characters by the sound of it, though neither lasted very long. Miss Rosa Stockwood was the sole United States representative, famous for the fact that two years previously she had run a spike into her foot but insisted on completing the round on crutches.

Molly McBride, the Canadian, was a chain-smoker and had a cigarette in her mouth throughout her round, even when playing her shots. She had the dubious distinction of losing by seventeen with fifteen to play in the Canadian Open, to no less than Cecil Leitch.

Cecil had suffered an injury to her hand whilst in America and it was to give her trouble for the next two years, but it did not prevent her proceeding through all the rounds to the final, beating Gladys Bastin by six and four in the semi-final. JW's successes included a seven- and- six win over Miss McCulloch, and a five- and- four win over Joan Stocker in the semi-final.

This was the fourth knockout championship in succession that had resulted in a Wethered/Leitch final. There was no seeding of players, so they were totally at the mercy of the luck of the draw. The odds against Wethered and Leitch not being drawn in the same half of the draw for four tournaments in succession makes one wonder. Surely the ladies of the LGU weren't cooking the books, so to speak? If they were, they were providing just the finals the spectators wanted to see.

Cecil appeared unusually nervy in the final, and allowed a boisterous crowd to affect her concentration. She was particularly upset by photographers clicking their cameras at the wrong moments. Let us hear what JW has to say about the match:

Cecil and I met once more in the final. A gale was blowing for much of the day, and we had to walk with our eyes shielded against the sand. As far as I was concerned, the more frequently we met, my chances would improve. Unlike Cecil, I was still considered the underdog and therefore I had nothing to lose. It is exciting to know that one has a chance to unseat the champion. By the time we reached the turn in the morning round, I knew that I was at least making a match of it and that was a great relief. At the end of the morning round I was one up and there had been little to choose between us. Cecil's recoveries were disconcertingly brilliant. Her chipping and putting were admirable and she has always possessed the faculty for sinking a long putt at the appropriate moment. I was kept on tenterhooks for most of the time. As a matter of fact I had gained very considerably in length since the Turnberry days. So far from being out-driven I proved, I think, to be the stronger player of the two, in being able very often to play iron shots where Cecil was compelled to play a wood.

That last statement would have given Joyce considerable satisfaction. You will recall that when she won at Sheringham, she had admitted that Cecil hit the longer ball and had conditions not been so dry, allowing a deal of run on the ball, she would have been hard put to take the title. By dedication and practise, by watching others and imitating their swings, she had advanced on to a plane of her own. She was good at all departments of the game and she was one of the longest hitters to boot. I think Cecil, who had held the British title for eight years (including the war years when play was suspended) knew how much Joyce had improved and feared the worst, even as she stood on the first tee of this final. She was unaccountably and uncharacteristically nervy; a lady who usually exuded confidence and struck fear into the hearts of her opponents.

In the afternoon round, Cecil collapsed. How would Joyce describe that?

The result I attribute to two reasons. For one thing, I was definitely a longer player from the tee and through the green than I had been [she was really chuffed about that], and secondly Cecil was suffering from arm trouble which would keep her out of the game for the best part of two years. My belief, however, is that her play was not seriously affected in the morning, nor had it been through the week, as her spoon and brassie shots were so accurate and deadly that I gained little advantage, if any, in using a shorter club. What effect it had on the collapse in the afternoon, I cannot say. For my own part I saw my chances in sight, got a good start and was able to put on a little extra pressure in consequence. The run of the game changed completely and the close tussle of the morning lapsed rather dismally. Cecil halved the first, won the sixth and left me the rest and the match finished on the eleventh green.

What Joyce omitted to say was that she played exceedingly well in the afternoon. She was on the 411-yard second in two, holed a twenty-foot putt for a three on the short third, and laid her spoon at the 200-yard fifth within ten feet of the hole; and this was in the face of gale-force winds. Meanwhile, Cecil went to pieces. She was on the 480-yard sixth in two to win the hole, and temporarily halted the rout, but a camera clicked as she was at the top of her swing on the very next hole and she topped her drive. She had let the audience get to her and appeared almost relieved to concede the eleventh and her title.

In July of that year, Cecil brought out a book which had been written in advance of proceedings at Prince's. It is evident from what she had to say about Joyce Wethered that she already had an admiration for her and knew that she was a very great threat to Cecil's previous supremacy. Cecil wrote:

She is absolutely at home with any club, and the game is no trouble to her. I have met her on five occasions, and on each she has treated me to an exhibition of her ability to secure a sequence of holes in or under par figures. She never knows when she is beaten; in fact she appears to be at her best when down. Her wonderful temperament is that of an experienced veteran, and she never shows a sign of nervousness. There can be little doubt that Miss Wethered's accuracy and length are largely the result of a straight left drive throughout the swing.

In a chapter devoted to putting, she says:

If I were to name the lady golfer whom I consider to be the best and soundest putter, I should say Miss Joyce Wethered, without a doubt. This wonderful player has a sound method of hitting the ball, which appears to be the result of study and practice. The firm stance, the still head, the short straight backward movement of the club-head, the decided hit, and the short follow through are clearly demonstrated in Miss Wethered's method of putting, and the results prove the soundness of it.

There is even more tribute to Miss Wethered's morale in a crisis. Referring to Sheringham, she writes, 'She seemed oblivious that she was fighting out the final of the first championship in which she had ever taken part... She showed herself to be in the possession of the real match-playing temperament.'

It is incredible that the indisputably best player in Britain for the last decade should write in such terms about a relative newcomer, a twenty-year-old. The fact that these tributes come from Cecil Leitch can only indicate what an impression JW was making on the golfing world. They also indicate that Cecil entered the Prince's final with at least a great deal of apprehension, if not fear, that she was about to meet her match. It wasn't true that Joyce did not suffer butterflies in the stomach like almost every other competitor in sport. She just had the good sense not to display them.

In 1922 Joyce Wethered was 'formidable', as the French would say. Strangely, the same word in English carries nowhere near the same authority. She had won the Surrey title for the second year running. In April she had won the Ranelagh Challenge Gold Medal, one of the most prestigious amateur events in the country. In October she would win the Worplesden Mixed Doubles, playing with her brother, the most important event of that type in the amateur calendar. She had taken the British title from the former holder, and a little later she took the English Ladies' title for the third year in succession. I expect that she won a host of lesser events, also, but the records of those have not come to my notice. She really did appear to have become invincible. Walter Hagen wrote on JW: 'When she is playing only mediocre stuff for her, she can still give strokes to any woman golfer in the world. When she is at the top of her game, there is not another woman player in the same class.' And that was from a man who was not only a champion himself, but someone who coached the best ladies in America.

Not content with demonstrating her golfing prowess on the field of play, Joyce now took up the pen and put her methods and ideas into print, and, as I keep reiterating, this girl was still only twenty. Imagine a twenty-year-old today writing a book on how to play golf – however good he or she might be, it would be treated with outrage. 'Who does she think she is?' and stronger remonstrations would rain down upon her. Sergio Garcia gets a bit cocky at times and the wrath of the press and elder statesmen soon put him in his place. But to write a book of instruction? I don't think even Sergio would contemplate that.

So, if Miss Wethered was the shy retiring sort of person I have maintained, why was she writing a book of golfing instruction, before she had even come of age? There is a simple answer and it is this: her brother Roger had established himself as one of the best amateurs in the country. He had contested the British Open itself at St Andrews the previous year. He had always been fascinated with the theory of the game and mixed with the elite of amateur golf, with whom he debated the finer points. More importantly, he had a reputation for good sense and was quickly being accepted as an authority on the game. He enjoyed the debating and contributed articles to golfing magazines exploring one theory or another. He must have discussed these theories with his father, who was a reasonable golfer himself. Now,

Herbert Newton Wethered was an author. Indeed, later in 1933 he would write a book himself, entitled *The Perfect Golfer*, and he would write a book in 1929 with the well-known golf course architect, T. Simpson, on *The Architectural side of Golf*. Without a doubt, Roger would receive considerable encouragement from his father to put his thoughts into print.

How did Joyce become involved? The Wethereds were a close-knit family. Roger and Joyce had been privately educated at home. They were both still single and living at home. Joyce may have been somewhat reserved in company, but she had a mind of her own and would not have been slow to throw in her ha'p'orth of opinion when a point was being debated. We can only surmise how the dual authorship came about. Perhaps their father (or mother) suggested it. Perhaps Roger invited Joyce's participation. I am fairly certain that the idea did not come from Joyce herself. She was too modest to have promoted herself to that degree at such a tender age. However, the decision was made, and of one thing I am absolutely certain, when Joyce agreed to play her part, she would have done so in the knowledge that she could carry out her task competently. She was not the sort of woman to blunder into a commitment without being confident that she could produce the goods.

Joyce's decision to help write the book illustrated the confidence which she had in knowing how to play her shots. She was not a boastful person, she would certainly not write for the pleasure and self-satisfaction of seeing herself in print. She would write factually and honestly, making a record of her methods. To do that meant that she fully understood why she was executing the strokes as she did. She may have grooved her swing by watching and imitating those she admired, but she knew why that type of swing produced as it did, and what would result if various amendments were made. In short, she was not just a natural ball-player, who could score well without really knowing why. She was a player who understood the theory of the golf swing. I feel that this is one very good reason why she was the greatest lady golfer of the twentieth century. She had to use her brain to take her to the pinnacle of achievement which she reached. She was not a natural golfer or a child prodigy; she had to work hard, with both muscle and brain, over a number of years to accomplish her skills. The reward was that, when she hit a good shot, she knew exactly why she had done so, and when things went awry, again she knew the reason. After that, it was mostly a case of concentration to put into practice all that she knew; and there was nobody, but nobody, better at concentration than Joyce Wethered.

The book which the two Wethereds wrote was called *Golf from Two Sides*, produced in 1922; the publishers were Longmans, Green and Co. of 39 Paternoster Row, London, EC4. The dedication at the front is to their mother, with the words, 'In recollection of numerous games and much affectionate encouragement.'

There is a delightful photograph, as frontispiece, of them both in the golfing clothes of the time. Roger sports plus-twos with tartan socks, a hacking jacket with patch pockets, shirt and tie and tweed cloth cap. His sister wears a heavy mid-calf length tweed skirt, a white blouse with a large collar, a long woolly cardigan, and a brimmed hat. They present a handsome, smiling pair. Roger was well over six-feet tall and Joyce was not more than an inch or two off six feet. Both were of slim build.

The first chapter of the book, written mainly by Roger, exposes their mutual great delight in the game of golf and utter dedication to the pursuit of its pleasures. It is not intended to consider the contents of the book at length, and the instructional part hardly at all, as Joyce later wrote another book which benefits from several more years of experience. There are one or two sections, however, which warrant comment.

At one point, Joyce compares tennis and golf for ladies and the needs and impacts of the two. She concludes that golf results in more nervous strain, and thinks that the physical exhaustion which is often felt may be as much due to this as to the more protracted exertion on a golf links. I wonder what the tennis players thought of that. She certainly played tennis, but not to championship standard, though it was rumoured in 1925 when she withdrew from championship golf that she would be taking up tennis. Modern tennis certainly requires better physical fitness than golf. I won't enter into a debate on which causes the most nervous strain.

She reveals that women were regarded as inferior to men in several ways. Strength and power are perhaps acknowledged even today, but in 1922 women were considered to be intellectually unable to appreciate the science and mechanics of the game. Don't forget, it wasn't many decades previously that women of class were discouraged from anything requiring any physical effort. Joyce commented on her brother refusing to answer her questions on certain aspects of the game. He said that she should find out for herself, and in that way she would benefit. A bit hard, but I suppose it is correct that to know 'how' to do something is good, but to additionally know 'why' makes you much wiser and able to benefit.

There is one lovely piece in the book, a chapter on 'Boys and Girls' golf. After a round of golf, Roger would resort to the library to try to reason out a problem. He expected Joyce to exhibit the same zeal for discovery. Her feeble attempts to play a correct shot would bring forth, 'Oh Joyce, you will never play golf; you won't study the game.' She says, 'It was rather severe to expect a mere girl of eleven to play mashie shots in the manner prescribed by J.H. Taylor!'

Joyce had this to say about her brother's attitude:

> Roger said that it was no use telling me anything, since I should never be any good until I found out things for myself. The warning might not have been too acceptable at the moment, but the principle he expressed was sound. How often one hears on the links the question asked: "What am I doing wrong?" The expectation is an answer which will supply a cut-and-dried remedy, some specific which will immediately effect an infallible cure. This cannot be done, or very rarely. The playing of golf is an art, and just as art is a matter that closely concerns the individual, so it is necessary for everyone to discover the nature of their own faults. The principles of the game require a lucid explanation, but the working out of their application must be largely self-taught.

Can I be bold enough to disagree with Joyce on this occasion? For a person of her abilities and ambition she may be correct, but there are many people who would never fathom out a correct procedure if left to their own devices. She goes on to say:

> My feeling is that ladies are too inclined to seek for mechanical excellence. Lessons from professionals rather tend to foster this inclination. Not that the professional is in any way to blame if he teaches on the lines of a drill-sergeant. It is difficult to see what other course he could very well adopt. Much can undoubtedly be learnt in this way; but to acquire that extra knowledge which is essential, there is probably not one lady in twenty who will try to penetrate to the root of her troubles and work out her own golfing salvation. With even the best players, whoever they may be, it is a

continual fight against one fault after another; and it is necessary to have at one's disposal the power and means of remedying these faults before they take too firm a hold.

JW had only the occasional lesson; indeed, it is often written that she had only one throughout her career, though that is incorrect, but she became a champion and the reason is that she had all the basic abilities to become a champion, including the ability to work out her own salvation. Many people do not have that ability.

JW's thoughts on practise might be surprising and not accord with the opinions of many of the best professionals. She states:

It is common to see players take out a number of balls and produce the same shot repeatedly in the belief that practise makes perfect. Theoretically this should be so; but practically I have found it worse than useless to repeat shots in practise when once the correct result has been found; you are only wasting good strokes. By all means take out a club which has been giving trouble and endeavour to cure any mischief which may have arisen. But, having once hit upon a satisfactory remedy, do not for the moment try to improve upon it. It may appear paradoxical to say so, but I nevertheless believe it to be a fact that the more often you play a shot, ball after ball, correctly, the greater the certainty that presently some error will make its appearance, and the excellence of the discovery which corrected the stroke will have lost half its efficacy.

Mmm! This is what she thought at twenty. Later, we will hopefully learn what her thoughts were on the same subject at thirty-two, when she wrote her second book and after another twelve years of experience. In the joint book, Roger startled readers with the theory that there was an American style of play, which he considered in many ways to be superior to that of the British. He had the benefit of a prolonged visit to the United States in 1920, when he was able to witness at first hand both amateurs and professionals. He, no doubt, was prompted to write about American golf because of the impact which they were making on the golfing scene. His conclusions were that they had sought to extract the essential principles of the various strokes and to establish a particular style – a style constructed upon orthodox lines, but cutting out all 'frills' and unnecessary trick shots, thus making the game simpler and more easily repeatable. He was much taken with the American ability to play shots with backspin, and noted that they played shots with 'draw' rather than with 'cut', which was the accepted method in Britain. He thought that they had a different method of swinging the club, more likely to preserve rhythm, which is a prime requisite of any golf shot, whilst also going for strength and distance. This was achieved by cultivating a large and deliberate backswing with a correspondingly long recovery in the follow-through. He acknowledged that their courses were more often inland than in Britain and less prone to the wind often experienced on our links courses, but still considered that their method would benefit British players. At that time, there was a good deal of unorthodoxy, particularly amongst amateurs in Britain. To incorporate a twirl at the top of the swing or an exaggerated waggle at the address was almost a way of putting one's signature on a swing, so that it could be distinguished from the swings of others.

Returning to the championship golf of JW, we travel to Hunstanton, the venue for the English Ladies' Championship in 1922. Could she make it three in a row? Her chief memories of that particular champion-ship were regarding the course itself. She remembered it as being ideal for ladies, in that a succession of holes required two good shots to reach the green. Particularly she remembered the first hole with affection, because it had character and challenge, probably two good reasons that most of the ladies remembered it without affection. Quite correctly, she recalled how many courses start with a rather dull hole devoid of interest, often designed as such to ensure few hold-ups, I imagine. At Hunstanton, the opening hole required a drive over a large and inviting bunker, 'which was calculated to strike terror into the heart of a player or else inspire an invigorating sense of adventure.' It would certainly have been the latter option in Joyce's case. With the wind against, the first drive at Hunstanton required a full-blooded blow; no chance of scurrying one straight but half-heartedly to find the security of the fairway.

Joyce did win her third successive English title, but not before she had weathered (or wethered) Molly Gourlay in a very tight semi-final. She had been three up at the turn, but Molly had taken the next three holes to equalise the scores. Following a ding-dong battle, JW had the opportunity to take the lead on the seventeenth, only to miss a two-foot putt. Miss Gourlay almost holed a birdie on the last green, which would have taken her through to the final. 'Almost' is the magic word of golf, rivalled only by 'if only'. How many have at last retired to their beds, exhausted from the memory of what might have been, only to rise on the morrow with renewed vigour and determination; hope lies eternal. Molly had missed her chance. The duo returned to that first hole, and the very sight of that gaping bunker, which might have cowed a lesser mortal, inspired Joyce to hit a stormer right over the top and down the middle. Molly was undone.

The other finalist was Joan Stocker, and history has it that she did not sleep a wink the night before the match. Joyce had never suffered from such problems, but she did reveal that she sometimes had nightmares when her backswing would remain obstinately aloft and refuse to return to ground. Ever positive in thought, Joyce decided that she would prefer the odd nightmare to tossing and turning when sleep will not come.

Joyce had an excellent opening eighteen holes and went round in seventy-four to give her a lead of five holes at lunch time. Her modest report of the remainder states, 'Though I began by losing the first two holes in the afternoon, the match came to an end on the twelfth green.' Another resounding victory!

4
HALCYON DAYS

By 1923, Roger Wethered was casting around for suitable employment, no doubt in the realisation that there must be more to life
than golf, golf, and yet more golf. It is not clear whether he seriously
contemplated a political career, but he took up an appointment as
secretary to the Hon. F.S. Jackson, who in the new government had
been appointed financial secretary to the War Office. This was the
selfsame F.S. Jackson who had captained England at cricket. There
were many light-hearted comments when Roger's appointment was
announced, from irreverent friends, suggesting that the real object
of the appointment was the improvement of the financial secretary's
golf by a little quiet practise over the winter in Whitehall, chipping
paper balls into waste-paper baskets and the like. In fact, Jackson was
already a very good golfer, playing off a handicap of +1, so the jokes
were a little wide of the mark. It is interesting to note that Roger's
appointment carried no salary, so perhaps he was simply gaining
experience of life in politics and he was seriously considering a career
in that direction.

A small extract in *Golfing* magazine has reminded me that America was
in the time of prohibition, not something that was popular with all its
residents. The magazine included a four-line stanza:

> *Four and twenty Yankees, feeling very dry,*
> *Went across to Canada to get a drink of rye,*

When the rye was opened the Yanks began to sing,
To blazes with the President! God save the King!"

It is quite amazing to realise that the prohibition laws were not repealed until 1933. How would our lager louts today have survived in that administration?

It was also the year that Jack Hobbs scored his 100th century in first-class cricket.

The Golf Hotel at Woodhall Spa was typical of many such establishments, as it advertised for customers with the enticing statement that there was 'electric light throughout.' Down in the South-West, the Mullion Cove Hotel claimed to be the only first-class licensed hotel on the Mullion Coast. What is more, it boasted five single fireproof lock-up garages (asbestos, I suppose), and declared its 'sanitation and water supply unexceptional.' Work that one out, if you can!

Silver King golf balls advertised the 'Green Dot' (floater), made in two sizes. The smaller was suitable for skilful golfers of middle age, men or women, as its size enabled experts to reap the benefit of their skill when playing into the wind. It appears that it must have been permissible to use different size balls in those days.

A new money-spinner had just been unearthed by golf clubs, municipal authorities, seaside resorts etc. – the putting green, or putting course, as it was called. One company which researched this innovation in a professional marketing manner concluded that, 'even at 2d per round, there is always a big credit balance at the end of the year.'

Further information on the cost of living reveals that Three Nuns cigarettes of pure Virginia tobacco cost 6d for a packet of ten. I expect Woodbines undercut that by a margin. A new Harris or Shetland tweed golf-suit could be purchased from Alderton and Sons (Tailors) for £6 16s 6d. At North Berwick, Burgh Golf Club advertised for 100 new members with no entrance fee required and annual subscriptions of only £1 5s, including green fees. How did they do it?

Joyce Wethered, now established and acknowledged by all as the best lady golfer in Britain and still only twenty-one, now had another superb year, albeit not without one stutter, at least. She revealed earlier that she was subject to occasional nightmares, and now we discover that she was also a mite superstitious, though she would have strenuously denied it. When she won the British Open at Prince's, she went to her room in the interval in the final, and lying upon her bed was a black cat which she had never set eyes upon previously. The fact that she recalled the event suggests that she was not immune to the superstitions which beset most of us. Moreover, she recalled that the following year, when the British Open was held at the seaside links at Burnham and Berrow, she was somewhat disturbed to see a vase of peacock's feathers standing on their sitting-room mantelpiece. 'They struck me immediately I saw them as not the best of omens.'

It is typical of Joyce that she remembered much more about this week in her life due to her brother's exploits than her own. But let us first see what happened in Burnham. The British Ladies' Open should have been held there in 1919, but it had to be cancelled due to the railway strike. The very means of opening the country to more travel and easier access to sporting events also had the power to control and curtail such activities. Joyce had an easy run to the semi-finals, winning her matches by 8 and 6, 7 and 5, 6 and 5, 7 and 5, and 2 and 1. In the semis she met the redoubtable Mrs Allan Macbeth, who clinched a closely fought contest with a birdie two at the seventeenth hole to win by two and one. For most ladies, reaching the semi-final of an event would have meant success, but for JW it would be comparative failure. Unfortunately for Mrs Macbeth, on the following day, she lost the final on the last green to Miss D.E. Chambers. After overcoming the favourite, she could have expected something better. 'If only...'

The Men's Amateur Open championship was being played in the same week, at Deal in Kent. Roger Wethered had proceeded through the preliminary rounds, emulating his sister at Burnham. The men's competition was played over a period one day longer than the ladies, and the final of the men's therefore fell on the day after the final of the ladies'. Family loyalties meant that Joyce was just as keen for her brother to do well as she herself, but although she had failed in the semis, she was much too polite to abandon the ladies' final at Burnham and get over to Deal. However, having watched the ladies' final, the news came through that Roger had beaten the great American amateur Francis Ouimet, and would be facing Robert Harris in the final the following day.

The Wethereds, in other words, Joyce and her father and mother, who had been with her in Burnham, sat down to dinner that evening as civilised folk do. I haven't discovered whether it was a formal dinner laid on by the Ladies' Golf Union or whether it was an informal family affair. It doesn't matter. The British upper middle classes of the period knew their priorities, and dinner was enjoyed. Immediately thereafter, the family motored to London. Joyce said that it was a beautiful moonlit night and they wasted little time in reaching London. I wonder, with the cars and roads of those days, how long it did take. Whatever – they arrived in the capital at about five o'clock in the morning, snatched two hours sleep and then caught the eight o'clock boat-train to Dover. A chartered car took them along the coast to Deal, and by the time they arrived the final had reached the thirteenth hole. As they arrived, a ball descended with a thump, literally at their feet. It was by way of Roger's greeting. He was already several holes up and proceeded to an easy victory by seven and six. The weather was atrocious, as sleet, hail, wind and rain vied for dominance, but the Wethered camp was happy, another championship was in the bag.

It is a strange fact that although Joyce and Roger won through to a number of British Open finals and semi-finals, there was only one brief period of ten days in 1924 when they both held their crowns simultaneously.

The English Ladies' Championship in 1923 was played at Ganton, near Scarborough. Joyce's mother, it will be recalled, was formerly Marion Lund and hailed from Yorkshire, and therefore Joyce knew the area around Malton well as she spent many holidays in her childhood staying with her cousins, playing in the woods, building log cabins, having paper chases and similar childhood pursuits. She was similarly accommodated for the championship. Her cousins were not golfers, they were of the hunting set, and Joyce suggested that the two hobbies of golf and hunting seldom went together. I suppose she is correct. Joyce travelled each day to Ganton and then returned to the bosom of the family at Malton, where the younger cousins didn't quite appreciate the seriousness of the situation and were treating her golfing ambitions in a very light-hearted manner. The weather was foul for part of the week, with gale-force winds blowing. Some of the lesser competitors found it a terrible trial and holes were even halved in double figures.

In the second round, JW was taken to the seventeenth green before overcoming Daisy Hartill by three and one. It might have been closer, as Daisy lost her cool at the second hole and picked up her ball when in fact she still had a putt for a half. A description in *The Times* of the pair playing the short fifth hole that day read:

At the short fifth, an iron shot of 153 yards, with the wind blowing at terrific force across the hole, was a test of one's golfing ability to control the ball. Miss Hartill's shot was blown like a shuttlecock away to the right and in the end was further from the hole than when she started. Miss Wethered on the other hand played a push iron shot into the wind with such perfect judgement that the ball fell lifeless within five yards of the pin.

Class will usually tell. To be fair to Miss Hartill, a report on the match in the *Morning Post* stated that Miss Hartill often outdrove Miss Wethered.

In the next round JW was, as she put it, harried all the way to the seventeenth green, before disposing of Joan Charles by two and one. The 'stymie' played a major part in the outcome of this match. At the sixteenth hole, both players cut their tee shots, but whilst Mrs Charles' ball was buried in gorse, Miss Wethered's was playable. However, Mrs Charles recovered to reach the green and lay Miss Wethered a dead stymie. Joyce lofted her ball over that of her opponent and left it right on the edge of the hole, thus stymieing Mrs Charles in turn. She apologised to her opponent, but had won the hole and, as it proved, the match. Thereafter things became a little easier for Joyce, and she won her succeeding rounds by 6 and 4, 6 and 5, and 7 and 5.

JW's iconic status is demonstrated by a piece in *The Times*, when the championship had reached the quarter-finals: 'Chief interest centres on the match between Miss Chambers and Mrs Macbeth, because whoever wins will, in all probability, meet Miss Wethered in the final on Friday.'

In the semi-finals appeared Mrs Macbeth, who, it will be remembered, eliminated Joyce at the same stage in the British Open earlier in the year at Burnham. On this occasion they were in opposite halves of the draw, and Joyce admitted to some relief when Mrs Macbeth fell to her opponent, Mrs Lodge. The latter lady was a Surrey player and therefore well known to Joyce. The young cousins were still having their fun at Joyce's expense and gravely predicted that Joyce would have to be at her very best to beat Mrs Lodge, who they had watched in the semi-final and who they declared to be playing extremely well. In the event, Mrs Lodge had a day when every bunker seemed to attract her ball and the match was over halfway through the afternoon round, with Joyce winning by the convincing margin of eight and seven.

Mrs Lodge had a handicap of five at the time she played in this event, so she did exceedingly well to reach the final. JW's figures for the final make impressive reading:

Morning round   4 5 4 4 3 5 6 4 5 = 40
                       3 4 4 4 5 6 4 5 4 = 39

Afternoon round   4 5 4 4 4 5 5 5 4 = 40
                     3 4

They are a model of consistency, taking into account the atrocious weather, and you will be interested to learn that the bogey, equivalent to the Standard Scratch score, at Ganton at the time was eighty.

Joyce particularly remembered that championship win for her victory speech. This was a part of the proceedings she did not particularly enjoy; she would have preferred to have taken her trophy and quietly slipped away. Indeed, more than once, she referred to prize-givings as 'very trying occasions.' I suppose most of us would love to have to suffer such trauma – just occasionally! At Ganton, she gave her usual polite but brief address, thanking and applauding others whilst totally ignoring her own achievement. Afterwards, her uncle declared that she had missed a golden opportunity to refer to her Yorkshire extraction on her mother's side, and she immediately appreciated her omission, a fact which stayed with her for the remainder of her life. A huge win by a Yorkshire lass in front of a Yorkshire crowd!! She could have milked that for all it was worth; and the majority went away not even knowing that they had been watching one of their own.

Newspaper reports of the time said: 'Even Harry Vardon at the zenith of his fame did not occupy a position of such isolated splendour as does Miss Wethered in golf. It may well be that only W.G has stood so pre-eminent in his own domain as does Joyce Wethered in hers.' That is some tribute. The great Dr W.G. Grace is still regarded by many as the best English cricketer ever.

'Frequently she reached greens of 500 yards in two.' Sometimes the reports went a little over the top, witness *The Times* correspondent at the Ladies' Autumn Foursomes, played at Ranelagh, under the sponsorship of the magazine, *Eve.* 'It was not merely that Miss Wethered never made the semblance of a bad shot. So far as I saw, she never made an ordinary one. They were all winners.' This competition was a handicap, so that JW and her partner, Mrs Hambro, found themselves giving shots in each match they played. The newspaper reports of the time illustrated Miss Wethered's unique position with comments such as, 'It was soon evident that the result of Miss Wethered's game was a foregone conclusion so that it was not worth following it any further...', and '...her opponents seemed overawed by the occasion.' In the semi-final, it was reported that she was again at her very best, '... she retrieved every slip that Mrs Hambro made, slips that severally and collectively must have proved fatal with any other partner.' Needless to say, the redoubtable pair won the competition (in miserable driving rain) and each received silver cups which would not have fitted on any but the largest of mantlepieces.

In the Worplesden Mixed Foursomes that year, JW had her first hole-in-one, but we will return to that because the Worplesden Foursomes played a major part in her life over a long period, far beyond when she had finished with Open Championships and the like.

There was much more golf in 1923, of course, but we will dwell upon only a selection of the happenings. In the autumn, Cecil Leitch returned to competitive golf after eighteen months on the sidelines with a troublesome arm. The Wethered/Leitch encounter at the head of the Surrey/Middlesex match was anticipated with eagerness by the golfing set. Unfortunately, at the last minute, Cecil, who had a very bad cold, was advised by her doctor to withdraw from the encounter. The golfing public who had been deprived of a battle royal did not have long to wait, for the return match took place the following month at Northwood. A thousand spectators turned out to watch this county fixture, or should I say to watch the Misses Wethered and Leitch. The result was a convincing win by five and three for Miss Wethered.

Did Miss Wethered ever lose? Well, yes, she did. Not often, mind you. There had to be exceptional circumstances. Mrs Cautley, captaining Kent ladies against Surrey, achieved the impossible on one occasion. Kent lost by six matches to one, but the win over JW was so unexpected that it almost appeared that they had won. Mrs Cautley played inspired golf over the first nine holes, including three threes, and most of the remainder were fours. She was six up at the eleventh and needed only one more hole to record a fabulous thrashing of the great Joyce Wethered. But great players do not roll over and die. By the fifteenth, she had reduced the margin to two holes. As they stood on the eighteenth tee, JW still trailed by one hole; she had to win the eighteenth to take the match into extra holes. Nobody would have gambled against such a happening, but it was not to be. Mrs C. had a five-foot putt for a half and the game, and to her great credit she did not shirk the responsibility. She had had her day and the affable Joyce did not grudge her it, but the following year, on a bigger stage, she would get her come-uppance in style; more on that later.

By now, it had become the custom to hold an annual ladies v. gentlemen match. It was as much a social occasion as anything, but the golf was played with no quarter asked or given. Apart from that, each lady received six bisques (she received six strokes from her opponent and could take them when she so wished). She did not have to make a decision on any particular hole until both players had holed their putts. The matches were played from the men's tees, and some ladies needed the six shots and more. There was not a man alive who could afford to give Joyce Wethered six bisques, and the results confirmed that fact. In 1923, her opponent was none other than Bernard Darwin, the golf correspondent of *The Times*. Joyce duly dispatched him by six and five. In other words, if she had played him off level, it would have been a good match.

Another annual fixture was the home internationals meeting at Ranelagh, which combined an international match with a medal-play competition over two days. All the players took part in the medals and each of the four countries selected four players to represent their countries in the international match. England won the international event very convincingly, with Joyce Wethered leading the way with rounds of sixty-nine and seventy-one. Ranelagh was not a long course, but that kind of scoring was quite exceptional. However, she was not top of the field in the medal competition and that honour went to none other than the redoubtable Mrs Cautley, who had not even been chosen for the English four! She produced a sixty-eight on the first day (a course record) and followed it with a seventy on the second day. Her immaculate play earned her no less than four scratch prizes, that for the first day, that for the second day, that for the combined two days, and the Kitcat gold medal for the best scratch round of the competition. Not a bad haul for two days' work. Oh dear, Joyce, this lady needs taking in hand. In actual fact, Joyce had achieved the self-same feat as Mrs Cautley the previous year. You just could not better this lady.

An article in the *Illustrated and Sporting News* of November 1923 stated:

> *Miss Joyce Wethered is no longer a subject of interest among women only. She is one of the two or three dominating personalities in the whole realm of golf. Ever since Miss Leitch was constrained to give up the game temporarily, Miss Wethered has been undisputed queen of her kingdom. There have been few monarchies so absolute. At the present moment there are only two other people living who can compete with Miss Wethered in regard to being in a class of their own in their particular line. Mlle Lenglen and Jack Dempsey are both for the moment serious rivals to Miss Wethered, whose record alone is sufficient testimony to her position...*

Incidentally, her handicap was +1 at this time.

As a fashion note or foul weather note, it was observed that several players, in bitterly cold weather, had started the American practice of wearing soft, pliable leather jackets, which are 'windproof and rainproof'. Gortex wouldn't make its appearance for many years yet.

1924 was an historic year politically. On 22 January of that year, the illegitimate son of a Scottish serving girl was asked by the king to become Prime Minister of Britain's first Labour government. James Ramsey MacDonald hired court dress from Moss Bros (I wonder if they really sent him a bill) for his visit to Buckingham Palace, where George V urged him to exercise prudence and sagacity. The advice was not necessary; MacDonald's cabinet of twenty included eleven with solid working-class backgrounds, two Tories, a Liberal, and only one left-winger. He knew from the beginning that he did not have the overall working majority which was necessary for him to function properly. Indeed, many left-wingers urged him to give a resounding socialist speech and then resign. MacDonald was made of sterner stuff, and in any case, he said, that would be a betrayal of those who had voted for the party. He admitted that Labour 'was in office but not in power', but he said that it had to show that the party was fit to govern. To his credit, Macdonald was resolute in governing with moderation, but the election of a Labour government represented nothing less than a social revolution in Britain. For the first time, the ruling elite of the public schools and Oxbridge were out. But, by November, Macdonald and the socialists had gone, replaced by Baldwin's Tory government.

1924 was also the year that Mallory and Irvine were lost on Everest, a story which continues to fascinate the makers of documentaries to this day.

In 1924, JW was totally unbeatable. The British Open was across the sea in Ireland, at Royal Portrush. Some felt that the championship as a spectacle was reduced by the fact that the tees were set well back, making it difficult for the ladies to reach the greens in two shots. The result was that many holes were halved in fives, rather than won with a four. JW progressed as usual through the various rounds without too much mishap, winning by 5 and 4, 3 and 2, and 6 and 5. This brought her up against Cecil Leitch, who had been out of competition for the best part of two years, with a troublesome arm. Joyce had already beaten her in a county match, but the game over the first seven holes was absolutely even, all holes being halved. Joyce confessed that had Cecil putted better she could have been in the lead. The two were now feeling the strain, each hoping that she would not be the one to concede first as that could be fatal. That is exactly what did happen. Joyce took the eighth and followed it with the ninth. Cecil's day was over; she went to pieces and Joyce came through an easy winner by six and four. How misleading a scoreline can be! Over eighteen holes, that sort of result suggests a one-sided game, and yet for almost the whole of the first half, there was nothing to choose between them.

In the semi-final JW played a good friend, Eleanor Helme, and beat her by four and three, thus qualifying to meet Mrs F. Cautley – yes, Mrs Cautley – in the final. The Kent ladies' captain had the temerity to beat Joyce in a county match, it will be remembered. This was another day on a bigger stage. There was never any doubt who the victor would be, and gradually Miss Wethered built up a lead which had reached three holes by the end of the first round. With a light lunch inside her, she turned the screw and ran out the winner by no less than seven and six. The match finished in a downpour and the two ladies were pleased to escape to the clubhouse. Their ordeal was not yet over, because they had to stand wet and cold throughout the prize-giving ceremony. JW said that the few remarks she could conjure up became a more painful business than usual, and felt sorry for the Irish hosts who were enthusiastic to the end. She distinctly remembered the pleasure of wallowing in a luxurious hot bath. Sorry, 'lying', not 'wallowing'; Joyce would never wallow.

Joyce arrived at that year's English Championship with the unenviable position whereby anything less than a win would be regarded by all and sundry as a failure. The championship was held at Cooden Beach and I confess that I had no idea where that might be. Apologies to Cooden Beach! 1924 seemed to be one of those years when it was always raining, and the 'English Ladies' was no exception. On the low-lying course, fairways became very heavy; but let it rain, let it shine, it was all the same to Joyce Wethered. She just took it all in her stride, and what a stride. Her winning figures for this championship are unbelievable. Did she never have an off day? Not many, that is a fact. Again, I must emphasise that all of these championships were of the knockout format. You had to be up to the mark each day and every day, not only in the morning, but also in the afternoon. Not one lax or even slightly under-par round could be afforded. Relentless, consistent play of the highest standard was necessary to win. In the championships of today, played over three or four rounds in medal-play format, you can have an off day and recover and survive and even go on to win.

Her figures at Cooden Beach were as follows: in the first round she won by nine and eight. That means that her opponent did not win any holes and halved just one. In the second round she won by seven and five. That means that her opponent won three holes at the most, and probably less as there could have been some halves. In the third round she won by seven and six. That means that her opponent won two holes at the most, and probably less, as there could have been some halves. In the fourth round, she won by seven and five again. The same facts apply as in the second round. In the quarter-final she won by four and three. She must have felt sorry for her opponent that day.

In the semi-final we are back to a six and five win. Incidentally, one of those vanquished in the earlier rounds was none other than Madame Defarge – sorry, Cecil Leitch. I expect she felt like taking up knitting after that one, but Cecil had her days also.

Whatever happened in the final, you will be wondering. Well, what could happen? It was all so unfair. This woman was not real. She was certainly in a class of her own. Do you remember how old she was? She was just twenty-two! This could go on for years. Dolly Fowler was the other finalist, and she was not one to keel over easily without a fight. Besides, she had met JW a number of times before and had always given a good account of herself, though she had not actually won any of those encounters. Dolly certainly did her darnedest, but it is difficult playing against a phenomenon; Joyce duly cantered away to an eight-hole victory with seven to play.

I have said that Joyce was a modest young lady. This is what she wrote in her book: 'This match was the last I have played in an English championship and it brought to an end, by what I can only regard as an extraordinary run of good fortune, a succession of five wins in this tournament.' Excuse me, Joyce, but that is poppycock. She won, if my arithmetic is correct, thirty-five successive matches over a period of five years, against the best lady golfers in the country. Good fortune does not come into it. She was just the best.

Incidentally, I came across a 1924 newspaper cutting concerning the Royal Dornoch Club ladies' tournament, from which I was delighted to note that Joyce was a competitor, as indeed she had been for the previous four years. Apparently she had returned to Dornoch each year and each year she had won the tournament. Her score of seventy-eight was one better than the Scratch Score of seventy-nine, fully justifying her handicap of +1. She had obviously retained her love for her childhood course, and there is little doubt that each year the members of Royal Dornoch would have given her a royal welcome.

A.C.M. Crome wrote about the subject of balance in 1924:

The balance of the golfer differs radically from the balance of the runner or cricketer. Mr Abrahams or Hobbs [note that he was a professional, so he did not get accorded his 'Mr'] balance themselves as tigers preparing to spring. Miss Wethered and Mr Bobby Jones, whatever appearances suggest, stand solidly like Martell towers on Felixstowe links. Others may acquire something of this solidity, if the accompanying graciousness be beyond them, by thought and practice. Professor Coue has disclosed the method of thought. Let the erratic golfer persuade and constantly remind himself the balance is the thing that counts. For practise I suggest that he should swing a club backwards and forwards, exercising at least three-quarters power, over a fixed point, and note whether the momentum set up tends to drag either foot from its position. When he can do this ten times consecutively, without feeling any tendency to shift his feet, he has got his balance. It is then up to him to memorise his sensations and repeat them on the last teeing ground when he needs a four to win.

So there you have it. Is it my imagination, or did they stand with their feet further apart than is the norm today?

In January 1925 came the announcement that Roger Wethered was engaged to be married on 29 April at St Margaret's, Westminster. His wife was Elizabeth Cavendish-Bentinck, whose father was Charles Cavendish-Bentinck and mother formerly Cicely Mary Grenfell. The liaison was to lead to a career in the City. On his retirement in 1951, Roger wrote a record of his memories with Grenfell and Co. It is an interesting insight into life as a stockbroker. He had started his career with six unsuccessful months on a trial basis with Rowe and Pitman in receipt of 0.375 commission. His mentor, one Lancelot Hugh Smith, succeeded in getting him transferred to Francis and Praed, a large firm of gilt-edged jobbers at a salary of £1,000 per annum, for doing practically nothing as a 'blue button'. He then transferred (possibly with the help of his mother-in-law) to Grenfell and Co., where he had twenty-five happy years.

Roger and Robin Stratford QC were at Oxford together, and remained friends thereafter. Robin's father was Chief Justice of South Africa. At the same time, Brigadier Stubbs of Mitford Castle, near Morpeth, Northumberland, was Chief Justice of the African Dept. His daughter, Marjorie Mitford Stubbs, married Robin Stratford.

Many years later, both Roger and Elizabeth and also Robin and Marjorie divorced. Eventually, Roger and Marjorie were married and lived until Roger's death in 1983 at Garnet House, Wimbledon. Marjorie, known to her close friends by the unflattering but understandable name of 'Stubby', moved into in the adjoining Coach House. She confirmed that Roger had inherited his father's love for art and was himself something of an authority on paintings.

Neither marriage nor work meant that Roger gave up his golf, and he was yet to experience many successful days in various championships and competitions, but 1925 belonged indisputably to his sister. The Ladies' British Open that year was scheduled for Troon, made eminently accessible by the development of the railways and their hotels. Joyce always loved the Scottish links courses; they took her back to her youth at Dornoch. The championship that year had one or two additional elements to it to excite the spectator. Firstly, there was another prospective confrontation of Wethered/Leitch, and although this was nothing new, the press were building it up to a battle royal.

Again they were drawn so that they could meet in the final should each progress that far. Was some unofficial seeding taking place? I haven't read anywhere that official seeding was in force.

There was also the prospect of seeing Glenna Collett, the American star. How would she measure up to her British adversaries?

Royal Troon conjures up vivid imaginations in most golfers' minds of a golfing Shangri-La. Everyone wishes to go to St Andrews, and afterwards there are a handful of courses which vie for second position, with Troon right up there among them. Strangely, although it came into being in 1878 and we tend to think that Open championships have been held there since time immemorial, it was not until 1923 that it hosted its first British Open. Ayrshire has a number of wonderful courses, and the late arrival of Troon on the championship scene is without doubt due to the fact that Prestwick, just down the coast, was the location for the first Open ever. Indeed, the first twelve Opens took place there, commencing in 1860. It was not until 1923 that Troon wrested the initiative from its ancient neighbour.

It is surprising how one hole can fire the imagination, and give even the best of courses that little bit of extra oomph which lifts it to a higher plane. This happens with several of the championship courses throughout the world. At Troon, it is the eighth hole, called 'The Postage Stamp'. It is said to be the shortest hole in Open golf, at 126 yards, and it earns its name because of its tiny green. For amateurs, it is a hole to strike terror into the heart as both sides of the green are defended by deep bunkers. Observers are often treated to an exhibition of ping-pong as some unfortunate goes from bunker to bunker across the green and back again. History records an Open contestant in 1950 as running up a score of fifteen doing just that. It sometimes bows to the famous, however; and the great but diminutive Gene Sarazen scored an historic hole-in-one there on the fiftieth anniversary of his first appearance in the Open championship. It was 1973 and Sarazen was seventy at the time. I wonder what that cost him in the bar afterwards! JW was a friend of Sarazen, and to the day she died she regretted that she did not send a congratulatory telegram to him to acknowledge his wonderful feat. Alas, most of us have been there at some time or another!

There is a delightful limited edition print from an oil painting of the eighth hole by Annie MacGregor. The background to the hole is the Firth of Clyde and Ailsa Craig.

I thought that I would have a quick look on the internet to see what might be available regarding information about Royal Troon. Firstly, I learned that the motto of the Club is '*Tam arte quam marte*', translated to 'As much by skill as by strength.' Very true; I suppose that could apply to all golf courses. It also said that ladies were not permitted on the Old Course. I haven't checked that, but I would be very surprised if it is true (see later). Then I discovered a website, sponsored by American Airlines, which gave assessments in terms of marks out of ten for various aspects of the course... greens, tees, rough, etc. People were invited to submit their assessments, presumably for the benefit of prospective American visitors. The site contained about eight or nine of these assessments, which at best proved little and at worst were quite slanderous. At the top was the gentleman who gave the course ten out of ten for everything and avoided such items as the moderate practise facilities by putting N/A, thus ending with an overall score of ten out of ten. He declared that the hospitality was great and it had been the thrill of a lifetime. He had played fourteen Scottish and Irish courses in eighteen days, and the caddies at Troon were the best of them all. Remember that statement.

All but one of the other assessments followed the same pattern. Apart from the practise facilities, everything was hunky-dory; the staff were welcoming and a great time was had by one and all. Now we come to the exception. It transpires that this gentleman lost his wallet and £200 whilst at the course. He scored the course quite well (I expect he scoured it quite well also), but accorded the staff only one out of ten. Apparently, he considered that they should have been more helpful in assisting him in recovering his lost money. Moreover, his statement was quite unequivocal in that he considered that his hired caddie had pocketed the loot. Is it helpful that one person's opinions, biased or not, should have such publicity afforded by use of the internet?

At Troon, it was noticeable that ladies' skirts were on the way up. At the turn of the century, the leg had been covered down to the shoe. By the early part of the 1920s, the hemline had risen to well above the ankle, and at Troon there had been a further adjustment to calf-length. 'Bad' influences were coming in from America, said the stick-in-the-muds. The Charleston had arrived to fortify the Roaring Twenties, and 'everybody was doing it', even the Prince of Wales – especially the Prince of Wales. Bright young things were dancing the night away with tangos, foxtrots, and the Black Bottom, whilst they puffed away at their Craven A's and sipped cocktails. Good Lord, some young gals had even been espied applying lipstick in public! Neither were the men exempt from these modernisations – no, not the lipstick – not yet anyway! But Oxford bags, Fair Isle sweaters, and caps were all the rage, and of course the inevitable cigarette between the first and second fingers. It seemed so innocent.

In America, steel-shafted clubs were legalised. It would be another five years before Britain followed suit. We like to give these matters proper consideration – a few committees to go through, vested interests to be considered, etc. We get there in the end.

As was the custom of the time, the Open championship was preceded by the Home internationals. Each team comprised nine players, and singles matches were played against each other team. The domination of the English was amply demonstrated when they beat Scotland eight to one, Ireland nine to nought, and Wales nine to nought. It had been sixteen years since any other team had won, but this was the most convincing win of them all. JW had no troubles in her three games, winning by seven and six, five and four, and seven and five. She certainly shouldn't have been tired after many of her matches, so many of them barely went into the second nine holes. I noticed in the team photographs that all of the competitors wore the tie of their country with the exception of Miss Wethered, who sported an exquisite silk neckerchief over a fine angora jumper and what appeared to be a pearl necklace. Was she making some mild demonstration? Would there have been a quiet word in the ear afterwards? It would not have come from the captain, because she was the captain. It has to be remembered that, although she was captain, she was still by far the youngest member of the team. Perhaps she considered some of the dress requirements a trifle fuddy-duddy…

The championship started in warm though grey May weather. The previous day there had been a thunderstorm and casual water still lay on the course and on one or two of the greens. Press reports of the event clearly indicate that the early rounds were suffered by the golfing intelligentsia only as a preliminary to the meeting of Wethered and Collett in the third round and Wethered and Leitch in the final. Joyce had acquired such a reputation. It must have been stressful to have had to win everything or otherwise to have been considered to have failed. When one considered the draw, she had no easy route to the final as we shall see.

In the first round her opponent was Miss Wardell from Dublin. *The Times* correspondent described the occasion as not so much a match as a public execution, conducted in an expeditious and Christian manner. JW started with a three and a four, her shots rifling straight down the middle of the fairway. Poor Miss Wardell must have been hoping for a miracle, but the luck of the Irish failed to materialise and she was duly dispatched on the twelfth green by seven and six. The misses Collett and Leitch both successfully negotiated their prospective opponents, Miss Leitch with consummate ease and Miss Collett a little less certainly. A feature of the round was the first appearance at the tender age of fourteen of Enid Wilson, the pigtailed champion of Derbyshire. She lost but acquitted herself well, and would have many victories in the future.

The draw now meant that JW would have to play three ex-British champions and one American champion in successive rounds if she was to progress towards the final! Her second-round opponent was none other than Doddie Macbeth, who had eliminated Joyce in the semi-finals at Burnham-on-Sea two years previously, and by so doing had kept her out of the British or English finals for the only occasion over a period of five years. That sentence alone surely underlines her dominance of the golfing scene at that time. Joyce recalls that she decided to adopt a certain grimness of demeanour for this meeting, which she confessed was not easy with a lady as likeable as Doddie. She believed that Doddie was probably secretly amused by Joyce's ploy, but at the same time she hoped that it showed her that she held her in respect for her quality of golf. The game was played in a downpour and was most uncomfortable for both competitors. JW steadily drew away from her adversary, and even when she put her tee shot into a bunker at the Postage Stamp, she expertly extricated herself and popped in the putt for a three. *The Times* correspondent seemed quite elated to have seen JW in a bunker. 'As a rule her wildest shots only drift a yard or two off the bee line.' The game came to an early end on the thirteenth green, Miss Wethered having played the preceding holes in level fours. The victory was by six and five. Meanwhile, Cecilia was busy equalling that feat in disposing of the Irish lady, Mrs Cuthill. And what of Glenna Collett? She also came through, by five and three, and played well enough to make *The Times* correspondent revise his original opinion that JW would easily beat her, to that she would win, but not easily. Her weakness was alleged to be her chipping and play just off the green. The Americans were more used to courses where high pitches into the green were necessary, rather than the chip and run of a links course. I was amused to read that after her victory she was overwhelmed with congratulations from some of her compatriots, 'who even went to the extent of hugging her in full view of the assembled crowd.' I say! Whatever next! Thank goodness the correspondent does not have to witness Saturday afternoon on the football pitches of the Premier League.

The third round provided what the audience had been awaiting – Wethered *v.* Collett, Britain *v.* America. The two ladies were of similar demeanour, both quiet and undemonstrative, 'nice' people. Joyce would have hated me using that word; even in later life, her associates remember that she could not abide the word 'nice'. Neither could my old English master, at least, not when it was used in the incorrect manner. 'Nice means exact', he would say. But times change, and the *Concise Oxford Dictionary* of today cites, 'pleasant, agreeable, satisfactory, good-natured, kind (archaic – fastidious)'. On that basis, they were both very nice people.

Joyce was not much under six feet tall (officially, I have seen five feet ten inches quoted), and slim and wiry. Glenna was two or three inches shorter, and perhaps a little stockier – at least, compared with Joyce. They were both attractive ladies, inside and out. They reported to the starter at twenty minutes past ten in the morning. JW was dressed in a white blouse, tweed skirt, and cardigan. Glenna sported a thick Fair Isle sweater (perhaps bought locally) over her blouse and tweed skirt. Both wore the accepted headwear of the time – cloche hats with small brims. I can do no better than let you read the words of *The Times* corre-spondent:

Whatever may be the issue of this championship, its great moment is past. Miss Wethered beat Miss Glenna Collett in the third round by four holes up with three to play. In the exuberance of the moment, it is difficult to avoid overstatement, but trying to be as cool and collected as possible, and after comparing opinion with good and experienced golfers, I hereby declare that more flawless golf than Miss Wethered's has never been played by anybody, man or woman or demi-god. It would be easy to write pages about her, but the real story is this: that she twice took three putts on the green in the first nine holes. Apart from that there was not a single shot that one could criticize. Every tee shot was right down the course. At the short holes she was right in the middle of the green. Every long iron shot was either on the green or within a yard of it, and every chip from off the green was left stone dead. It was magnificent, supremely magnificent, but hardly golf as ordinary persons understand the word.

Miss Collett is a very fine golfer and the Americans are rightly proud of her. She played her game but she was a human being with the frailties and fallibilities of our common humanity. Her wooden club play, for example, was just as long and accurate as Miss Wethered's, except for this, that she smothered two tee shots, and each mistake cost her a hole. She was just as good with her long irons, except that she put two of them into bunkers and bang went two more holes. On the way out she holed two long putts and had something of the better of it on the greens, but on the way back she was out-putted. She did make one or two bad mistakes but before anyone ventures to criticise her let him try to imagine how he would have felt against that glorious, ruthless golf which was not only without fault but never seemed capable of fault. Miss Collett showed signs of a collapse in the middle of her round, but she pulled herself together nobly and against any other adversary she might have got the holes back, but her recovery made no more impression on Miss Wethered than it would, let us say, upon my Lord Nelson on the top of his column in Trafalgar Square. Nobody who did not see it can imagine the utter hopelessness of her task. The weather was perfect from an American golfers' point of view; warm, still, with slow greens, but in spite of the easy weather it seemed quite possible that with such an electrical atmosphere of excitement both parties might play nervously and badly. In fact both started as though they could not make a bad shot....

He goes on to describe the match, hole by hole, and it is evident that JW's golf was near flawless rather than flawless, but she was obviously at the very top of her form and wowed the crowd with superlative golf. Her scores for the holes played were: Out 4, 4, 4, 5, 3, 5, 4, 4, 4 = 37, Home 4, 3, 4, 4, 3, 5. The match finished on the fifteenth green, and Joyce had triumphed by four up with three to play, an exhibition which enthralled *The Times* correspondent and several thousand spectators.

It is obvious from reading that Joyce Wethered had as much respect for Glenna Collett as for any of her antagonists. I believe this is as much due to Glenna's personality as to her golf. Indeed, when you read Joyce's appreciations of Glenna, it is as though you are reading an appreciation of JW herself. She admired Glenna because she held the same values as Joyce. Concerning Troon, she said that it was her privilege to meet Glenna, and she later recalled her matches with the American as some of her pleasantest memories in championship golf. As an opponent she was unequalled in the generous-minded and sporting attitude that she displayed. She never moaned about her misfortunes, and took her defeats in the same manner that she accepted her victories, with a calm philosophy that nothing can change what has been. I quote Joyce:

> *Of all the great players I have known, Glenna presents the most detached of attitudes in playing a match. She intrudes her presence to the smallest degree upon her opponents. I would even say that she appears to withdraw herself almost entirely from everything except the game, and her shots alone remind one of the brilliant adversary one is up against.*

Now, who does that remind you of?

Joyce felt that there were days when Glenna was just not with it, her mind elsewhere. 'Her charm to my mind as a golfer and companion lies in a freedom of spirit which does not make her feel that success is everything in the world. Those who are so generous in defeat are the people most to be envied.' Joyce, herself, did not have many opportunities to demonstrate that particular virtue!

Joyce acknowledged that the golf she played on that particular day was probably the best that she has played in her life. Strangely, another train story comes from this match. They were playing the eleventh hole, when an engine puffed slowly by, sending clouds of smoke behind the green. Joyce recalled that she certainly noticed this particular train, but decided to continue with her putting as she was sure that a Scottish engine driver was unlikely to proceed on his way until he had seen the outcome of the hole. She holed a long putt, which placed her three up and the match finished soon after. Meanwhile, Cecil Leitch won her third round, again convincingly, by five and four.

Glenna acknowledged Joyce's superiority, and said that if she cared to go to the States, she would start a raging favourite for the American Championship, and that she could not see how she could not win. The American public took all of this with a pinch of salt, because they had not had the opportunity of witnessing Joyce in action. Glenna, however, had no doubts whatsoever, and said, 'Hagen would have been hard put to it to beat Miss Wethered, so what chance had I of winning? Even fours for fifteen holes (Miss Wethered's score) is as good as any first-class professional can accomplish, consequently I have nothing to be ashamed of.'

It is a sobering fact that later that same year, Glenna Collett won both the American and French Opens, Joyce taking part in neither.

It was about this time that a new edition of the book (priced 6s) written by Roger and Joyce, *Golf from Two Sides,* appeared. On the subject of footwork, Joyce presented a change of view on her old contention that the left heel should remain on the ground throughout the swing. In her own words:

The habit was acquired almost unconsciously; and at the time I was inclined to think that it possessed certain advantages in the matter of steadiness. Possibly this may be found to be the case with some players – there is nothing injurious in the principle – but any benefit that might have attached to it I have since discarded for a freer method which I think is more pleasurable to the player and productive of better results, both in length and direction.

Joyce Wethered in particular had made ladies' golf popular, and British Railways had made the championship courses accessible to more and more spectators.

Administration of these major sporting events had lagged a little behind the playing of them. This was particularly noticeable in crowd control, or lack of it. There were 5,000 people present to witness the Wethered/Collett clash. Perhaps it had not been realised that Glasgow was so close to Troon. There were no stands, as there are at current Opens, and people did not like to pay good money and not be able to see. Moreover, the event was treated as a day out, for the family in some cases, including the dog. The result was anarchy on the field of play, with players buffeted by surging crowds, as officials tried to maintain some semblance of order. It is to the credit of those who organise such events that they soon identified the problems and took appropriate steps to deal with them, but for a time it made life difficult for the players.

It seems strange that not many years previously, it had been argued that ladies were not sufficiently strong to play games such as golf, and yet here they were engaging in two rounds of eighteen holes per day for several days in succession. The fourth round of this particular championship took place that same afternoon. JW hardly had time to savour her morning achievement, have a bowl of soup and spend a penny before she was on the tee again. In fact, she had played only fifteen holes in the morning and her afternoon opponent only thirteen, so they both benefited from a slightly longer break than would have been the case had their matches gone the full eighteen holes.

Joyce's next opponent was the 1923 champion, Doris Chambers. Once more the weather deteriorated in the afternoon; firstly into mist and drizzle, a typical haar, and this gave way to pouring rain. Waterproofs were still a thing of the future, and the ladies squelched their way round in soaking woollies, a bedraggled force urged on by the fact that they had made it through to the fourth round and glory might lie ahead. Far from being spent after her morning exertions, Joyce continued in her rich vein of form, though not quite to the standard of the morning. She had to combat two stymies, but still managed to win by the comprehensive margin of five and three. She had played four matches and hadn't played the last three holes at all. Cecilia Leitch could go one better; until the fourth round she had not played the last four holes at all.

The competitors had now been reduced to the last eight. The unlucky one to face Miss Wethered was Mrs Jameson. She suffered the same fate as her predecessors, crushed by five and four. Joyce must have been longing to play the sixteenth by now. And what of Cecilia, presumably she had disposed of her opponent in like fashion? Not a bit of it. Cecil had faced a lady from Ireland, Miss Jackson, who sported the country's colours in a green coat. She had started like a good 'un, with 4, 4, 4, 4, 2. Poor Cecil did not know what had hit her. Miss Jackson should have gone three up at the next hole, but three putted from fifteen feet and gave Cecil a half in seven. Miss Jackson had suddenly realised what she was doing, she was thrashing the great Cecil Leitch. The realisation was too much for her and she started to three putt the holes with regularity. By the fourteenth some semblance of order had returned to her game, but she was now one down. The next hole was a tragic-comedy. Miss Jackson missed two shots completely and her sixth hung on the lip of the hole. Today, it would have been marked and she would have scored seven. Cecil had two putts from four feet to win the hole. Just as she lined up her putt, Miss Jackson's ball decided to drop into the hole. Totally unnerved by this eventuality, Cecil looked to high heaven and closed her eyes in disbelief. She then missed the first putt and the hole was halved. The sixteenth was halved in sevens after more adventures than in a boys' comic. A putt of four feet for a three at the seventeenth would have won the hole for Miss Jackson and sent the players to the last hole all square. Alas, it hit the back of the cup, jumped up and stayed out. There was no way that Cecil would not get a half at the last hole and she did, but whew! – that was close.

The afternoon semi-finals were like chalk and cheese, so different were they. JW faced another ex-champion, Gladys Dobell. She had won the title back in 1912, just down the coast at Turnberry. At that time, before marriage, she had been Miss Ravenscroft. Now, I know that it is nonsense but what a wonderful name for winning. It is the sort of name that you expect to win things. With due respect to holders of the name, Dobell does not provide the same expectation. Dobell, to me, suggests the possibility of a duffed shot or two; Ravenscroft suggests ramrod straight drives and an inherited history of winning. I haven't searched for other such examples, but one jumped out of the newspaper reports of the same championship. Rhona Adair! I wonder if she was in any way related to Red Adair, who used to go round the world putting out oil-well fires which had defeated the efforts of others. A wonderful name for exciting adventures and meritorious achievement! If you were choosing a partner for a four ball, you would go straight to Rhona Adair. She had won the championship as long ago as 1900 at Westward Ho!. Well, of course she would; with a name like hers she had a sense of occasion and a sense of location. Moreover, she didn't win just any old championship, she chose a date to be remembered, 1900. Rhona Adair at Westward Ho!, it stirs the imagination. You can imagine her with a long stream of red hair flowing in the wind behind her as she stood, unconscious of the elements raging around her, and purposefully surveying the scene ahead. She might then have stroked a niblick 400 yards and left the ball within inches of the hole. She could have taken on all opponents with one arm behind her back, with a name like that. In the following year she again reached the final at Hoylake. Not content with that, she created her own fairy story by winning again in 1903 at Royal Portrush. And where was her home club? At Royal Portrush, of course. She was indeed a lady with a sense of occasion. When she was young, with another champion of the past, Mary Hezlet, she used to do a round trip of twenty-four miles on her cycle to the course at Portrush and play thirty-six holes in between. Rhona Adair certainly lived up to her name. And then she got married, and became Rhona Cuthill. I'm sorry, but it just isn't the same you know.

Just imagine, Miss Ravenscroft and Rhona Adair coupled together as a pair. You wouldn't want to meet them; they would probably skin you alive.

Joyce Wethered could be pretty frightening, too. The reincarnated Miss Ravenscroft never quite knew what had hit her that afternoon of the semi-final. Having slain two of the Graces of Cheshire in the preceding rounds, she set about poor Mrs Dobell as though she had offended her. It wasn't that the latter played badly, she simply had the misfortune to come up against a superior being, who displayed skills seldom seen on the golf courses of the country. JW went out in thirty-three! Glory be! Even 'Ravenscroft' wouldn't have been enough to save the day.

Mrs Dobell was an unorthodox golfer, who held the club with her right hand right under the grip. In her younger days she putted in the style of some of the early golfers, standing facing the hole with the ball outside her right foot. On the day of the semi-final, she was driving well, but she was playing her second shots more like a right Gladys, and she could ill afford to play anything less than immaculate golf if she wished to hang onto this phenomenon's coat-tails. Even when she seemed to have a glimmer of hope, the fates conspired to determine otherwise. At the fourth hole she hit the green with two beautiful shots, but the phenomenon laid her third shot dead and poor Gladys putted her ball to just behind that of the phenomenon, thus leaving herself with a hopeless stymie. Four holes played, Wethered four up. Gladys thought she had been badly done to; more so at the next hole when Joyce had a two. Another glimmer of hope at the sixth, JW had made a mistake and was still off the green, whilst Gladys put her shot beside the hole for a gimme. She can't get out of this, one can she? Oh yes, she can. In went the chip for a half! The phenomenon took the seventh with a perfectly played four, and placed her tee shot at the short eight straight onto the green. Suddenly, it was Miss Ravenscroft out there –a two, a two, a two. The gallery went mad. They loved Joyce Wethered but an underdog with the pedigree of Mrs Dobell should not be made to suffer so, it just wasn't right. They craned forward to watch as JW sized up her putt. She would obviously sink the thirty footer, no doubt about that; but they couldn't see (although they half anticipated it) how she was going to get down in none! The hole went to the afflicted and she received a roar of approval, a mixture of delight and sympathy. She really was playing like Miss Ravenscroft now; it was Sohrab *v*. Rustum.

I can imagine the thoughts flowing through Gladys' mind as she made her way to the ninth tee. 'I'm not playing too badly now. I've got it back to five. There's still hope if I keep plugging away. She can't keep on like this.' Oh dear, oh dear. It was a par-five, but JW turned it into a three, courtesy of another holed chip. One spectator, with beautiful understatement, described her as 'an awful woman', and was surely justified. JW's card for those nine holes was 4, 4, 4, 4, 2, 5, 4, 3, 3 = 33. The fight was o'er, the battle done. Three of the next four holes were halved, and Gladys, looking for some respectability in the scoreline, won the twelfth, when JW was, to the amazement of all, bunkered. The winning margin was six and five. Now was the victor's triumph won! Joyce had still not played the last three holes in the whole of the championship. All week she had been playing, morning and afternoon, and she still had not played sixteen, seventeen, and eighteen at all.

In the second semi-final, there was a much closer affair of a rather lesser standard. How could it not have been? Cecil Leitch was playing Miss Brown of Formby, and it was nip and tuck all the way. Miss Brown hit a good long straight ball and putted well. Her weakness was the short irons, when a high floater was required. She much preferred a low chip and run, which wasn't always a practical alternative. Cecil went two up early in the round, but by the seventh it was all square and it was still so at the ninth. At the eleventh Miss Brown went one up. Her big opportunity then went begging. Cecil had a bad twelfth, and Miss Brown needed to get down in three from just off the green to take a two-hole lead. She contrived to stymie herself and take four. She was still one up with three to play, but alas, she fluffed one of those little pitches and the match was all square. Cecil played the seventeenth as Cecil did. She was in a bunker, but in the words of *The Times* correspondent, 'she hewed the ball out of the bunker'. Cecil was one of the breed who believe in giving the ball a good whack – the 'if all else fails, hit it' philosophy. She followed this by firmly sinking a four-yard putt. She was up for the first time since the eighth hole, and unlikely to relax her grip now. Sure enough, her second putt hit the back of the hole with authority. The hole was halved and the match won. The press and the public had what they had desired, a Wethered/Leitch final.

The final was always played on a Friday in those days, over thirty-six holes. The crowd which gathered for the morning round was about 6,000 strong. For the afternoon, it would swell to 10,000, as the shipyards and schools and shops closed and an afternoon out for the family was declared. The large crowd was to cause some problems and heartaches as the stewards, many of them players in the earlier rounds, strove to retain control. JW vividly remembered years later, one very large man, red in the face, with a little girl astride his shoulders. He was hurrying along, elbowing his way through the crowd, and replying to the many indignant requests to refrain from pushing with the words, 'No, I won't. Haven't I promised Elspeth that she shall see every shot of the match? And see them she shall.' There were men with dogs, ladies pushing perambulators, scurrying schoolboys. By the afternoon round, the players were having difficulty in finding the room to play their shots, and as soon as they hit them the crowd would surge forward to the vicinity of where the balls fell. In consequence, the players saw where their balls had landed only when they had been allowed through the enveloping throng.

It was five years since Joyce Wethered had announced her arrival on the golfing scene by beating Cecil Leitch in the English championship at Sheringham. Since that time, the pair had met in seven finals and JW had won five of them. Indeed Cecil had not beaten her young opponent since 1921. Joyce seemed to have been top of the tree for so long, that it did not seem possible that she was still only twenty-three. Cecil was ten years older. There was no doubt who was the favourite in the eyes of those placing bets. Few gave Cecil a chance, the odds were three to one in favour of Joyce. Indeed, some thought they should favour Joyce by even more, considering the way in which Cecil had played in the quarter and semi-finals. But Cecil, like all the best sportspeople, was inspired by a final and seldom failed to rise to the occasion.

Joyce, for her part, has freely admitted that she did not particularly relish games against Cecil, more perhaps due to her personality than fear of her golf, though that also could be quite fearsome. Joyce was convinced that she was successful against her because she always followed the rule that she must ensure that she shut out of her mind any disturbance, particularly that of a fellow competitor, and that she played the course and not the individual. Great golfers have different opinions on this subject, but Joyce was never in doubt that her method was correct. It was a method which was particularly appropriate against Cecil, who had a very dominant personality and was invariably the centre of attention wherever she might be. Her apparent confidence had won her many a match when her opponent had been overwhelmed by her very presence. Joyce wrote, 'To have allowed myself to watch her strike the ball with her forceful and individualistic swing would have been destructive to my own sense of rhythm, as the timing and delivery of the shots were founded on totally dissimilar lines.' It was often said that JW proceeded through a round of championship golf, seldom speaking to her opponent, quietly playing her shots and unhurriedly following them, with little attention to her opponent's endeavours. It was a conscious attempt to concentrate and give herself every chance of success. In purely social games, where the outcome was of less importance, she could be as chatty as others. She also revealed that she considered the acquiring of an early lead extremely desirable, and thought that Cecil lived by the same belief. Her friend and famous amateur golfer of the period, Cyril Tolley, sometimes stated that the first six holes didn't really matter, but Joyce certainly did not subscribe to that idea, and she thought that against Cecil the first sign of weakness of either gave added strength to the other.

Joyce appeared for the final much as she had been dressed throughout the week, wearing a heavy, mid-calf length skirt, white blouse and single string of pearls, a long cardigan, and cloche hat. Most of the ladies opted for laced shoes, but Joyce played in shoes with two buckled straps across the instep. Cecil sported her club tie and a loose woolly rather than a cardigan. They presented the same picture as when Joyce had played Glenna Collett. Joyce was tall and willowy, Cecil a couple of inches shorter and of slightly stockier build. Cecil soon showed that she was 'up for it', holing a twelve-yard putt for a birdie three on the very first hole. Game on. The next two holes were halved, and Cecil was bunkered on the fourth. However, she came out of it well and JW failed to win the hole. At the short fifth, both had five-foot putts for par. Cecil missed, Joyce holed, and the match was back to all square. The long sixth resulted in JW having one of her few sixes of the week, and Cecil regained the lead with a par-five. Murmurs emanated from the crowd. This was not really going as everyone had predicted. Joyce was making a few mistakes and Cecil was looking good. The seventh was halved, and, at the eighth, Cecil was again bunkered off the tee.

Incomprehensibly, Joyce missed her tee shot, took five, and Cecil again recovered well to win the hole. Two up. More murmuring from the crowd. Indeed, the fainter hearts in the Wethered camp were already starting to predict a catastrophe. Blimey, we've only just started. She didn't seem to be herself, though. The ninth was halved in good fours. Joyce had played the first nine in seven more strokes than in the semi against Gladys.

Cecil played two superb shots to the tenth green and came off it three up! Quick, get a saver on Cecil, before the bookies close their books! A sort of constrained silence fell upon the crowd. It was not that they did not want Miss Leitch to win, but that they could not believe that Miss Wethered was three down. She had not played well. You can't often say that about Joyce Wethered. Now, she began to play well. She had a rock-solid par-four on the eleventh, but Cecil equalled it with another long putt for a half. Undaunted, Joyce came at her again, with one of the most exquisite birdie threes you could wish to see. This time Cecil had no answer. Two halves followed, and then another fine pitch and a single putt reduced the deficit to one hole. Cecil was giving nothing away, Joyce had simply raised her game and made her own chances. The crowd was getting noisier again. This was good stuff, we've got a real game on here. The faint hearts, the very same ones of a few holes back, were now reassuring everyone that they knew that Joyce had only been biding her time. Cecil momentarily crumbled on the sixteenth and four-putted. All-square. Cecil was not finished, and re-established her lead on the short seventeenth. She followed it with a perfect par- four at the last hole, but the last throw of the dice for the morning round went to Joyce when she rattled the back of the tin with a birdie three from all of twenty feet. Joyce had never had the lead all through the morning and must have been fairly satisfied to have gone into lunch all square.

I'm sure you would love to know what the competitors lunched upon, and I have searched the writings of the time, but to no avail. A little smoked salmon, perhaps? Today, I would hazard a guess at a ripe banana, but I don't think the sustaining qualities of these particular fruits had been acknowledged at that time.

Out they went to the first tee once more. At least Joyce had now had the benefit of playing the last three holes, which had evaded her throughout the week. Would she now stride away from her opponent as had been expected? Would Cecil revert to her less accomplished play of earlier rounds? It had become obvious to everyone that nobody could predict the outcome of this absorbing battle. There had been one or two disturbing signs for Miss Wethered's supporters. She had actually been seen running on two occasions to try to see the outcome of her shots. Never had that been witnessed before. She was the lady who remained cool and calm through all and any situation. Meanwhile, Charlotte Cecilia Pitcairn Leitch, who always effused confidence, was literally brimming over with it. When you have a hatful of names like those, you have to be good.

Cecil took the second hole when Joyce, with the adrenalin pumping, was too strong with her approach and went through the green. Two halves followed in par figures. At the short fifth, Cecil was bunkered from the tee. Joyce went straight for the flag and the ball landed barely a yard from the cup. A birdie two and the match was once more all square. Both contestants played the next two holes in a perfectly orthodox manner and were rewarded with their pars. Another short hole and Joyce found herself stymied and lost the hole. At the next hole she was stymied again, though only three feet from the hole. She needed the 'putt' to win the hole, but Cecil's intervening ball was a mere four inches from the hole. A little bit of magic followed, the likes of which we no longer see in modern golf. Joyce extracted her mashie-niblick from the bag and flipped her ball over her opponent's and into the hole. It was pure magic and, if she had failed, it would probably have resulted in Cecil winning the hole and going two up. Overcoming stymies was fairly commonplace business, but not when the other ball lies so close to the hole, leaving absolutely no scope for error. Most people would have putted up close and settled for a half, but this was a match of the titans. It was a gesture of almost scornful bravery and it had its effect. Cecil's heart must have missed a beat, though there was no outward sign of such. But at the next hole she foundered and succumbed to a par. It was the twenty-eighth hole of the match and the first time that Joyce had been in the lead. Cecil started to wobble.

She missed her second to the twenty-ninth, but recovered beautifully to gain a half in four. She then almost totally missed her tee shot and could not recover. A bad hole for Cecil. A good hole for Joyce, a perfectly played three. Two up and six holes left. The boisterous crowd pushed and shoved. This might soon be over; they did not want to miss a moment of it. 'Make way for the players please'. '****** the players. We've come to see the match!' Joyce didn't like it, but she was made of sterner stuff than to let it deprive her of the match. The amazing thing was that the golf became even better. Neither side would give an inch over the next three holes. Par, par, par. This was not for faint hearts. The standing of women in the world was done no harm, no harm at all, by this exhibition.

So we came to the last three holes, the three holes which Miss Wethered had played only once, that very morning, throughout the whole week. She still retained that two-hole lead. Surely it was all over now? Wasn't it? Let us hand over to JW herself to take us through the final phase.

The mistakes began at the long sixteenth. First of all, Cecil pushed her third shot into the rough to the right of the green and I was left with a medium iron to reach the green with the like. No doubt I realised the position of the match too acutely, hurried my shot in the anxiety to see the ball on the green and pulled it into a bunker. The hole ended in a half where it so easily might have seen the end of a gruelling contest. Dormy two still looked a fairly promising state of the game, but a missed opportunity is like a mistake at bridge; the cards never forgive. Cecil played the seventeenth – a most difficult three – perfectly. That brought me down to dormy one. Feeling far from happy now, my second shot at the last hole over intervening bunkers was truly deplorable. With Cecil finding the green in two, out we went to the first tee once more. I remember how depressed and downhearted I felt when again I was faced at the thirty-seventh hole with the same length iron shot as the two last I had played so disastrously. How I loathed the sight of the club! But I could see no alternative. Fortunately I had the advantage of seeing my opponent play first [so much for the philosophy of playing the course and not the opponent] *– a shot that was none too good, short of the green and to the left.* [In fact, Cecil hit a low hook which hit the top of a bunker and just managed to roll clear]. *With this encouragement I am thankful to say that my shot just reached the edge of the green and I was able to scramble down in two more to win.* [In fact, her first putt was superb and left her with less than three feet for the win. Cecil's pitch had been short and her long putt skirted the hole].

It was all over. Well it was as far as the crowd was concerned. They had enjoyed a cracking day's golf and now the huge mass of people divided, some to witness the presentations, others to catch their trains back to Glasgow, Paisley, Ayr and other destinations. Largely they had been a good-hearted throng, but at times, particularly in the concluding phases of the match, their enthusiasm to see the action had turned them into a stampeding herd. There were moments when the stewards were swept aside by a tidal wave of humanity, and there were several occasions when the proceedings had to be halted whilst order was restored. The effect upon the players in such circumstances is difficult to ascertain; I suppose it depends upon the nature of the player. Cecil Leitch thrived upon the attention of a large audience, she was an extrovert and the adrenalin never ran stronger than when she was the focus of attention and adulation. This had been demonstrated in the early holes of the match. Her indifferent form of the day before had been replaced with a grit and determination to carry the fight to her opponent. She might possess inferior armaments to those of her antagonist, but by golly, what she did have was going to be used to the full. In her dreams she probably likened herself to Boadicea at the helm of her chariot, moving ever onward against the might of the Roman foe. I can imagine her in those final holes, elbowing her way through the crowd, or more likely demanding passage in a stentorian voice, and the crowd unfolding in passive obedience to allow the queen to enter through.

Joyce, on the other hand, would be quietly making the best of things, relying on others to find her a way through the throng. She would be neatly side-stepping the hurtling bodies, her big eyes wide open to avoid contact with stumbling intrusions. She wouldn't have liked it at all, but neither would she have complained.

It is reported that both players arrived at the last green looking decidedly pale. They had experienced a hard and gruelling battle. Thirty-six holes of golf is tiring at any time. In pure walking terms we are in the region of ten miles. They must have been physically exhausted; a tiredness which would have been hidden from them by their desire to win. It is when the battle has been lost and won, that complete fatigue overcomes the beaten party and even further strength and energy carries the victor forward, all thoughts of tiredness banished for a further hour or two.

Cecil strode quickly across that thirty-seventh green and sportingly congratulated Joyce. She then disappeared into the arms of her supporters, lit a cigarette and drew deeply upon it. She was bitterly disappointed but kept that inside her; she was a lady and could lose like a lady. She must have derived some satisfaction from the performance which she had given. The bookies had given her no hope at all; hadn't she lost to this same Joyce Wethered in previous British championships by nine and seven at Prince's Sandwich, and by six and four in the quarter-finals at Royal Portrush? Yes, Cecil must have been disappointed, but she must also have had her faith restored in her own ability to win again, at the very top.

The presentation of the prizes was made by the captain of the Troon club, one W.P. Stewart. He commented upon the fine play throughout the week and particularly the final. He indicated that it had given the members of the Troon club very much pleasure indeed to have the hosting of this championship and he hoped in some future year the ladies would come back. He paid tribute to the Executive Committee of the Ladies' Golf Union and their very able secretary, Miss Macfarlane, for the excellence of their arrangements. They were all pleased to hear that the players had expressed themselves as highly delighted with the course and the arrangements made for their comfort by the club. An article by Liz Kahn in the *Daily Telegraph* golf supplement yesterday has made me think more about this, because ladies are still, in the early years of the twenty-first century,, not made totally welcome at all golf clubs. Headlines were made at Royal Wimbledon, one of Roger Wethered's old clubs, recently, when ladies were allowed into the AGM for the first time. Apparently, after the meeting, six of them went into the former men's bar and were bought drinks. I take that to mean that they are to be welcome in the bar at any time hereafter; otherwise it would be a very hollow victory for equal rights. They are certainly permitted into the bar at my club at any time, but I do hope that they don't expect to have their drinks bought for them all the time. What has brought about this change in men's attitudes so that they are opening up to the ladies? Old-world charm perhaps, new-found courtesies? Not a bit of it, it is a case of the old spondulicks. Lottery cash can be claimed only by those practising equal opportunities. Nothing is more guaranteed to alter the attitudes of golf-club members than the likelihood of some intervention to prevent or reduce increases in their annual subscriptions.

There are still clubs for men only. At Royal St George's, there are no ladies' tees and ladies can play by invitation only. There used to be a notice in the club's luncheon room, stating, 'Women are admitted to play only on sufferance and must at all times give way to members.' That notice would have been hanging there when JW won the 1922 championship at the adjoining Prince's course. At Muirfield, women are 'welcomed' but must play with a man. Prestwick treats women just the same as male visitors, but to be a member you must be a man.

Well, what about Troon, where the captain of 1925 hoped that the ladies would return? He meant it, but with reservations. Members are male, women can play only as visitors, and women are normally permitted only in certain parts of the clubhouse. Not too much of an advance there. Perhaps they will want a lottery grant to restore the clubhouse!

It is intriguing to wonder about the arrangements in 1925, and for that matter in other years, at other championship courses, where constraints on the ladies would have been equally substantial. Presumably they were allowed to use the locker rooms and accepted the facilities as they were, provided for men rather than women. Were they allowed to eat there in the dining room? Were they allowed into the bar and could they order a drink? One wonders why a club like Troon would invite the LGU to hold their championship there at all. It couldn't have been a financial venture, and I can imagine the views of the members on having to give up their course for a whole week.

Many golf clubs have been male bastions since they were incorporated, but times are changing, albeit very slowly in some cases. The R&A itself remains predominantly a male institution. The clubhouse, the home of golf, remains barred to women. All former male presidents of the United States Golf Association have been made honorary members of the R&A, but, in 1997, the USGA appointed its first lady president. You can imagine the long hours of R&A committees poring over that one. In the end, they gave her a diamond brooch.

I love the R&A rules for admission to membership of the society. You have to be invited, you need a proposer and a seconder and at least twenty members supporting the application and – here comes the good bit – no member against!

At the presentation ceremony at Troon, Joyce had her usual task of thanking the club, officials, and all those who had helped in administering the event. She said that one of her greatest desires had been to win a championship in Scotland and she considered it the greatest of her achievements. The chairwoman of the LGU included in her comments that the officials had dealt expertly with the very enthusiastic crowd. No visible sign of disagreement showed on Miss Wethered's countenance. Cecil Leitch was also called upon to say a few words and stated that she had never played before a more courteous or sporting crowd than on that day. She said that she was sure Joyce would join her in saying that. She then went over the top a little by thanking them for their great kindness and consideration. Still, Joyce's face betrayed no contrary opinion. Indeed, unless in private to her most intimate associates, she never expressed more than mild concern, even though she had found the boisterous proximity of the crowd quite worrying. 'I am bound to say that keenness to see the play can frequently cause not a little discomfort to players and onlookers alike. Still, it is generally worth it', was the most she would allow herself.

There is no doubt that the experiences of this tournament had a lasting effect on JW. The final tested her resolve to the utmost. She had always suffered nerves inside as most people do, but unlike many she could withhold any sign of these to outward appearances. To her opponents she appeared totally at ease, which had the effect of heightening their nerves, much to their distraction and usually destruction. After a tournament Joyce would often withdraw from the limelight for a while to regain her strength, and to allow her hidden emotions to subside to a more normal level. To hold these in check throughout a week of championship golf can be quite debilitating. Several years after, she admitted that that game had made her take up a more dubious attitude over what should normally be a fairly comfortable and encouraging position. She had been two up with three to play and nearly let it slip from her grasp. Afterwards, she never allowed herself to relax in a similar position. Indeed, she couldn't, because the memory would come floating back to her.

It is likely that before the championship started, she had decided that it would be her last. She had consistently won for a number of years, with only a very occasional hiccup, and she didn't see the point of putting herself through the mental strain. She wasn't playing for a living. She had no pretensions at creating records of achievement. She had always played because she enjoyed golf and because she felt it incumbent upon herself to prove herself at the topmost level. To prove this to herself, you will understand, not to glorify in her dominance over others. In her words:

After this rather hectic finale I was only too glad to feel that the following year would not call for further efforts on my part. Not that I would have missed any of the thrills for worlds. I am only too grateful for the fact that I got as much fun as I did out of what cannot be described as unmixed pleasure. At the same time I felt that I had had a sufficient experience to make me wish never to be other than a carefree spectator in the future. A less active role has always suited me perfectly. I can enter into the emotions of the game and enjoy them just as I like without having to preserve a state of elaborate calmness as a player over incidents which are in reality causing me acute excitement and probably no little apprehension and alarm.

'A less active role' is a bad choice of words. It gives the impression that she was happy to laze around. Nothing could be further from the truth. Throughout her life she pursued her interests of the time with vigour and determination. The interests might change but she was never without them and was always enthusiastic about them, sometimes to the extent of exclusion of other activities which she enjoyed. Later we shall hear something about her life at Knightshayes Court, where she and her husband created wonderful gardens to complement the Victorian house. Not far away runs the river Exe. Knowing of Joyce's great love (and expertise) of game fishing, I asked of one of her friends of that period whether she often fished the Exe. Not at all apparently, because that would have been to divide her attention, and detract from her dedicated work in restoring and extending the Knightshayes gardens.

When she withdrew from championship golf, she was still only twenty-three. She had played in ten consecutive English and British championships, all of them knockouts played over several rounds, and had won eight of them, and been in the final and semi-final of the other two. Even Tiger Woods would have difficulty in measuring up to that sort of record. She would be back, as we shall see later, in one of the most astounding comebacks of world sport.

In one of JW's scrapbooks, which I have been privileged to have been loaned, there are notes in the margin, some I believe made by Joyce and some by Roger. After the Troon victory, there was considerable specula-tion as to how Joyce would fare against certain leading male players of the day. It was generally agreed that not many would have the beating of her. A hand-written note in the margin beside newspaper cuttings of her success stated, 'Tom Fernie asked if Joyce would qualify in the Open. Qualify! She'd damn well nearly win it.' Brotherly love and respect!

The magazine *Golf Illustrated* had at this period a person of poetic bent, known by the initials H.R.B., who regularly graced its pages with an offering in verse on the latest epic event. This is what he wrote of the battle of Troon:

The Golf Queen

What thoughts surge 'neath that mask serene,
Whose placid, calm, unruffled mien,

No fear betrays, no sign doth show
Of wrathful fires pent up below…
  Methought in spirit I o'erheard,
  (Or was't some whispering little bird)

  'I cannot shake her off,' she said,
  'Whether a live weight, whether dead,
  I know not; she clings like a leech,
  And at each birdie hurls a peach.
  She challenged me to combat dire,
  Who doth to my fair throne aspire,
  And, with her gauntlet, this threat hurled,
  'I will be queen of all the world!'
   Now to the death I will defend
  My title to the bitter end,
  I thirst for vengeance, and will take it
  E'en to the thirty-seventh to slake it
  So she and all the world shall own
  No two queens e're sit on one throne
  Come one, come all, J'y suis; J'y reste
  Let Saint Cecilia do her best!

  And there she sits unconquered Queen
  Unruffled, smiling and serene,
  Though if I be not much mistaken,
  She feels the crown a little shaken
  For what firm throne can bear the shock
  Of battering rams, with ne'er a rock?
  To few on earth shall it be given
  To reach the thirty-seventh heaven…
  And all of us rejoice to know
  Cecil sits but one tier below,
  While scribes angelic pour sweet balm
  Into her wounds, to soothe and calm,
  Who from the cup of victory quaffed
  A moment's nectar – precious draught
  The while with eager hand she gripped
  It, for a second – 'ere it slipped.

Ummm – yes. Not quite Keats or Shelley, but you can see what he was trying to say! It was an appropriate tribute to the two contestants of Troon.

As I have indicated previously, Joyce led a privileged and comfortable life. She had many friends of the upper classes and indeed the aristocracy. Some originated from the Oxford days of her father and brother. Many were acquired on the golf course and at the social functions associated with golfing events. As a champion, she would be in demand at house parties, her presence a coup for the host and hostess. There is very little doubt that Joyce would have the minimum of difficulty in separating the wheat from the chaff, or to put it more kindly, the sincere friends from those of a more flippant nature. After the Troon championship, she did not have to travel far to a refuge, to regain her strength and equilibrium. One of the good friends of the family was Lt-Col. Dalrymple Hamilton, known to friends and readers of his occasional contribution to *Golf Illustrated* as 'Snatch', a sobriquet attributable to his lightning golf swing. The Colonel's seat was just down the coast from Troon and a little inland in a lovely valley not far from Turnberry. It must have been an ideal haven for Joyce to relax, fish, and perhaps even play an occasional round of golf. She once said that the happiest three days of golf she ever experienced were when she was staying with the Hamiltons, played five rounds on the New Course and one on the Old Course at Turnberry, and at the end stood at one over fours!

On this occasion, her main relaxation was fishing in the Girvan and its tributaries, and it was the first time that she had landed a salmon. She went with a gillie to a swift-running pool known as Donald's Wield, and lo and behold, the very first cast she made she landed a twelve-pound salmon. She was supposed to be relaxing from the strains of the previous week's golf, so she was somewhat taken aback that as soon as she and the gillie had dealt with the first salmon and she had returned the fly to the water, a second salmon seized it and made off down the river. Her arm was already aching from the fight to land the first fish, and here she was in combat once more, for this fish was a fighter, and a clever fighter to boot. He twisted and turned, accelerated and stopped, and used every trick in his knowledge to dislodge the taken lure. The fight lasted for all of fifteen minutes before Joyce cried out to the old keeper that she was spent and would have to give in. Not if he could help it, he was already in position with his gaff, prepared for action. In desperation that the fight should not be ceded, he groped for words which would energise his young charge to further efforts, 'Aye, and imagine it's Miss Leitch you've got hooked at the end of the line.' Joyce was so surprised by his exhortation – she did not know that he had even heard of Cecil Leitch – that she hung on and was rewarded five minutes later when a fat salmon lay on the bank.

In reminiscing about the event, she was not naïve enough to think that the gillie was one of her golfing admirers. She shrewdly observed that had the fisherwoman been Miss Leitch, it would have been Joyce Wethered to have been imagined as the fish on the end of the line.

1925 was a sweet year and it was still not halfway through. A little later that summer, on a different field of play, the great Jack Hobbs of Surrey and England, down in cider country at Taunton, was making cricketing history as in consecutive days he took hundreds off the Somerset bowlers, to first equal W.G. Grace's world record of 126 hundreds in first-class cricket and then to surpass it. Hobbs was forty-two at the time, but there were no thoughts of retirement for him. In fact, before he hung up his bat he notched another seventy centuries!

Neither the Ladies' Open at Troon nor the Hobbs hundreds at Taunton were broadcast on the radio, or wireless, as it was known at that time. But this newest of technologies was beginning to transform communications, and at the end of the year over 1.5 million ten-shilling licences had been sold. The BBC were selling crystal sets at £2 to £4 a go. It sounds extremely cheap, but that was a significant sum at the time and many people were making their own. Lord Reith, though he was still only John Reith at the time, the general manager of the BBC, said that he intended to lead public taste, not follow it. Mmmmm! I hear his words and agree that the radio is a fine medium for furthering the education of the people and making them aware of their cultural heritage, but whilst you can take a horse to the water, it is not always easy to make him drink. Nor did Lord Reith have any competition from other stations at that time. He would be appalled at the influence of listening and viewing ratings on the compilation of programmes today.

5
THE INTERMISSION

So, which nunnery did Joyce Wethered enter? Well, none actually. She had said that she was finishing with golf championships, and that is exactly what she meant. She never hinted that she would give up golf or disappear from view. She simply wanted to play her golf for pleasure and perhaps also turn her attention to other things. Apparently she was something of a natural ball player, because she was pretty efficient at many games, including tennis, table tennis, and squash. It was even rumoured that she was giving up golf to concentrate on tennis with a view to reaching similar high standards in that particular game. She was an all-round sportswoman who enjoyed fishing, and winter would usually mean a visit to the ski slopes at St Moritz. She enjoyed the occasional hand of bridge, and was an excellent needlewoman. She inherited this last skill from her father, who produced some truly excellent tapestries. As has been indicated earlier he was also a very good artist. I have unearthed no evidence of Joyce's abilities in this direction. We know little of her mother's attributes; she seems to have been the home-maker, the reliable, always available, mother and wife who quietly and undemonstratively provided a secure base and probably an attentive ear.

What about the men in her life, I hear you say? If there was one matter which Joyce guarded most jealously, it was her privacy. The newspapers and magazines of the time were not so inquisitive as those of today. Sensational revelations were still infra dig. Newspapers reported the news as it happened. They didn't search out titbits of titillation. It must be remembered that the radio had only recently been commercially introduced. Television was many years away. Travel abroad was restricted to the few, unless of course they were shipped there to wage war. Communications were limited. Even without these barriers to rumour and tittle-tattle, I doubt whether much of note would have emanated from a watching brief on Joyce's daily activities. I believe she was slightly prudish. Even when she toured America and Canada in 1935, she was accompanied by a female companion as chaperon.

Study of her dress shows that she was always careful and never outrageous, though I hasten to add that she could look quite divine when she chose to adopt higher heels and dress for the occasion. Commenting upon female golf attire, she said that she was pleased that the long inhibiting skirts and high-necked blouses of the early part of the twentieth century had now given way to more practical clothes as the 1920s advanced to the 1930s, but she was unhappy when skirt lengths started to go above the knee. That was taking things too far.

When she toured North America in the 1930s, her outfits looked somewhat outdated. This could have been an economy measure because the family wealth had disappeared by this time, and she may have been dipping into last year's wardrobe. But she was the star attraction and did not appear to realise that she could have wooed the American public with other than her golf. She was a delightful shape, tall and willowy, and there are a number of photographs which show how attractive she could be with a little effort, but she seemed to want to play down her physical attractions, modesty taken to the extreme. Whilst the Americans thrilled over her golf, it was evident from the reporting that they regarded her attire as a little frumpish and her looks as pleasant rather than attractive. Presumably that is what Joyce wanted, but it is such a pity.

I have spent more than a few minutes considering what Joyce would have said had she been alive today and I had asked about the men in her life. I don't think she would have declared the subject taboo, because she was a very sensible person and would have realised that a biography, even an essentially golfing biography, could not ignore this aspect of her life. But she would surely have wanted it dealt with in a matter-of-fact manner, with few embellishments and as briefly as was practically possible.

When she was thirty-five she married Sir John Heathcoat-Amory, but we shall be saying a good deal more about that later. She had at one time been engaged to marry Major C.K. Hutchison. The major was much older than Joyce. He was elected a member of the R&A in 1903, when Joyce was only one year old. He seems to have devoted a good deal of his life to golf, and was obviously a very good player because records reveal that he won two medals at the R&A, the Silver Cross in 1914 and the George Glennie Medal in 1919. He served on the Rules of Golf Committee from 1906 to 1939. He was a member of that most prestigious of clubs, The Honourable Company of Edinburgh Golfers, playing at Muirfield. He lifted many trophies at the club, including Gold Medals at the spring meetings of 1908 and 1910 and also at the autumn meetings of 1907, 1912, and 1922. Added to those achievements, he took the Silver Medal at the spring meeting of 1909, and at the autumn meetings of 1909, 1910, and 1920. I can imagine some of the members in 1914 saying, 'Thank goodness he has gone off to war.' But, as can be seen from his results, he was still a force to be reckoned with when he returned from the war fray to the golf fray some years later.

Major Hutchison played for Scotland against England in nine successive years from 1904 onwards. These international matches were usually played before the British Open Amateur event; and in 1909, with the Open being played at Muirfield, there were no less than four of the Honourable Company in the quarter-finals, including the good major. He survived to the final, where he played another of the Honourable Company, the famous Robert Maxwell. The thirty-six-hole final was not decided until the very last green, when Maxwell won after being one down with two to play.

In 1932, 'the Amateur' returned to Muirfield, and *The Times* deplored the slow play of the final, which took six and a half hours for the thirty-five holes played. That seems pretty good to me; it is just as well that *The Times* reporter has not had to witness some recent major championships, when five and a half hours are needed for just one round! However, the reporter had taken as his yardstick the 1909 final of Maxwell and Hutchison, when they apparently completed the thirty-six holes in four hours! They can't have taken a lot of time lining up their putts on that occasion. As they were both members of the championship course, they probably knew every green like the back of their hand, and had no need for prolonged study.

The notice in *The Times* to would-be competitors for the 1909 Amateur Championship revealed that the entrance fee was one guinea, and the value of the Cup was stated to be £100.

Joyce Wethered, in her book, mentioned Major Hutchison only once, and that was to recall a game she played at Muirfield, partnering the Major against Robert Maxwell and J.E. Laidley, all three of whom had been in that last eight contesting the 1909 final. It is possible that Joyce came to know the Major through her father's interest in golf-course architecture. Major Hutchison was well known in this field, and had a hand in the design of several important courses. He first became prominent in 1913, when together with James Braid he designed and supervised the construction of Gleneagles. In 1910 the general manager of the Caledonian Railway, Donald Matheson, spent a holiday in the area and was so taken with it that he decided to build a luxury hotel and golf course. Hutchison and Braid were appointed to design the golf course and the architect of Turnberry Hotel was appointed to design the hotel. Hutchison and Braid visited the area in December 1913 and in the following April were appointed to design and supervise construction for a fee of £120 plus expenses. The work was done by Carter's, the seed merchants, at a cost of £5,500. The King's Course and the Queen's, intended as a ladies' course, were completed by the end of the war and opened in 1919, which begs the question of whether the good major could have been on active service.

In 1925 Major Hutchison was joined by Sir Guy Campbell and Colonel S.V. Hotchkin in a company which became one of the foremost golf-course design consultancies in the country. They numbered amongst their successes Woodhall Spa in 1925, Royal West Norfolk in 1928, North Berwick in 1930, and West Sussex in 1930. Certain of those were alterations and extensions to old courses. The highly successful partnership came to an end in the late 1930s on the advent of war and due to Hutchison's failing health.

I have told you more about Hutchison's golf architecture than I have about his relationship with Joyce Wethered. The only reference to him in her writings was as a partner in that friendly four ball at North Berwick. She played her personal cards very close to her chest. It is conceivable, though I admit borne out of sheer speculation on my part, that they realised a common interest in golfing activities alone would be insufficient to sustain a long marriage and the engagement lapsed accordingly.

There is also a rumour that Joyce came close to marrying a member of the peerage. Perhaps it is no more than rumour. Close friends included Lord Charles Hope, a family friend with whom Joyce and Roger played quite frequently, but I have no evidence to suggest that there was ever anything more than friendship.

I am sure that Joyce had many eligible partners at the social events of the year, and as her successes on the golf course multiplied so would have her admirers, but I would hazard a guess that she kept them largely at arm's length, and they would have to earn her friendship, too. She was too sensible to suddenly fall head over heels in love with a passing gigolo. She'd had a protected upbringing and found her pleasures largely in the bosom of the family. It would require someone very special to prise her away from home.

And so Miss Wethered departed the championship scene. Some did not believe it; at twenty-three, how could she? They clearly expected that she would regret her decision and rue the loss of the challenges that the championships had presented for her over the previous five years. The *Daily Express* thought the occasion warranted deeper investigation and so sent a special correspondent to interview her at the family home in Witley. The response he received to his question of 'Why?' was that she was tired of it. 'You can't go on doing the same things for ever, can you?' was the uncompromising response. 'I have no reason for my decision that would appeal, I suppose, to a logical and masculine mind. I am stopping playing, simply because I choose to. I am tired of it for the time being. I was not particularly keen on playing last year as a matter of fact. There is no deep mystery about it. I have not decided suddenly to emigrate or get married. That I know would make a pretty excuse, but I am afraid that you must be satisfied with the fact that I have simply exercised a woman's prerogative, and have decided to do something without the slightest regard for what anyone thinks, and just because I want to please myself.'

Well, it wasn't quite the scoop that the correspondent was hoping for; it was Joyce at her down-to-earth, no-nonsense best, perhaps slightly miffed that she couldn't make a decision without all these people harping on about it. She was an intelligent woman, who perhaps did not know quite what she did want out of life. Her brother had married and that must have brought home to her that family life as she had known it must inevitably change. Others in her circle were querying their future. Cyril Tolley, friend and golfer of the highest order, had intimated that he may give up golf to concentrate on tennis. It was all quite disturbing. But essential to any thoughts was the fact that she had no interest in hero-worship at all. Some thrive on being in the limelight and enjoy the adoration which they receive from their supporters. They like to be recognised as they walk down the street, to make heads turn, and perform well before a large audience. Not so, Joyce Wethered. The crowds frightened her a little. She was playing for herself, not to please an audience. She had always preferred to be in the background; anonymity didn't trouble her, indeed she almost welcomed it. She played the game at the highest level because that was the only way she could prove to herself that she had reached the highest targets which she had set herself. Now she had more than adequately demonstrated to herself that she had achieved her ambition, and at the same time she realised in so doing that she had made herself public property, which was not really what she wanted, so she called a halt and withdrew from the limelight.

There were those who thought that she was going to withdraw to a much greater degree than she actually did. It was their fault for not heeding her statement. All she wished to do was not play in the championships. That did not mean that she would retire to a convent and relinquish all golf. She still intended to enjoy the pleasures of social golf up to the highest level.

Her successes meant that she had become famous. It is sometimes said that a person has become a legend in their own lifetime. In Joyce's case, she had become a legend before the majority of her lifetime. This meant that she had many invitations to social events and she was pleased to honour such invitations by opening village fêtes and garden parties, declaring new putting greens open, and unlocking the doors of new clubhouses. She had certainly not withdrawn from view.

Some were surprised when she entered for the autumn ladies' foursomes at Raneleigh. Had she reversed her decision of earlier in the year? Of course not, she had always enjoyed the social atmosphere of the Raneleigh event and had always had every intention of being there. It was not a major championship. She played with Miss Hunnewell and in the third round they encountered the Cheshire pair of Mrs Macbeth and Miss Chambers, who defeated them on the final green.

The *Golf Illustrated* Gold Vase was played on JW's home course at Worplesden, and her knowledge of the course was amply demonstrated when she won the competition by eleven strokes with rounds of seventy-seven and seventy-six. The sponsors had been sensible enough to rule that no competitor could win more than one of the prizes, otherwise she would have scooped the board. She won both the scratch and the handicap competitions for both eighteen and thirty-six holes.

That winter JW could be found in St Moritz, enjoying her skiing. To what standard she aspired I know not, but I would be very surprised if she was not to be found on the black runs with the experts. She never did anything by halves; it was not in her nature. If an activity appealed to her, she would do all that was necessary to enjoy that activity to a high standard. There are those who think that too much effort or practise means that you can't enjoy something. They are usually the poorer players, those who achieve only a low standard of accomplishment. It is usually the dedicated who come out on top, not only in achievement, but also in the enjoyment which they receive from their efforts.

It is a strange fact that most of Miss Wethered's successes on the golf course in her early years had been achieved with one or two flaws in her style of play. American ladies, who, unlike those in Britain at that time, had almost all received many hours of tuition and who had been grooved into the acknowledged swing, were amazed to find that Joyce played with her left foot firmly flat to the ground on her backswing. Indeed, her early book, written in co-operation with her brother, advocated this as a means of ensuring that she remained steady throughout the swing. In later editions she amended this idea and acknowledged that the raising of the left heel on the backswing allowed her more freedom of movement resulting in a more fluent swing and greater power and distance. The Americans also wondered at her lack of pivot, but she did pivot and their comparison with their own swings was without doubt due to the fact that many of them were apt to overdo an exaggerated pivot.

Obviously, JW's swing received a great deal of attention from all quarters, not least because of the successes it had brought her. Another peculiarity was that on a full-blooded shot she would finish on her toes. It was a peculiarity which she shared with that other great golfer of the 1920s, the immortal Bobby Jones. Everyone has a hero and Joyce was no exception; her hero was Jones. Strangely, the reverse was almost true also. It is common knowledge that Jones declared her to be the best golfer, man or woman, that he had ever seen, and on one occasion when they had been playing together he had said that he had never been so humbled on a golf course as he was on that occasion. A mutual admiration society developed between them.

I think that it was Bobby Jones who unconsciously brought Joyce back to the championship golf she had forsaken, be it ever so briefly. She had the minimum of tuition throughout her career, preferring to study others and then take what she saw as being good in them and try to use it to her advantage. She watched Bobby Jones with more interest than she paid to anyone else. She was a champion and she could recognise a champion. His influence on her was so great that she decided to change her swing to a more upright plane.

Robert Tyre Jones Jnr was born only a few weeks after Joyce Wethered. Joyce has often been referred to as the female Bobby Jones, and she admired him so much that it is doubtful whether she would have been annoyed by the comparison. In some ways, particularly in their achievements, they were similar, but in other ways they were very different. In stature for example, Joyce was tall and willowy, whilst Bobby was short. Throughout her life Joyce was composed and affable, but in his early days Bobby could be very temperamental and was a club-thrower of the first order. In his first visit to Britain in 1921 to play for the United States in the very first amateur international match between the two countries, he played very poorly and then disgraced himself in the ensuing Open by tearing up his card during the third round after a run of bad holes. Matters were made worse in that the venue for the Open that year was no less than the home of golf, the Old Course at St Andrews. It was an action which he bitterly regretted for the rest of his days, though he did set the record straight by later becoming the darling of the British golfing public as well as that of the States, and declaring St Andrews his favourite course. Strangely, the fates conspired in 1921 that, as Jones blotted his copybook, Joyce's brother Roger Wethered was having one of his greatest days. It was the year when he tied with Jock Hutchison in the final, only to lose in the play-off.

Bobby started playing golf at an earlier age than Joyce and showed evidence of his talents by the time he was fourteen. That year he was entered for the US Amateur Championship, and caused a minor sensation when he carded a pre-qualifying round score of seventy-four. He progressed through several rounds of that knockout competition.

He continued to show his enormous talent but, by 1922, he had not succeeded in winning one major championship even though he had been a competitor in eleven such competitions. That year he had tied for second place in the US Open at Chicago, losing out to another small man, Gene Sarazen. He had high hopes in the National Amateur at Brookline and started full of confidence, only to be demolished by Jesse Sweetser by the huge score of eight and seven. Golf was not his whole life; he had just graduated from Georgia Tech. and now enrolled at Harvard to sit for an MA degree, but he was beginning to wonder when that elusive title would be his, much as Phil Mickelson and Colin Montgomery, to mention but two, have in recent years. He was still only twenty years of age.

Meanwhile, of course, in a manner of speaking, he had been overtaken by JW, who recorded her first victory in the English Championship in 1920, and by 1922 had added two more plus a British Open.

It was 1923 in the US Open when Jones broke the drought, and, as often happens in nature, once broken the drought was followed by a flood; but in Bobby Jones' case by a flood of championship victories. It is worth dwelling on that first victory for a short while, because it demonstrates just how difficult it can be to lay a bogey, if you will excuse the expression. Bobby had a lead as he entered the final round of this stroke-play competition and proceeded through the first half without too much trouble, but the nearer he approached his goal the more stressful he became. He started pressing to ensure that nobody could catch him, and inevitably the course bit back. He finished 5, 5, 6 against three par-fours. He thought that he had blown his opportunity, but found that his score was sufficient to take him into an eighteen-hole play-off against Bobby Cruickshank. It was a terrific contest, nip and tuck all the way to the final hole. Cruickshank opted to play his second shot short of the lake guarding the eighteenth green. Jones then had to decide whether to do likewise, or go for the green two hundred yards away. Like a true champion he decided on the latter and ripped a long iron all the way to the flag, where his ball came to rest not six feet from the pin. He must have been a very relieved man. I remember Christy O'Connor Jnr doing the selfsame thing at the Belfry in 1989, to clinch a tie with the Americans, thus ensuring that the Ryder Cup was retained by Europe, who had won it four years previously after twenty-eight years of American domination.

In both 1924 and 1925, Jones won the US Amateur championships and was runner-up in the US Opens of those years. In 1926, the Walker Cup was destined to take place in Britain at St Andrews. As became the custom, the US team entered the British Amateur and Open championships. Jones had been dying to return to Britain and to atone for his indiscretions of five years previously. He played sub-par golf in the Amateur event but had the misfortune to come up against Andrew Jamieson in the sixth round and bowed out to the Scot. The final was eventually won by Jones' old tormentor, Jesse Sweetser. Jones played well in the Walker Cup to win both of his matches and help the United States to a convincing win. He looked good and was getting better. The qualifying rounds for the Open were played at Sunningdale. He carded a superb sixty-six, with neither a two or five on the card. The final itself was played at Royal Lytham and St Annes. Jones won with a total of 291, which equalled the record lowest score for the Open at that time, held by James Braid since 1908. The British press and public alike took him to their hearts. How wonderful that national bias does not always prevent the appreciation of someone who has something special to offer. On his return to New York, Bobby was awarded a ticker-tape parade down Broadway and a welcome home from the mayor on the steps of City Hall. A short time later he also won the US Open and his greatness was confirmed.

Amazingly, by this time Joyce Wethered had assembled five English Championship titles and three British Open titles, and taken her clubs and departed from the championship scene.

Jones returned the following year to defend his British title at St Andrews. He did so successfully and in so doing reduced the record total from the previous year by six shots for a four-round total of 285. More than that, he made his peace with St Andrews, feeling that he had treated the Old Course with the courtesy that it deserved. He continued to take titles and when he returned once more to Britain in 1930 as the captain of the US Walker Cup team, he was the holder of the US Open from the previous year. The Grand Slam in those days before the advent of the US Masters and USPGA was regarded as the Open and Amateur championships in both Britain and the USA. It wasn't referred to as Grand Slam. It wouldn't be in those days, would it? It had a title more fitting to the times, of 'Impregnable Quadrilateral.' I'm beginning to think I prefer Grand Slam, after all. Bobby Jones was aware that he was capable of being the first man to bring off such a feat. The first of the four competitions was the British Amateur, which by coincidence was scheduled for St Andrews. He had some shocks in the early rounds of the competition and almost capitulated on several occasions. In one round he had been four up with five to play and squandered the lead until he had to hole a putt on the last green to stay in the championship. He had been two down with five to play against another opponent, and he had stymied Cyril Tolley at the nineteenth to win that round. In the final, however, he played well and overwhelmed his opponent by seven and six. And who was that opponent? Roger Wethered! It was most fitting in that they should meet in the final, as they were the respective captains of the two teams in the Walker Cup that year. It was the last of Roger's three Amateur Open finals of which he won once in 1923 before losing in 1928 and 1930.

Jones immediately repaired to Hoylake to prepare for the British Open. At that time, two rounds were played on the final day. (Imagine that in this day and age). At lunch-time he had lost the lead to Archie Compston, and then he took seven at the eighth hole. However, the wheels came off Archie's wagon and he crashed to a final eighty-two. Bobby had won with a four-round total of 291, the same total as he had achieved at Lytham four years previously.

Back went Bobby to America, and don't forget it was a case of sailing in those days. It is a moot point whether the enforced rest was to the player's benefit. As soon as he arrived in America he went to Minneapolis, where he had two weeks to prepare for the US Open at Interlachen. He had his share of luck during the championship, such as when he hit a shot into water and it skidded off the surface and onto the green, where he took advantage of his good fortune by sinking a birdie putt. That must have made his playing partners bite their tongues. He went into the last round five shots clear of the field, but not for the first time he squandered strokes in a major event, including taking double bogies on three short holes. On the last green he was under the impression that he needed to sink a forty-foot birdie putt. In it went, only for him to discover that his opponents had capitulated. He was still on course for the impossible, or 'impregnable'! Three out of four and still going strong, ignoring the occasional hiccup, none of which had been fatal to date.

He had a long wait until the fourth and final hurdle, the US Amateur in the autumn, and when it came he progressed in much the same style as in the British Amateur, building leads and then letting them slip, but holing the crucial ones to keep his hopes alive. Thus he arrived at the final. It was as though his cares fell away; he played beautifully and his opponent, Gene Homans, was a beaten man long before the eventual finish on the eleventh green, soundly thrashed by eight and seven. The first Grand Slam (Impregnable Quadrilateral) in golfing history had been achieved. Had I written this last year, it would have read the only Grand Slam, but as we all now know an even greater Grand Slam has been recorded by today's wonder boy, Tiger Woods. Was Jones as good as Woods? Oh no, better not start that. Woods certainly doesn't squander shots as Jones apparently did, but perhaps he didn't have as many strokes advantage to be able to do so. Tommy Armour probably got it right when he said, 'It is nonsense to talk about who was the greatest golfer in the world. All you can say is that there have been none greater than Bobby Jones.' Another wise head would add '…or Tiger Woods.' Yet others would claim a place for Jack Nicklaus, and so it goes on....

After 1930, at the age of twenty-eight, Jones retired to his law practice. He was an amateur, after all. He had nothing else to achieve. He had set himself targets in the same way that Joyce Wethered had. They simply wished to demonstrate that they could achieve the highest level. For Joyce, it was definitely to demonstrate to herself; with Bobby, there was sufficient of the showman in him for him to want to show the world. They had both suffered physically at the major events, though both kept that largely to themselves. Jones's friend and biographer revealed that in a tournament Bobby might lose as much as a stone in weight. The inner emotional stress drained him, and Bernard Darwin recalled watching him after the 1930 Open at Hoylake, as he waited to discover whether he had triumphed. He had to hold his glass in both hands as he shook with emotion and threatened to spill the contents all over the room. Joyce would retire after competition for a week or two, to comparative seclusion, until her emotions had settled back to normality. Jones and Wethered were both well liked for their modesty, quietness, and good humour.

The record books are not the only witness to Bobby Jones's greatness; he built a golf course called Augusta. At the time, it was mainly to provide a venue where friends and rivals of his playing days could meet to compete and demonstrate their skills whilst, no doubt, indulging in a little nostalgia. Although remaining a private course with an invited membership, it soon became the scene for one of the great tournaments of the world – the US Masters. It had previously been an indigo plantation and was then converted into a nursery. It was a wonderland of tall pines, magnolia, camellia, azalea and dogwood. Jones and the Scottish designer Alister Mackenzie produced a course with few bunkers, but where the troubles lay was around the approaches to the greens. The first 'Masters' was played in 1934, though it had not adopted that title at that time. Jones very reluctantly agreed to play and the American public swarmed back to watch their hero of yesteryear. His old faithful putter had been donated to the R&A Golf Club Museum, and he failed to find the touch with his new model and so the fairytale return never quite materialised, but the Masters was launched and has arguably become the best TV viewing championship in the world. Superb golf played in superb surroundings!

Bobby Jones had been a delicate child in his early years and seldom enjoyed perfect health throughout his life. By his early 1930s he was already becoming affected by a wasting disease of the muscles and spent many years in a wheelchair until his eventual death in 1971.

As has already been written, Joyce Wethered and Bobby Jones had a mutual admiration of each other. They both had a long, flowing, apparently effortless swing which was a joy to behold, particularly when they were playing with someone who preferred to propel the ball by force, and achieve much less. Hal Rhodes, a Canadian teaching professional who did not become a pro until he was forty-four years old, had graduated from a hacker to a reasonable player by minutely studying a cine-film of Bobby Jones' swing. When Joyce went over to America in 1935, she permitted Rhodes to shoot a similar film of her own action. She stated that Bobby had done a lot for golf and if an instruction film of her own action could be of benefit to others, she would be pleased to oblige. Rhodes claimed to have used the film for over thirty years. There are several interesting points about this. The first and most important, and revealing, is that Rhodes claimed, 'Joyce Wethered's swing matched Bobby Jones's almost frame by frame in a remarkable manner.' I suppose we should not be surprised, as she did freely admit to having admired his swing and tried to model herself on it – apparently very successfully. Joyce Wethered claimed later in life never to have seen herself in action, so it appears that while many others did and benefited greatly from it, she never saw the film herself. Amazing! The final point is that Joyce was not paid for the film, and by this time she had become a professional by playing exhibitions for money. Where was her agent?

During the 1920s, Bobby was continually coming up against Roger Wethered in tournaments and Joyce would usually be in attendance. Bobby knew of Joyce's great record of championship successes, of course, and a friendship developed between them. Indeed, when Joyce went to America the two people she most wanted to meet and play with were Glenna Collett and Bobby Jones, and they were equally anxious to oblige. Perhaps the greatest tribute to Joyce's playing prowess came from Bobby Jones in 1930, the year in which he achieved the Grand Slam. He played in a four ball at St Andrews, where he partnered Joyce against her brother, who a week or so later he would beat in the final of the Open Amateur event over the same course, and T.A. Bourn, a well-known amateur of the time. They all played from the back tees and there was a strong breeze blowing in off the sea. Joyce carded a seventy-six and Bobby a seventy-five. In fact, she had been two strokes up on him with three holes to play but had then lost her putting touch, including taking three from twelve feet at the seventeenth. After the match, Jones declared, 'I have not played golf with anyone, man or woman, amateur or professional, who made me feel so utterly outclassed. It was not so much the score she made as the way she made it. It was impossible to expect that Miss Wethered would ever miss a shot – and she never did.' Praise indeed, and even if there was an element of courtesy included in it, Jones admiration could not be denied. It reminds me of that lovely story of the conversation between Dr Rowland and Andrew Kirkaldy, when the former related to the latter that Joyce had just gone round the Old Course at St Andrews off the back tees in seventy-four:

> '"What do you think of Miss Wethered's seventy-four?'
> 'Here?'
> 'Yes.'
> 'On The Old Course?'
> 'Yes.'
> 'By Gawd!"'

Whilst the golfing public enjoyed the triumphs of Bobby Jones in 1926 and took him to their hearts, it shouldn't be forgotten that golf was still very much a middle-class sport. True, the general public, or those of them in the large conurbations conveniently situated and connected by rail to courses where national events were taking place, might pour forth for special occasions, but mostly golf was the sport of the privileged. There was still a great divide between the classes. In Britain, in 1926, it all came to a head when the TUC called a general strike. It happened on 3 May at midnight and was the first time that this had happened in Britain. It was brought about by proposals of the mine owners to cut the miners' wages and increase their working hours. Talks to avert the strike had broken down when the TUC had refused to repudiate action by printers at the *Daily Mail*, who refused to print an anti-union editorial. A state of emergency had been declared and troops were deployed as class warfare was feared by many. The response from the working men had been solid in their support of the strike, but middle-class volunteers had come forth to try to keep the services operating. After little more than a week, and following promises from the government regarding a national wages board, the TUC called off the strike and averted a nasty possibility of civil warfare.

I imagine that JW in Surrey was largely insulated against the troubles. Her family had not yet felt the effects of the growing depression. She was not without occupation in her retirement from the championship scene. After all, such events had comprised a relatively small part of her life. She continued with the rest of her golf, playing for pleasure rather than for titles, though I would hazard a guess that she played to win, whatever the circumstances. She would be surprised if anything other was suggested. 'Do I play to win? But, of course. You do, don't you.'

Her fame brought other duties. She was in demand to open new clubhouses and putting greens, and to attend garden parties and other social occasions, to declare events open or cut the ribbon with silver scissors, play the first official shot etc. Whether she attended the ladies' championships which she had forsaken I have been unable to discover, but she was certainly a regular attendee at the men's national events, where her brother was continuing to perform with distinction.

There were a number of annual golfing events supported by the top amateurs in the country, and therefore Joyce was not devoid of good competition. One of the more famous of these was the Worplesden Mixed Foursomes, always played in October, the end of the season, as it were, before winter set in. It is appropriate to dwell on Worplesden for a while, as it is a good indication of top level amateur golf at that time.

Worplesden lies between Guildford and Woking, and Joyce had transferred her allegiance there quite early in her golfing career. Indeed, in 1922 she was lady captain and was president of the club from 1963 to 1977. She may well have retained her membership at West Surrey also. Her brother Roger was president of the Woking club for twenty-one years. He maintained membership at a number of clubs in the area, and it is possible that Joyce did likewise.

Worplesden Mixed Foursomes was on the calendar and there was a waiting list for those aching to join what was a social event in addition to a golfing event. It was all started in 1921 and, as Bernard Darwin, the golf correspondent, said, 'Once a Worplesdonian, always a Worplesdonian.' The meeting took place over four days and house parties in the surrounding area were part of the event. On the first day there was a good deal of back-slapping and bonhomie and, not unnaturally, comment on partnerships of the previous year which had been dissolved and partnerships of the current year which had been formed. One topic of conversation after the first few years related to who would be JW's partner that particular year. Joyce attended the event most years, from the commencement of the competition until the outbreak of the Second World War, when play was suspended whilst Jerry was dealt with. She also played immediately after the war with her husband, now of course under the title of Lady Heathcoat-Amory. She won the event with her partner on no less than eight occasions – with seven different partners. It was notable that whenever she reached the final, she usually won. On only two occasions did this not happen. The first occasion was the very first year that the event was held and Joyce played with brother Roger. They maintained their partnership the following year and were successful. The Wethereds didn't tolerate too many failures.

The second time she lost in the final was twenty-seven years later in 1948, playing with her husband Sir John Heathcoat-Amory. Sir John was not in Joyce's class, but he was a single-figure golfer and a win would have been extremely popular, but it was not to be. It is a strange fact that no husband/wife combination managed to win until the famous Bonallacks, Michael and Angela, brought it off in 1958.

How was it that JW played with so many different partners? It is an intriguing question. It was not as if she played with one partner for two or three years and then moved on to someone new. She and her partner won in three successive years from 1931 to 1933, but in each year the partner was different. Had she become so famous that no man felt it right that he should request her company on more than one occasion? I am sure that she did nothing to offend them, and I can't believe that she would simply give them the push. A study of the records of Worplesden suggests that the answer is no mystery at all. Worplesden was like one big happy family, and in the manner in which a good hostess will ensure that she mixes with the guests and tries not to show too much favouritism to one particular guest, so the participants at Worplesden, Joyce included, mixed and matched from year to year. In addition there were, of course, the enforced changes brought about by circumstance. One year, for example, Joyce was due to partner Bernard Darwin, who contracted a rather bad dose of flu at the last minute. Richard Oppenheimer stepped into the breach, and that explains the background to the selection of one of her partners. Mr Oppenheimer was rewarded by accompanying Joyce through to the final of the event and winning it.

Joyce's own comments on the formation of her partnerships are not particularly revealing:

> For a time many of the couples in the field were composed of family collaborations, mothers and sons, fathers and daughters, husbands and wives, uncles and aunts with nephews or nieces. Since those early days the family tradition has flagged a little and a freer exchange of partners is the general rule today. Now it is looked forward to as a pleasant and effective finish of the season where partnerships change frequently and championships are for the moment lost sight of. The foursomes have pleasant memories for us, as we lived not very far from the course and always collected amusing house parties for the week, some members of which, it was hoped would survive to the finish.

In 1927, Joyce played with Cyril Tolley, one of the best amateurs of the time and a friend of Roger's at Oxford. She had previously played with him in 1923, when they had been successful. In 1927, Cyril was staying with the Wethered family at 'Tigbourne' for the week of the tournament. Also at 'Tigbourne' were Simone de la Chaume (later Madame Rene Lacoste) and her mother. Simone was the current British Open champion, and she was partnering Roger in the foursomes. It must have been a very jolly affair, for Joyce and Cyril, and Simone and Roger all progressed through to the final. One can imagine the talk and leg-pulling at the dinner table at 'Tigbourne' on the evening before the final. Madame de la Chaume had no doubts that she was supporting her daughter and partner. Mrs Wethered was in the difficult position of not quite knowing which side to support. In the event, Joyce and Cyril triumphed by three and two after a closely contested game which apparently included more than a touch of humour. Here again we receive a taste of Joyce's modesty. She recalled that 'Madame was by far the most excited member of the party, but Simone was the coolest and most collected.' Always a congratulatory word for the loser!

Joyce's record of achievement at Worplesden would have been even better had she not teamed up for a period with Colonel Dalrymple Hamilton. He was a friend of the family but not quite up to the standard of some of the other players, and Joyce could not carry him through to victory. They tried on three occasions without success. She described him as a keen ally, but thought that his chief concern might be that she would take the game too seriously for his peace of mind. I wouldn't think that he was far off the mark there. To Joyce, it was a game – a game to be won.

1923 Worplesden provided JW with her first hole-in-one. This was at the Pond Hole, a medium iron over the water. Perhaps more entertaining that year was the performance of a somewhat eccentric New Zealander, who played with a tee-peg nine inches high, comprising a piece of wood with a nail in the end with which to stick it into the ground. On the top of the wood was a rubber tube, at the summit of which he placed his ball. He argued that it was no recipe for disaster to have to play one shot nine inches off the ground and the next one on the ground, as it simply made the player concentrate all the more, and in concentration lies the 'secret' to successful golf. Nice one! We shall not be entering into any correspondence on this last point. Nor did I think it worth the trouble to try to find out how far the New Zealander progressed in the tournament. I am willing to wager that he made an entertaining house guest.

One of the loveliest stories I have read about JW has nothing to do with Worplesden, except that it was included in an article on Worplesden written by Bernard Darwin. It recalls that there was a foursomes' competition due to take place one afternoon at North Berwick, which was a mixture of all ages. A small boy was to have the great Miss Wethered as his partner. He disappeared in the morning and his parents were getting somewhat agitated when he failed to turn up for his lunch. A little later he arrived looking very hot, tired and dishevelled. On being asked what he had been doing, he replied, 'Practising getting out of bunkers.' Beautiful!

In case you have the idea that Worplesden was a social occasion and therefore the standard of play would have suffered from a surfeit of wining and dining, I should disabuse you of any such thing. It was not unusual for a pair to play round in even fours, and Joyce recalled nine holes playing with Cyril Tolley in driving rain when they went out for the first nine holes in thirty-two, which would have been thirty-one had they not been stymied on the last hole. You did not win at Worplesden unless you were on the top of your form and played well, and even then often needed a little luck. Oh! It also helped to have Joyce Wethered as your partner.

Whilst Joyce enjoyed her well-earned break from the national championship scene, golf continued to flourish, as did other sporting activities. Gradually, more and more of the population were finding themselves with a little more money to spend and more leisure time in which to do just that. The first greyhound racing track opened in Manchester in 1926, and the following year London sported no less than three such entertainments, at Harringay, White City, and Wembley. Malcolm Campbell and Henry Segrave were engaged in taking the world land-speed record from each other. Segrave was the first to exceed 200mph, but Campbell had held the record three times already and was confident that he would soon have it back. On his last attempt the wind force had knocked off his goggles, temporarily blinding him. In glorious understatement, he declared that 'It was most testing'!

On a more ominous note, the newspapers revealed that Britons led the world – in cigarette smoking. 'The cigarette held between slim fingers has become one of the symbols of female emancipation, while lighting a girl's cigarette is fast becoming a romantic cliché.' The consumption of cigarettes had trebled in twenty years. It was a curse of the twentieth century, when I had always assumed that smoking had been widespread since the time of Sir Walter Raleigh.

In 1926 Sam Ryder had persuaded the American and British Professional Associations to play a semi-official match which was played at Wentworth, the British team winning by the extravagant margin of

13.5 to 1.5. The following year, in America, the tables were turned when America won the first official biennial match by 12.5 to 2.5. The Ryder Cup was born, a huge step forward for professional golf. It is interesting that the expenses for the British trip were raised by appeal via George Philpott, the editor of the magazine, *Golf Illustrated*. In these days when all sporting events of any note are supported financially by advertising, it is easy to forget that there was a time when that source of funding was small and elusive. Indeed we shall see later that international matches for the ladies were delayed several years due to the lack of finance and the consequent need for any participants to find their own finance.

Although JW had retired from the fray for a while, her brother Roger had done no such thing and continued to keep the Wethered flag flying. Apart from his exceptional record against the Americans in the Walker Cup matches (only three losses in nine matches), he was also a regular winner of the January Oxford and Cambridge Golfing Society annual tournament at Rye – 'the President's Putter.' He achieved success on no less than five occasions. This was a major tournament at the time (many will say that it still is), because the preponderance of the top amateurs were Oxford and Cambridge men. The title of the tournament derived from the fact that the trophy was indeed the putter with which Hugh Kirkaldy won the 1891 British Open. The tradition was that the ball of the winner for that year should be attached to the putter by a silver band and chain. The first winner of the event was Ernest Holderness, British Amateur champion of 1922 and 1924. He won the first four 'putters', and later added a fifth. Holderness, incidentally, was an extremely dour man, especially on the golf course. One of his opponents recalled that he spoke only three sentences throughout the match: 'I think that's three up', and 'Thank you very much. That's five and four.'

Roger Wethered was to equal Holderness's feat in the late 1920s and 1930s. On one occasion he tied with A. Storey. They had been tied after eighteen holes and had proceeded through extra holes nineteen to twenty-four, halving each, by which time it had become too dark to see and therefore the match was declared a draw, and two balls hung from the old putter that year. Bernard Darwin, *The Times* correspondent, used to wax lyrical about 'the Putter' and quoted Dr Watts, 'I have been there, and still would go; 'twas like a little heaven below.' Having noted the kind of weather the doughty competitors have to contend with on occasion, that sounds a mite inappropriate; but Bernard was a convivial soul and there is no doubt that it would be the event rather than the golf to which he was referring.

In 1928 Roger again reached the final of the British Amateur, with Joyce in supporting role among his entourage, but it was not to be his day and he lost to a Midlands golfer, Philip Perkins, at Prestwick by six and four.

6
ST ANDREWS

As the decade drew to a close, with the advent of 1929, my research through the newspapers lighted upon the statement, 'Jerusalem. The British declare martial law in a bid to quell clashes between Arabs and Jews which have left sixty dead.' The problem of the Middle East, as with the Irish problem, seems to have no end or solution.

Of less worldly importance, but to some of great golfing significance, was the fact that the Ladies' British Open Championship was scheduled for the home of golf – St Andrews. I do not know how far in advance Joyce Wethered had decided that she would return to the fray, but it was not a spur-of-the-moment decision. St Andrews was her favourite course, as it should be for any golfer worth his or her salt. For a lady who had always strived to reach the top of the tree, this was an opportunity not to be missed. To win the British crown was an achievement of the highest order, but to win it at St Andrews would be a pinnacle unsurpassable.

Those in the know were aware that Joyce was making her preparations diligently, practising with more purpose, playing with even greater control. The signs were there to tell that this was a serious attempt. For the first time for several years, she was the Surrey champion again.

Steel shafts to clubs had now been made legal in Britain, but Joyce stayed true to her hickory shafts, as did Bobby Jones when winning his four championships the succeeding year. Steel shafts reduced the tendency to slice the ball. Bernard Darwin wrote, 'Never again would anybody be able to write, as did a facetious friend of mine, to the maker of a patent club, "It has added fifty yards to my slice."' The introduction of steel shafts was to the disadvantage of the old club-makers. With wooden clubs, each one was crafted individually and the more discerning could tell the name of the maker from simply looking at the clubs, not reading the label. Steel shafts permitted the introduction of matched sets. It wasn't long before the old timers were out of work. Of course, the new materials did not eliminate the myriad of problems associated with the golf shot. As the old Scots pro said, 'Whatever clubs you have, the ball maun be hit.'

When the golf correspondent Lewine Mair interviewed Joyce she was in her eighties, but she still had fond memories of St Andrews. It still excited her to recall the Old Course, the Town, the People... 'The magic everyone talks about at St Andrews really does exist. I have always loved the way you meet the same people on the streets as on the fairways, the way in which town and course are one.'

Those are not the murmurings of a dear old lady dreaming of yesteryear and looking back through rose-tinted spectacles. Those words are every bit as true today as they have been for countless years. Anyone who has any interest in golf at all simply must make a pilgrimage to the home of golf. It is wonderfully incredible that the Old Course is so accessible to anyone. There are even public footpaths and a road across it. You couldn't gain access without the appropriate ticketing during a championship, of course, but for ninety per cent of the year you can stroll around to your heart's content. There are many courses where access is denied to all but the members or those willing to pay a large green fee, and where security is frightening, but not dear old St Andrews. It is the peoples' course; and it is so near to the town that it is part of the town. You can literally walk off the street and stand beside the eighteenth green. There is nothing pretentious about the town. It is a pleasant university town with all the usual amenities that a town would have, plus the added attractions of an ageing castle and a ruined cathedral.

I find it impossible to convey to you the immense feeling of content-ment which will come upon a golfer when he first arrives and parks his car, and discovers everything is within walking distance. In minutes he can be viewing the famous Swilcan Burn or inspecting the dreaded bunker (it looks much smaller but no easier than on the television) at the Roadhole, and then, feeling thirsty or hungry, can take a five-minute walk along the footpath adjacent to the eighteenth fairway, and he is back in the town.

When you first arrive, drive to the car park on the seafront, adjacent to the British Golf Museum on Bruce Embankment, and just behind the clubhouse of the Royal and Ancient Golf Club. Three minutes' walk and you are in front of the clubhouse, and the scene you see so often on the television during a championship stretches out before you, but with rather less people in attendance. If you are lucky there will be only a handful of like-minded folk gazing down the first fairway, most of them in silent contemplation, their thoughts conjuring up those magic moments when Jack Nicklaus, or Tony Jacklin, or Laura Davies were doing something incredible. The first fairway looks so incredibly wide that even though you are not going to play the course, you feel relieved that you could put your first shot somewhere upon it. Even the great players have admitted to jelly legs and queasy tummies as they have addressed their ball prior to that first drive. Please God, let me hit it... Unfortunately, there have been those who didn't. The new captain for the year of the R&A is aware six months in advance that he must face that most onerous of duties of new golf captains everywhere – the drive-in – when his drive, watched by a host of members, heralds the new golfing year. At least one captain of the R&A has been overcome by the event and the huge responsibility and has swung in vain, contacting nothing but fresh air, but was rescued from his dilemma by a quick-witted starter, who announced loudly, 'Good practise swing, sir. Now let us have the real one.' There is a story, and I am sure that it is only a story, but sufficiently entertaining to bear the re-telling, that one unfortunate man on that famous first tee caught his drive in the socket of his club to such devastating effect that the ball shot off at right angles between his legs and finished in the hole on the eighteenth green. 'Round in one, sir,' expostulated his incredulous old Scottish caddie. I have surveyed the scene, and it could be done!

At the end of the wide fairway of the first hole, sharp eyes can just detect a thin ribbon which denotes the Swilcan Burn protecting that first green. Then the course becomes a receding blur of seemingly flat greenery. A quick glance to the right at the white-capped rollers coming in to St Andrews Bay, and then look half-left and a number of well-known phenomena present themselves. In the distance stands the new Old Course Hotel, resplendent, where there once stood the old black railway sheds, beside the seventeenth fairway. There is the little stone-arch bridge over the burn on the eighteenth fairway, where the great players enjoying (or suffering) their last championship are wont to dally and wave to the appreciative crowd. There is the row of shops, houses and restaurants which borders the eighteenth fairway, with one shop in particular proudly boasting in large letters that it was once the shop of the great 'TOM MORRIS'. Tom Snr and his son Tom Jnr won the Open four times each between 1861 and 1872; Tom Jnr could and probably would have made it five times in 1871, but he had won the three previous years and had in consequence been presented with the championship belt permanently. The Prestwick Club, who used to organise the event at that time, embarrassingly had to cancel the 1871 event because they had not organised a new trophy in time!

You are still standing in front of the R&A clubhouse, and must now look left to the eighteenth green and the infamous 'Valley of Sin', a fold of ground which eats into the green, and has the nasty habit of trapping a shot to the flag which is so nearly perfect but not quite. In consequence, the ball rolls away and finishes many yards away, making three putts quite possible.

Now, looking behind you to the left is St Andrews itself. 'The Rows' is a street, facing the bay, of solid Victorian hotels and houses, many converted to offices, including the home of the Ladies' Golf Union. Golf Place leads into North Street and into the town, where hotels, restaurants, and shops serve your every need. It is as easy as that.

There are books which are devoted entirely to the Old Course and many others which give every detail of St Andrews. The town has a most informative website also, including a map, and comments on all the amenities. It is not my intention to attempt to vie with these various sources of information, but some comment on the golf course seems justified, particularly as it was Joyce Wethered's favourite course, and we have the benefit of observations which she made about it.

There are in fact four (it may be five) courses at St Andrews and the New Course would probably be a championship course if it did not have to compete with its elder sister. The Old Course is 6,566 yards long (though it is lengthened to something in the vicinity of 7,000 yards for major championships) and has a SSS of seventy-two. Not all players like the course, including some of the top professionals. JW states:

It is useless to try to pretend that St Andrews appeals to everyone. To some it may appear cold and unattractive; the links may seem a flat and dreary expanse, with too many blind holes, hidden bunkers and bad lies. An unfortunate collection of bad faults to begin with, you might say. To others it appears in all the glory of its past history, a battlefield that has been the scene of countless victories and a course requiring a never-ending stock of intricate and cunning shots to defeat the broken quality of the ground.

There is no doubt that, because so much is hidden as the golfer contemplates his shots, a good knowledgeable local caddie is a must at St Andrews, more so than at most courses, for any player trying to return a serious score. JW remembers that on her first round she eventually gave up trying to fashion her own destiny and put herself entirely in the hands of her competent caddie, following his direction to play towards a church steeple or some other landmark on the skyline. There is also no doubt that golfers warm to the course and its intricacies, the more they play it. This is because they learn the layout and realise how each hole has to be played. They come to realise that it is a test of skill all the way round and their admiration for it grows accordingly. There are a number of top professionals who do not rate it in their early association with it, but very few, if any, continue to berate it as they come to know it, and many fall in love with it. Bobby Jones, for one, declared that if he were allowed to play only one course, it would be St Andrews. Joyce Wethered, likewise. I imagine from knowledge of their mutual admiration that they would be more than happy if they were in the same four ball.

To hear from JW again:

To become a genuine lover of St Andrews needs plenty of time and experience. I stayed a fortnight on my first visit and the last week passed in a flash – one heavenly day after another. It took the whole of the first week to sort out the holes and even to begin to understand the links; but ever since then the Old Course has stood alone in my estimation and I love every hummock of it. When I saw all the famous holes which have so frequently been written about, I found that they were quite different from what I expected. I can safely say that the two holes which frightened me more than any others I have ever seen were the eleventh and seventeenth. There could scarcely be on any course two more alarming or awe-inspiring

*holes. I have played them both at very critical moments, so I ought to know
what a terrifying test they can be.*

Only the first, ninth, seventeenth, and eighteenth holes have their own
greens; the remainder all share huge greens with another hole, some not
very far short of 100 yards across. This is because the course is laid out
on a comparatively narrow neck of land. Originally, the holes coming
in were simply the same holes as those going out, but played in reverse.

Every hole has its peculiarities, and Joyce found it difficult to express
a preference for any favourites, but she did concede that, of the less
famous holes, she had an affection for the second and the thirteenth.
The second hole is a par-four of a little more than 400 yards. The easier
approach is from the right, but that is an area fraught with danger from
bunkers waiting to gobble up your tee-shot. The green slopes from
front to back and Joyce found that the only way to play the hole and
get your second near to the flag was to trickle your ball as slowly as you
dared over the little ridge in front of the green.

All the holes have wondrous names, as have many of the bunkers and
other hazards, something those with the job of marketing modern golf
would have been proud and delighted to have introduced. There are
only two short par-threes on the course, the first at the eighth, which
starts what is referred to as 'the loop', four holes which set the player
on his way back towards the clubhouse. It is here that players will be
hoping to make an impression against par, and, if they miss out, it is
awfully hard to make any headway on the return journey.

The eleventh hole is little more than 300 yards and is a real candidate
for a possible birdie, if one can avoid the many small bunkers which
are not apparent from the tee, but which become apparent when
one finds oneself in one. One of these is named 'The Admiral'. The
name derives from an experience of Rear Admiral C.H.G. Benson, a
stalwart of the R&A, who was traversing this particular hole one day
when his attention was momentarily distracted by the appearance of a
rather attractive young lady on the starboard bow. As his opponents
confirmed, one moment he was there, the next he was not. He had
disappeared, clubs, trolley and all, into a sandy retreat. Ever since, that
particular bunker has borne his name.

The thirteenth, a favourite of JW, is remembered by many non-golfers
or those watching an event on the television, for the three Coffin
bunkers and Cat's Trap which are lying in wait for any drive pulled to

the left. The Coffins leave no doubt about the fate of anyone unlucky enough to enter them, but interpretation of what might constitute a Cat's Trap needs a very fertile mind. JW comments:

A good drive should land one just to the right of the Coffin bunkers, under – but it is hoped not too near – the steep bank running across the fairway. Then comes a glorious spoon shot to be smacked right up to the large flat green, followed by a rush to the top of the hill to see that the ball is over the jaws of the Lion's Mouth and yet has not faded away into the Hole O' Cross bunker.

Well indeed, fancy Joyce Wethered 'smacking' a shot and 'rushing' to the top of the hill! This course must be something special; we are not used to Joyce acting in this excitable manner.

Hole fourteen rejoices in the title of 'Long'. It is about 567 yards. It contains a cluster of bunkers, famous the world over, 'the Beardies'. If these are evaded and your drive lands with satisfaction on the fairway, known as the Elysian Fields, you are faced with two more beauties, guarding the green and still some two hundred and fifty yards ahead; 'Kitchen', which is small, and 'Hell', which is not. The green is also difficult due to a steep fronting bank, and many has been the golfer who has taken seven, without, in his opinion, hitting a bad shot.

The sixteenth contains 'The Principal's Nose', which is a bulge in the ground right on the line you would like to play to the hole and containing three little bunkers, one on the tee side of the bulge and two on the other.

The seventeenth is the infamous 'Roadhole', which is a dog-leg right, and this necessitates that competitors have to drive over the out of bounds if they are to have any chance of reaching the green in two. Many decide to do it in three, and thus hope to avoid the nasty little bunker which protects the approach to the green. Even then, it requires the most delicate of pitches or chips if one is to negotiate the treacherous bank guarding the green which tends to gather the ball and guide it to the waiting bunker. Over-pitching is equally fatal, as one finds oneself on the road which lies directly beside the green. Stories are legion about this hole, perhaps more so than any other in Britain. Davie Ayton, an apparent certain winner of the Open took eleven there. In the 1921 Open a professional had thirteen. Richard Oppenheimer, a winner at Worplesden in conjunction with JW in 1932, reached the seventeenth in 1935 in the Autumn Meeting, only one stroke behind the clubhouse leader, and promptly drove three balls out of bounds in quick succession to record an eleven.

The eighteenth is a comparatively straightforward par-four if the Valley of Sin can safely be negotiated, but stresses and strains are likely to be at a maximum by this time and all but the most avaricious will be content with a par. Whatever the day or time, there are likely to be a few spectators leaning on the railing watching events at the eighteenth green. On the day I was there, I had followed a mixed four ball over the last two holes. Their standard was not high, but they were obviously enjoying the experience. On the eighteenth, one lady had the misfortune to top her drive and also her following shot. Her third shot placed her just within reach of the green. She played a long iron, which skipped happily on to the green and straight into the hole via the flagstick. The gathered audience roared its approval. 'Wonderful eagle 2,' said one gentleman. I hesitated and considered telling him of the events at the other end of the hole. But no, why shouldn't the lady enjoy the adulation, even if it was slightly suspect. I imagine she will still be recounting the story to this day.

It was to St Andrews that the London night express brought Joyce Wethered in mid-May 1929. She had that same feeling of excitement which she always experienced when she came north to Scotland. Edinburgh was just waking as the train arrived and the Firth of Forth beneath its famous bridge was hazy in the morning light. Battleships lay at anchor. Then on to St Andrews, and the town was visible over the last few miles, the various landmarks becoming identifiable as the train approached its destination. The track ran beside the golf course over its last mile or so and Joyce indulged herself in alertly spotting as many of the famous sites and hazards as was possible as they passed by the window.

She booked in to Russack's Hotel and permitted herself a visit into the town, more to just see it again, as if looking up an old friend, rather than for any specific purpose of purchasing anything. She didn't actually go in anywhere, other than the odd shop; it was more a tour of the streets and buildings, as if to make sure that they were still all in place. Only after this had been done did she contemplate anything to do with golf, though, as she mused to herself, St Andrews was everything to do with golf. You didn't have to be on the course all the time.

She wasn't sure how to approach the course as she returned down from the town, and inwardly chastised herself for being so stupid and melodramatic. In the end she opted to slip past the university library from North Street into The Scores, in the knowledge that she would be able to savour her approach as she passed the Bruce Embankment and the Old Course came into view between the houses and hotels on her left and the R&A clubhouse to the right. It was like looking down on heaven. She avoided the clubhouse in the certain knowledge that some-one would recognise her and she preferred for this first hour or two to be by herself. Then it was back to the hotel, feeling good inside and ready for the first practise session that same afternoon.

The first round of the championship started on the Tuesday in glorious sunny conditions – it was 14 May. Joyce was drawn against Phyllis Lobbett and was expected to see her off in no time at all. Never a comfortable position to be in – you can't really win, only lose. They teed off between one and two o'clock. A goodly crowd had gathered, but marshals were conspicuous by their absence. The result was that for the first three holes, pandemonium reigned. Bodies were flying everywhere, and the players and their caddies had to push their way through in the hope of locating their balls, which they amazingly did. This was not what Joyce wanted. It was precisely why she had vacated the championship scene four years previously. However, she realised there was little that she could do about it, and concentrated on concentrating. By the fourth hole an army of flag-waving marshals had gathered and some semblance of order had been restored. Phyllis, a good golfer on her day, was not quite up to the task, not helped by the fact that she was consistently fifty or sixty yards behind her opponent off the tee. Out they went, and the screw tightened on poor Phyllis. Joyce went round the loop 4,3,3,3. It was too much and the match finished on the fourteenth green with JW the winner by six and four. She had become so relaxed and was concentrating so much on her own game (the two are compatible), that she did not realise that she had won, and hadn't she always said that you should play the course and not your opponent?

The next day Joyce had to face an Irish challenger, Mrs Madill. The weather had changed and the contestants had to suffer the combined challenges of thunder, lightning, rain and even hail. Joyce did not start at her best and had a couple of fives, almost shanked a shot and actually lost a hole. She then settled down to work. Mrs Madill was out-driven at times by as much as 100 yards! The game was all over by the eleventh hole.

By the afternoon the weather had relented and JW had a comfortable five and four win over Mrs Garon.

The next round pitted her against Miss Skewan, who was playing her home course. She survived until the fifteenth hole, and it was generally agreed that this reflected great credit on the St Andrews lady, as the oracular Andra Kirkcaldy had been willing to bet that 'no human lady would take Miss Wethered past the corner of the Dyke.'

A final between Joyce and her old rival, the American champion Glenna Collett, had been forecast by certain 'experts', but forecasting the final of a multi-round knockout competition is not for the faint-hearted. It needs only one slip from either of the prospective candidates and that is that. Glenna was playing anything but champion's golf as she scrambled through, round by round. But the competition had whittled the competitors down to the last eight, and she was still there. There were still some tough cookies disputing the right to feature on the final day. Joyce had to play Molly Gourlay and Glenna had Doris Park standing in her way.

Joyce dealt with the situation by simply turning up the gas a little more. Her very good play of the previous rounds became almost perfection. Molly would have many successful days on the tournament circuit in the years ahead, but on that day in May 1929, she hardly knew what had hit her. She was, as she said later, quite dazed at the speed with which it all happened. Never had she felt so helpless. She just followed in the wake as HMS *Wethered* steamed ahead. It was all over on the twelfth green. She avoided the 'Coffin bunkers', but she had been buried out of sight, by seven and six. She must have wished that she could have done an Admiral Benson, and dropped out of sight into a very large bunker.

Glenna Collett, meanwhile, having disposed of Mrs Watson in the morning with the best golf she had played all week, came out for the afternoon semi-final and repelled the doughty Doris Park with a steadiness and consistency which belied her form of the early part of the week.

On this occasion, the 'experts' were right. Almost everyone had the final which they wanted. Joyce Wethered *v.* Glenna Collett; Great Britain *v.* the United States of America; the queen of English golf *v.* the queen of American golf. A fiction writer could not have set it up better.

Joyce had been out of competition golf for four years, but she had five English titles and three British titles to her credit and was still regarded as invincible by the British public. So what did Glenna Collett have to offer? The answer is, 'plenty'.

Glenna, like Joyce and many of the other golfers of that era, had been born into a wealthy family. That was in 1903; she was two years younger than Joyce. She was soon demonstrating that she could be good at almost any sport she cared to try, including holding her own in her brother's baseball team. She was an excellent swimmer and diver, but her parents didn't want a tomboy, they wanted a daughter and persuaded her towards more genteel sports such as tennis and golf. She took to golf and won her first American national title in 1922. She eventually took that title five times, and also won a French title and a Canadian title. In her playing career at the top level she won forty-nine championships. When she came to Britain in 1929 she was on a roll, which included three consecutive US Amateur championships in the years 1928-1930.

Glenna Collett was not only very good at golf, she had grown into a very attractive young lady who was very much in the image of the typical American outdoor girl. In addition, she had a lovely temperament. On the golf course, her peers, without exception, found her to be friendly, courteous and even-tempered. Glenna was more outgoing than the conservative Joyce. She was a natural athlete and more worldly-wise. But the two not only had a high regard for each other's golfing abilities, they genuinely took to each other and enjoyed the other's company. Indeed, two evenings before they were playing each other in the final of the Ladies' Open, they were dining together. When Joyce went on her American tour six years later, she had said that one of the things she most looked forward to was meeting up with Glenna once more. When their golfing days were over they kept in touch, and whenever interviewed, which was often, they always were most complimentary about one another. A sporting attitude was a key element of both characters. They weren't often defeated, especially Joyce, but it didn't matter whether they had won or lost, there was always the same courteous acknowledgement of their opponent. In victory, there were no high-fives, no boastful comment upon their accomplishment; simply a desire to make the outcome more palatable to the loser, by kind words or kind actions.

Glenna once explained that being a good sport was expected to go far beyond the golf course; the champion is expected to bow to the desires of all, sponsors, press, organisers, etc:

> *There are times when life can become slightly tedious... you are expected to do many things which in reality you don't give two hoots about, to*

go to parties when you long to be in bed, to be nice to all sorts of people who ask all sorts of favours. The champion, unless she has the skill of a diplomat, has no way of expressing her gratitude and at the same time refusing. Sooner or later the champion begins to realise that she is supposed to do this and that, either from a desire to be agreeable or an honest wish to live up to the sweet things said about her in the sports columns. So the title-holder becomes a bit of an actress, creating a professional manner. That's the insidious thing about being a champion. You change inside or outside. But you change, anyhow.

Well, that was a bit of a revelation, but all credit to Glenna that she was able to cope with the demands and requirements as she explained, and still retain her highest of standings in sportsmanship. The reason is simple enough – she was by nature a very pleasant lady.

Does Joyce express herself on the same subject? Well, yes, she does, but I would rather leave that until later when we consider her American tour, when the demands really homed in on her. Suffice it to say here that the nature of Joyce was really a case of 'what you see is what you get'. She became very professional in her dealings with people, but there was not a lot of 'acting' with Joyce. She did her best to accommodate the needs of others, but if she really needed to go to bed rather than to a party, she would say so. It gave her a slightly more distant, arm's-length sort of relationship with people, which meant she would be described as courteous and accommodating rather than warm and affectionate, as would be applied to Glenna.

It was only as the two great ladies grew older that they preferred not to have to talk about each other in detail. For nigh on sixty years they had done their duty. They had described each other's swing and recalled specific characteristics. They considered that they had talked themselves out, that they should be left to get on with life rather than constantly having to go back to days left far behind. Glenna played competitive golf right into her eighties, and continued to oblige her public, if somewhat reluctantly, right through to her death in 1989. She came to Britain in 1984 for the Curtis Cup match at Muirfield, possibly a celebration of fifty years of Curtis Cup. The surviving members of that first epic event were invited, and Glenna remembered that every time something of importance occurred, two chairs would be pulled out for her and Molly Gourlay, who was eighty-five at the time, and, as she put it, 'The two old dames would be pointed out to those attending.' Joyce had written to Glenna to tell her that she would not be attending; it would all be too much.

Glenna's contribution to golf was acknowledged when she was selected as one of the six ladies to be entered into the United States Hall of Fame of Lady Golfers, when it was inaugurated in 1951.

Back to St Andrews in 1929: the great final was about to be played. Could Glenna Collett at last lay her bogey, and beat the great Wethered? Could Joyce Wethered really return to her beloved St Andrews and lift the crown, after several years' absence from championship golf?

Bernard Darwin, *The Times* correspondent and friend of the Wethereds, had described Joyce's progress to the final as 'a triumphal procession.' He was in no doubt as to the outcome, but then, he wasn't having to play the match. Those diehard fans who had been at the championship throughout the week had seen Glenna, with a fortunately easier draw than Joyce, play some uninspiring golf, particularly with the putter. They had been singularly unimpressed. But they had been lulled into a false sense of security. Real champions, playing on an unfamiliar course, are not only using the early rounds to progress against more modest opposition, they are carefully accumulating knowledge about the course. Where not to play their ball, where a risk is inadvisable, where not to over-hit a putt. All negatives in a positive sort of way. Also, they become more confident which club to play, when they can go for a big one without too much danger as a result, and how the wind and weather can affect their play. I suppose any golfer must benefit by increased knowledge of a course, but a champion, who can most of the time play the ball to where she wants it to go, benefits tremendously from course knowledge. I often wonder whether it would be more productive for a professional to use a local caddie, steeped in the knowledge of that particular course, than to take a caddie on tour. You would then have a marvellous combination of one person who knew exactly where each shot should be played and a second person who had the ability to play the ball to that spot.

I can tell you what the weather was like on every day of that championship week, but for the final the various press reports for some curious reason omit to mention it. I believe it was dry because the lady assigned to 'guard' JW carried her mackintosh over her arm!

The two protagonists shook hands. Looking composed and relaxed on the outside, but somewhat wound up on the inside, they drove off, watched by a large gallery including a packed R&A clubhouse. Eleanor Helme, writing for one of the periodicals, stated that the gallery was gloriously impartial. Not a view shared by Miss Collett, who recalled that she could plainly feel that the crowd favoured Joyce. Joyce later confessed that she was always a bit jumpy around the green for the first few holes, until she sank a decent putt, after which she would relax a little and settle into her game. On this day of all days, an early success was not to be. Glenna put her first drive straight down the middle, second on to the green, two putts and a perfect opening par-four. Joyce's putt failed to drop. One down.

If you can be straight on the second, it is a straightforward par-four. Glenna was straight and her second shot was near enough to the flag to make a birdie possible. She didn't sink it, but Joyce came up a little short and recorded a five. Two down.

The third is a short par-four. Joyce put her second very close to the flag and sank the putt. She had to; Glenna played another perfect par-four.

The fourth is called Ginger Beer, after an old character known as 'old Daw', who used to sell refreshment there. It is probably the hardest par-four on the front nine but was halved in fours by these ladies, playing superb golf. Joyce, playing each hole perfectly well until she reached the green, had a par on the long par-five, Hole o' Cross. It was not good enough. Two raking shots from Glenna and confident putting gained her a birdie. Back to two down.

Shared par-fours at the sixth, and the contestants arrived on the seventh tee where there is a blind drive and the big Shell bunker to be cleared with the second shot. No problem for Glenna, another par-four to her credit. Joyce had to settle for a five. Three doon!

The first of the short holes came next. Both ladies were on the green from the tee. Two putts for a par for Joyce. One putt for another birdie for Glenna. The crowd suddenly realised that they were watching something a little bit special. Their champion wasn't playing badly, although, as they say today, 'she couldn't buy one with her putter.' But this phenomenon from the USA was playing, as they also say today, 'out of her skin.' She completed the front nine with yet another perfect par-four. She had played those first nine holes on the great St Andrews course in thirty-four shots, two under fours, and not one bogey to be seen. What is more, she was five up!

In her book, JW wrote:

Glenna's first nine holes of the match was the finest sequence of holes I have ever seen a lady play. By the ninth green I was faced with a deficit of five holes. It was not that I had played badly through the green but the putts would not go down and I frittered away my chances round the hole. If the touch of the putter leaves you at St Andrews on those fast and immense greens, then heaven help you. You are indeed lost until you recover it.

As all golfers know only too well, problems in putting are multiplied when the opponent is playing well. It seems that the fates are conspiring against you; and who knows whether even the great Wethered was suffering from the pressure put upon her by this charming opponent.

The next three holes were all halved. The tenth is called 'Bobby Jones'. I know not why, presumably he effected some miraculous shot in the playing of the hole, but there again he played so many miraculous shots that many holes could be named after him. Here, Joyce thought she had at last laid the bogey of her putting. The ball actually entered the cup, but contrived to screw itself out and remain on the lip.

The eleventh is the sort of hole where long handicappers wonder what all the fuss is about, not realising that on championship days, the flag gets placed right behind the little Strath bunker, which guards that part of the green. The Hill bunker to the left has also gained some notable scalps. In the 1933 Open, Gene Sarazen, defending his title, took six at the hole, three of them in the bunker. At one point, frustrated beyond recognition at his inability to extract himself, he waved his club in the air, and an over-zealous marshal assumed that he had played a stroke which would have made him seven. The committee accepted Sarazen's explanation, but he was mortified that anyone should have suspected him of cheating. The ladies both had par-threes.

It is amazing how frequently we hear that one hole, or one shot even, has decided the outcome of a golf match. It is generally accepted that events at the twelfth hole, dear old Admiral Benson's hole, decided the contest about which I am writing. Hear what Joyce said:

The twelfth to my mind was the crux of the whole game. I believe that Glenna missed her chance there of making the match almost a certainty. We were both on the green in two and my first putt was woefully short.

Finally, after I had missed the next, Glenna was left a putt of three or four feet to win. If she had become six up at this point of the game, due to my criminally taking three putts yet again, I do not think the result would ever have been a close one. But she let me off, missed her first putt of the match and left me a ray of hope.

The crowd was too polite to express themselves audibly, but the beams of satisfaction and relief on their faces told all. As often happens at times of high drama, a quick reaction results. There is tremendous encouragement for the person who has benefited from the gaff, whilst the leader, however strongly she is going, senses a degree of strain and uncertainty. It was the first loss of a stroke to par that Glenna had suffered.

On the thirteenth, Joyce gave Glenna more reason for concern when she holed a four-yard putt, her first real putt of the day. She bravely holed out for a half, but at the next hole, one of the most fearsome on the course, a par-five with out-of-bounds perilously close for anything with a little slice in it, she slumped to a six. She was still four up but the damage seemed to have been done. A four at the next secured a half, but she finished the morning round with three fives as opposed to JW's 4, 5, 4.

Two down at the interval was almost like a lead to Joyce who had once been within a whisker of six adrift. Perhaps more significantly, it sowed seeds of doubt into Glenna's previous confidence. She knew that the fight was far from over and wasn't sure that she could cope. The overall golf had been superb; playing over 6,600 yards, the two ladies had a best ball score of seventy-one.

I am unaware of what luncheon arrangements were afforded the ladies. I am aware that Joyce, when once told by the press that a certain champion golfer had little more than a glass of milk between the morning and afternoon rounds, and asked by the same pressman of her preferences, stated that she ate whatever was placed before her! Her nerves didn't appear to affect her stomach in that direction.

Out they went for the afternoon round, and the already large crowd had increased considerably. Word had gone round the town that there was a contest taking place. Whatever Joyce had for her lunch, it suited her fine. Straight long drive, iron into the heart of the green, and most significantly a longish putt rattled into the cup. It was exactly what the doctor ordered. How the confidence came flooding in! Glenna secured her par, but it was not enough. By the third the match was all square, and a hole later Joyce was in the lead for the first time that day. Back came Glenna with an excellent birdie four at the fifth, but she spoiled it all by taking six at the next. The Wethered was now going like a bomb, and finished the first nine, 4, 3, 3, to be four up, a position nine holes better than she had been when they passed the same point in the morning. She had played that front nine in thirty-five, almost emulating Glenna's thirty-four in the first round. There were many who there and then decided that it was all over.

Well, they may have thought that, and Joyce may have been feeling pretty comfortable, but Glenna Collett certainly did not think in those terms. Champions don't. Perhaps that is one of the things that separates them from the rest.

Bang, bang! Three, three, she went. The crowd stirred, became doubly alert, and rushed around trying not to miss a shot. The stewards were earning their corn now, and often the players had to wait until some order was restored and they could get to their balls, and then wait again whilst an avenue for them to play their shot was negotiated. This was what Joyce did not like about championship golf. How would it affect her? She may not have liked it, but she was made of pretty stern stuff, and there was no way that she was prepared to let it take the match from her.

We are now at the twelfth, and Joyce lies two holes to the good. Emotions were running high, but the two participants ground out matching par-fours. Joyce took the next with another par-four. Yes, said the knowing ones, she has the temperament, she is maintaining that composure, for which she is renowned. Oh dear! Out of the mouths of babes and sucklings.... Why didn't I keep my big mouth shut! The two ladies played the fourteenth, that notorious long par-five, as though they remembered its reputation and decided that they could not live with it. For the first and only time that day, they played as many people play most of the time – extremely moderately. As said earlier, the hole is difficult to the extent that players can record a six or even seven without feeling that they have played a bad shot. Glenna did just that – a seven. So that's dormy four is it – Joyce four up with four to play? Not on your life; the great Miss Wethered had recorded an eight. Many years later, the occasion still made her shudder whenever she recalled it. She confessed that she had lost the hole after taking a number of strokes which still made her blush to think of them.

So there was still a game to be won and lost. JW was two up with four to play, but realised that she could still lose. In her own words:

At the fifteenth, I sliced my drive and was unable to reach the green in two. A poor run-up left me still six yards from the hole. Glenna was lying practically dead in three. It looked very much like being only one up, and in such a crisis, with still three holes to go, anything might have happened. But the most opportune putt I have ever made came to my rescue. I holed the six-yarder for a half and kept my lead of two, which I was able to hold on to until the seventeenth green. I did not in the least feel like holing the putt, and even when it was on its way I scarcely realised that it was going in. Generally, there is an instinct about a putt which tells you what is probably going to happen. This time I had no such feeling. I only remember feeling distinctly desperate and hitting the ball rather hard as the putt was uphill; and then the hole gobbled it up. Thank heavens there are still such happy surprises in the world.

The next hole we halved to make me dormy two. Then at the seventeenth, a very exacting hole in any circumstances, I was relieved of the responsibility of playing it really well as Glenna took four to reach the plateau. All the same I shall not forget the anxiety of keeping the ball safely in play on nearing the dreaded green. It is the most trying of all experiences to keep cool just on the brink of winning; so easy to lose control and spoil it all. It was also impossible to ignore the pent-up excitement of the crowd which was ready to break out as soon as the last putt was struck. When the moment finally came, it threatened very nearly to destroy us. Glenna and I were torn apart and became the centre of a squeezing, swaying and almost hysterical mob, shouting and cheering themselves hoarse.

Thrilling as was the wild enthusiasm around us, I was gratefully relieved to find struggling at my side two stalwart officers of the law. After what seemed an eternity we were able to force our way, yard by yard, through the crowd to the road by the side of the green, and from there gradually to the steps of the hotel. How Glenna fared in the meantime I never quite discovered; evidently she escaped by another route.

It was on being escorted once more on either side by my two friends, the policemen, to the clubhouse, after the crowd had thinned a little, that I first realised the apparent ignominy of my position. Thoughts of stone passages, prison cells, and bread and water floated vaguely through my mind. The inspector, however, was reassuring: "Nothing so bad as that this time, Miss," he said with a smile.

It was only after the prize-giving and speeches were over that I began to feel really free once more. Then came the awakening to the fact that the greatest ambition of my life had been realised after all – the winning of a championship at St Andrews. As a finale of ten years from my first championship it seemed altogether too good to be true.

Glenna had lost to her nemesis once more and never would beat her in singles play. Later that year, Glenna won the United States Women's Amateur for the fourth time and would go on to take it twice more. Sound evidence, surely, that Joyce Wethered was someone very special in the golfing world.

Thirty years later, in the Commonwealth Tournament, no player bettered Joyce's score in the 1929 final, which is strong testament to her outstanding play.

I have read that Joyce and Glenna were destined never to become close friends, which surprised me greatly because Joyce has often talked and written of her high regard for Glenna, and not only for her golf. Then, the article went on to state that they never had the easy affection and shared confidences of true friends. On the contrary, I believe they did have the easy affection, one for the other, but it was 'the shared confidences' that made me realise that the article was probably correct. Joyce did not make close friends easily, she was far too careful for that. True friendship had to be earned, and I suspect that few could truly consider themselves to have aspired to that position.

Please do not translate the above to suspect that Joyce was not a friendly person. To the contrary, she was very friendly and affable, but sharing confidences was something else. Reflecting on her golfing career, she once remarked that it was not easy to cultivate real friendships when you were the champion. Fellow competitors felt that they could not treat you totally as they would any other competitor, and therefore friendships were abundant but close friendships were very rare. She added, extremely poignantly in my opinion, that there were probably people who would have become great friends if this situation hadn't arisen. It almost appeared to be a cry of regret.

Incidentally, a revealing postscript to the 1929 championship came from the lady correspondent of *Golf Illustrated*, where she thanked the R&A members for their kindness in opening the clubhouse for the competitors to view the trophy cabinet. On only one previous occasion had women been allowed in. I am still wondering whether she wrote with tongue in cheek, but probably not. Scraps from the rich man's table were very welcome. It begs the question of where the lady competitors got changed, but my researches have not gone that far – I apologise.

7
A SUPPORTING ROLE

Having achieved her ultimate ambition, to win at St Andrews, Joyce once more retired from the championship scene. The crowd problems in the final round would not have encouraged her to continue, but it is clear that she had determined to return for this one championship only, whatever the outcome.

She retired to the enjoyment of social golf, though she did still play in county events, so she was playing at a high level, and she was still regarded as the real champion of British ladies' golf. It was almost as though she had been mothballed, to be called upon when the necessity should arise.

Other ladies were making the news, and in May 1930, Amy Johnson, who had earned her pilot's licence only the previous year, became the first woman to fly solo across the world, from Croydon to Darwin in Australia, and she achieved her epic journey in a second-hand de Havilland Gipsy Moth.

In June of that year, the government rejected plans for a Channel Tunnel! The idea was encouraged, no doubt, by the proliferation of motor cars, which were entering onto the roads of Britain and which had inspired the production of the first Highway Code and the signature of the millionth member of the AA.

On the golfing front, the subject of international competition for ladies' teams was very much to the fore. The men had instituted the Walker Cup for matches between Britain and the United States amateurs in the early 1920s, and in 1927 the creation of the Ryder Cup did likewise for the professionals. The ladies fancied a piece of the action, but it was not all smooth going. There was the little question of finance. There had been home internationals for several years for England, Scotland, Wales and Ireland, but they had always taken place immediately preceding the British Ladies' Championship and the participants had been expected to finance themselves and to bear their own expenses.

If a team was to be sent across to America, who would pay? The best players were not always the most wealthy, and some would not be able to afford to pay for themselves. To take only those who could was beyond recognition. The chances of the team winning would be compromised and it would not be ethical. Besides, how would the Americans be hosted when they arrived in Britain? They could hardly be expected to shoulder all their own costs.

The Ladies' Golf Union decided to ask all the affiliated clubs to make donations of 2s 6d per member towards an international fund. It was not received well everywhere. Those who are going to enjoy and benefit from the occasion are the ones who should pay for it was the gist of the criticism. Understandable, if not commendable.

Joyce was not at all enthusiastic about the proposal for international matches. Apart from the tricky subject of finance, she seemed to think that such a development would not be good for the amateur status of the game. She thought that the winning would become more important than the playing, and feared that commercial matters would intrude and take over.

More Americans and continental players were coming over for British Open events all the time and it was really inevitable that the wishes for international competition would soon follow. The *Fairway and Hazard* periodical, which was the mouthpiece of the LGU, promoted the introduction of internationals with a full-page editorial explaining the meaning of internationalism and expounding its beliefs that it would all be for the good of nations. The prefix, 'inter', it was explained, meant a meeting between nations, and not nation against nation in a struggle for supremacy. Well, I don't know about that. Britain was still a place where you could find people who almost regarded practicing for an event as cheating, but, in general, the idea was to give the other side a damned good walloping. In the right spirit, of course!

Nevertheless, it is quite correct that, should nations meet on common ground with a common interest, this will lead to a clearer understanding of one another, and sport provides the ideal vehicle for this to happen.

In the spring of 1930, an unofficial match between Britain and America was arranged to take place at Sunningdale. JW was asked to captain the British team but declined, possibly because she was not yet convinced of the desirability of such fixtures. Her Surrey colleague, Molly Gourlay, was then asked to take on the duty and complied readily. Unlike Joyce, Molly would follow her playing days by becoming heavily involved in the administrative side of golf, and to her goes the credit of the introduction of the Commonwealth Tournament.

Molly selected the team herself and the outcome was an overwhelming victory for Britain of 8.5 to 0.5. Molly defeated none other than the redoubtable Glenna Collett, who, I believe, had by this time become Glenna Collett-Vare. It was an amazing victory, but more importantly, everything about the event indicated that this was what the public wanted and that it was confirmed as the way ahead. A crowd in the region of 5,000 attended the event and the press showed great interest. It was a good feeler and the LGU could now proceed with more ambitious promotions with much less opposition, particularly as they had demonstrated that such events could be self-supporting and not mean that the membership would have to dig into their pockets. Indeed, it was evident that such occasions could be money-spinners and actually spawn income.

The opportunity was grasped and very soon an official contest was instituted. The American Curtis sisters, great golfers in their own right, presented a simple silver trophy, 'to stimulate friendly rivalry among the women golfers of many lands.' The wording seems inappropriate to me, as it was intended to be a contest between Britain and America.

The unofficial match was probably the golfing event of the year to most ladies, but I suspect not to Joyce Wethered. She had other memorable doings on her mind. The Men's Open Amateur was scheduled for St Andrews. Was it too much to hope that brother Roger could emulate her success of the previous year? That wasn't the only excitement for her. Bobby Jones was coming.

In a fairytale manner, the captains of the two Walker Cup teams for that year were Bobby Jones and Roger Wethered. The match was played at St George's, Sandwich. We know that Joyce was in attendance, because newspaper reports indicate so. Surprisingly, it took place in the same week as the Ladies' Championship, and who do we find in the final of that event? None other than the illustrious Glenna Collett. She had battled her way through to the final, disposing of Miss Wilson on the home green in the semi-final, after a titanic struggle which neither contestant deserved to lose.

In the final, she faced Diana Fishwick, a nineteen-year-old young lady from North Foreland. She may have been young in years, but she was already far from young in experience. She had taken the girls' crown two years in succession, and the previous year had won through to the English Ladies' Final, before losing out to Molly Gourlay.

On a beautiful day at Formby, and in the first year that she was old enough to play in the event, Diana beat Glenna by four and three. Poor Glenna, was she never to take this crown? I'm afraid she wasn't.

It was interesting to read *The Times* correspondent the following day:

We have every reason to be proud of the showing that our ladies have made, and especially that of Miss Fishwick. For a girl to win the Ladies' Championship at the age of nineteen and at the first occasion that she has entered the competition, and against probably the second-best lady in the world, is an outstanding achievement.

He did not even have to name the best lady!

Back to Sandwich. *The Times* correspondent – it must have been another one, he couldn't be in two places at the same time – reviewed the British team and concluded that they had a fair chance of taking the spoils. Roger Wethered was back to full fitness after treatment for a pulled muscle in the leg.

It is strange how the British always hope for inclement weather on these occasions. There is a belief that the sun always shines in the States and that Americans can't play in cold or wet and windy weather. Yet every time that those conditions prevail, it matters not a jot to the results. On the day of the Walker Cup, after a cold spell, the temperature had risen and was even described as balmy. It was noted that certain of the Americans still sported mittens, whilst the British contingent were dispensing with their woollen cardigans.

At that time the cup comprised foursomes over thirty-six holes, and singles likewise on the following day. Captain Roger elected to lead the way and show by example what was expected of the British team. His partner was his old friend, Cyril Tolley, and they did lead by example, winning on the final green, after being two down after the morning's round. Unfortunately, the team failed to live up to their captain's expectations, and the United States took the foursomes by three matches to one. Bobby Jones and partner had a comfortable eight- and-seven- victory, after being five up at the halfway mark.

On the morrow, the two captains faced up to each other, and Joyce and her parents were keeping their fingers crossed that Roger's driving would be on song. It was a part of his game which could at times desert him, and his sister chastised him frequently for failing to practise more this most important aspect of the game. But Roger was an amateur of the old school. He would sit for hours and debate the theory of the game, but practise… well, yes, sometimes.

The two captains locked horns and, at the end of the first nine, they were equal. Not too bad for Britain. Unfortunately, Bobby Jones can always produce the goods when necessary. Suddenly, he went 4, 3, 3, 3, and Roger found himself three behind. The strain exposed Roger's Achilles heel and a bout of hooking off the tee resulted in Jones being seven up at the eighteenth. I have found nothing written about what his sister said to him at the interval. Probably something like, 'Keep at it, Roger.' There wasn't much else that she could have said, and it is doubtful whether it would have helped much anyway, for Bobby Jones had played the first round in sixty-nine. Roger lasted to the halfway mark in the afternoon, before bowing out to a demoralising nine and eight defeat.

With the exception of Torrance, who had a good seven and six victory over Francis Ouimet, the rest of the British team surrendered to the invincible Americans, though some fought like tigers for at least part of the match. Deserving of special comment was J.A. Stout, stout by name, stout by physique, and stout by character. He started his match as though he had come down from heaven. He had no less than six threes in his first nine holes. His opponent had played as a god himself and had gone out in thirty-two strokes, and still found himself a hole down. At the end of the morning round, Stout was four up. He probably ate a side of ham for his lunch; he was a big man. As they stood on the first tee for the afternoon round, his opponent, Moe, probably thought that he couldn't do that again, referring to Stout's morning start. If he did, he soon regretted it. Refreshed by lunch, Stout started with three threes! After three holes of the afternoon round, he was seven holes up.

He continued to play well, but now the overtures must pass to his willing opponent. He gradually overhauled his adversary and won the last hole with a birdie three, which also won him the match. He had played a sixty-seven to add to his morning sixty-nine. Poor Stout!

The British team, full of high hopes only forty-eight hours previously, had been beaten by ten points to two. At least it was a point better than the previous match at Chicago, when they had been trounced by eleven points to one. They had to wait until the tenth meeting in 1938 before they recorded their first win in this biennial contest – and then came the war, play was suspended, and when it resumed they were back to square one, losing time after time with only the occasional win to sustain their ambitions. But you can't fault the British for tenacity, and, in the last decade of the century, they started to give as good as they received. No longer is the result a foregone conclusion, and of course the interest in the two countries has spiralled upwards accordingly.

In 1930, the Walker Cup was followed with a gap of only one week by the British Amateur Open, to be played at St Andrews. Many of the Americans stayed on for this event, and it was obvious that the British were going to be hard pressed to keep the trophy in these isles. The caravan moved north from Sandwich to Scotland, and with it went the Wethered family, including Joyce.

The early part of the week was given over to golfing and socialising. Before that gave way to the amateur championship itself, and to battles of Britain *v*. America, the British had to indulge in their annual tourney between the home nations.

On the Friday a friendly four ball took place, the outcome of which would reverberate round the world of golf for evermore. The players on one side were Roger Wethered and T.A Bourn, a top amateur of the time. Their opponents were Bobby Jones and Joyce Wethered.

It was an occasion which Joyce enjoyed as much as any in her golfing career. To be playing with her hero was bliss in itself, but to be doing that at St Andrews was something of which she had dreamed. Word soon spread around the town, and a goodly crowd assembled to see the fireworks. The greatest male and the greatest female golfers in the world could be observed together, plying their trade in an unsolicited exhibition of their skills.

The two British gentlemen allowed Joyce to play with Bobby. After all, he was the best, and she was only a woman. It would make for a more even game! Joyce was playing in a game with Bobby Jones, it

didn't matter to her whether he was playing with her or against her —
they were playing together. I am quite certain that she was determined
to play at her very best on that auspicious day. She wouldn't want to
let the opportunity pass by letting the side down.

We don't have details of the play hole by hole, more is the pity. Joyce,
of course, disdained any suggestion that she should play off other than
the same tees as the men. Joyce and Bobby duly won the match, and it
was only because she three-putted the last two greens, when the heat
was off, that Bobby managed to score one less than Joyce for the round.

What did Bobby Jones make of all of this? He was a generous man,
but there was no undue generosity in his admiration for Joyce's golf.
'It is the best swing, man or woman, that I have ever seen,' said he,
and, 'I have never played golf with anyone, man or woman, amateur
or professional, who made me feel so utterly outclassed.'

Joyce must have blushed a little at such spontaneous commendations.
The world felt good. Her only problem now was, who was she going to
support in the forthcoming Amateur championship, Roger or Bobby?

In the England v. Scotland match, which England won convincingly
by eight points to four, Roger was victorious in his foursome partnered
by Cyril Tolley, and also in the singles when he won two and one. So
he appeared in reasonable form!

The Times correspondent looked upon the day or two before the start
of the 'Amateur', as the lull before the storm, so great was the interest
in the conquering Americans. There should have been much more
interest in the home internationals, especially as Scotland were playing
at home. Half an hour before the international match began, a four
ball, featuring Bobby Jones, the Provost of St Andrews, the chairman
of the championship committee, and the chairman of the greens
committee, set forth. The crowd which followed them was larger
than any of the groups which put forth with the international match
players. The correspondent then made the amusing, but nevertheless
true, aside, that had the four ball included Joyce Wethered as on the
previous day, there would have been nobody at all left to watch the
international match. It was nothing more than a statement of her
standing in the golfing world.

The course was stated 'to be good enough, if not at its silky best
such as we know in September'. A long spell of chill east winds had
stopped the growth of the grass and the greens were somewhat variable,
with one or two decidedly on the slow side. The ground was hard

and the ball would run, but the tees were as far back as they could be accommodated. If leviathans were to match their strengths then the Old Course would do its best to play its part.

There was a large field for the event, to the extent that a preliminary round had to be incorporated, and thereby, although the championship started on Monday 26 May, some of the competitors were not required to unsheathe their weapons until the Tuesday afternoon. The weather was kind, a grey morning giving way to a sunny afternoon, without a breath of wind. The British spectators bemoaned this, although it made their watching more comfortable because it gave those ****** foreigners a better chance!

JW was on the scene early on the first morning to give her support to a family friend, none other than the celebrated columnist Bernard Darwin. Bernard was a good player and had represented his country on several occasions. Indeed, he had once not only represented his country but had actually captained a British team against the Americans. It had happened when he had accompanied the British team out to the States, as correspondent for *The Times*. The captain of the British team fell ill, and into the breach stepped Bernard. How he came to take the captaincy as well as a place in the team, I know not. I suppose it was because he was an outgoing sort of chap, one willing to take the leadership when it was thrust upon him. His grandfather was the famous scientist Charles Darwin, discoverer of the principle of natural selection. He had five sons, all eminent scientists, and one can't but wonder whether grandfather would have been proud of Bernard, or whether he would have considered that a life devoted to the golf course was not that desirable for a Darwin. As Bernard was no more than six years old when his grandfather died, the problem did not arise.

Bernard was a good friend of the Wethered family and Joyce and her father were out that morning to cheer him upon his way. Unfortunately for Bernard, he had a very cruel draw in that first round as he was pulled out of the hat with the US Amateur champion, H. Johnston. The game proved to be exciting and competitive, with Bernard giving as good as he got. The match ended at the Roadhole in spectacular fashion, when Johnston, playing first, drilled a spoon straight at the flag. Surely he would be in the bunker or on the road, so small was the tolerance for error, but the ball climbed the bank and rested quietly but a yard from the pin. Bernard was out by two and one.

I imagine that Joyce enjoyed the morning round, though she would have been disappointed at the result. In the afternoon, however, she more than enjoyed watching – it was Bobby Jones. He had to perform well too. No, not because Joyce Wethered was watching, but because his opponent, S. Roper from Wollaton Park, threw everything possible at him. Jones eventually triumphed at the sixteenth, and he needed to be four under fours to do so.

The Amateur that year was a week full of incident. Tell me of a year when it isn't, you say. Fair enough. Many of the matches make thrilling reading, but we will hear about only a few because this book is dedicated to Joyce Wethered's memory, not brother Roger's, nor indeed the immortal Bobby Jones. It hardly needs to be said that Joyce shared her time between the matches of the two men.

By Wednesday morning and the third round, the weather had turned more 'British'. It was cold and windy and woolly cardigans and woollen mittens were much in evidence. Bobby Jones, out early, looked miserable. Perhaps those biased towards the British were right; the Americans didn't like the cold weather. Some of the greens had become very slick, the eleventh in particular, and the greens committee had made their pin placings to avoid farcical situations. Joyce was again lucky, in that Roger teed off some two hours after Bobby, giving her the opportunity to see something of both.

Bobby did not play well and went out in an inglorious forty, but he was assisted by his opponent C. Shankland, who wilted against the champion and did not take his chance to be able to sit his grandchildren on his knee in later years to tell them how he clipped the great man's wings. Jones won by four and three.

Roger played as though he knew he had an afternoon round to play later and wanted to be done with the morning's affair. He won by seven and five and deprived his sister of an hour's watching. In the afternoon, he continued his gallop, and disposed of his opponent by five and three. He started about an hour after Jones, but finished his match before him. Sister Joyce did not know where to be, as she followed Jones and another great family friend, Cyril Tolley, who had been at Oxford with Roger. The bush telegraph told her that her brother was not especially needing her that afternoon, and so she was able to watch a titanic struggle between Tolley, the previous year's champion, and the favourite to be heir apparent. Joyce knew Tolley's game very well. She had often played with him and her brother and other Oxford graduates. She confessed that much of her success was probably due to playing much of her golf with men rather than women. She had to play well to match them and their superior length made her work on that aspect of her game. Cyril Tolley had been Joyce's partner on two occasions when they had won the prestigious Worplesden Foursomes.

The conditions under which Jones and Tolley played their match was appalling – not the weather, but the crowd. It was a Dundee holiday and every man and his dog seemed to have crossed the Tay to see the golf. Marshalling had not reached the sophisticated level of today, and the crowd (rabble, *The Times* correspondent called them) ranged all over the course, with the stewards almost helpless. Most of the huge crowd wanted to watch Jones and Tolley, which meant that they had great difficulty in clearing the way for them to make a shot. But it also meant that the unthinking spectators got in the way of other competing couples, bringing them to a halt for long periods at a time. Those waiting at the greens sometimes would wait for over half an hour before the players could get to them. How Joyce Wethered fared in the turmoil I dread to think. She had departed the championship scene partly because she found the crowd problem exhausting. One description of the scene summed up the situation beautifully: '....Jones and Tolley played encircled by a mob. All the others played through, round, or over the mob.' The fact that Jones hit no less than four spectators with his shots that afternoon was only partly due to the close proximity of the crowd. He contributed to the tally with one or two slices also.

The match was a nip and tuck affair throughout, and the golf varied from ordinary to brilliant. On the sixteenth tee, Jones stood one up, but immediately drove into the Principal's Nose and the match was level once more. At the Roadhole, the crowd came to Jones's rescue. His approach shot flew fast across the green and would likely have made its way to the road, but the massed ranks of spectators blockaded its progress and a half resulted.

The eighteenth hole, and still these giants were locked in combat. Now, Cyril Tolley could hit the ball a country mile – not always straight, mind you. The previous year at this same eighteenth hole, in a competition, he had reached the green from the tee in two consecutive rounds. Many of the more knowledgeable amongst the spectators were aware of this ability, and they literally fought for position to witness what Cyril could produce. It was an anti-climax. He was well short, and yet another half.

Off they went to the nineteenth. Two superb drives. Jones played onto the green, but Tolley hooked left. Tolley played a superb pitch to four feet from the pin. Surely another half in four was imminent, as Jones was a long way from the hole. There then occurred one of those twists of fortune which shouldn't happen at such important moments. Jones's putt stopped short and in so doing laid poor Cyril a stymie which he was never likely to forget. He tried to swerve around Jones's ball with an iron, but it was not to be. The match was over in cruel circumstances.

Thursday hosted the fifth and sixth rounds. Jones had an avalanche of threes in a convincing morning win which didn't progress past the twelfth green. In the afternoon, he met a fellow American, none other than Johnston, who, it will be recalled, ousted Bernard Darwin in the first round. Jones won on the last green. Once more he benefited from a fortuitous stymie, though I hasten to add that it was not at the final hole. Fortune did appear to be smiling upon him, however. When genius and fortune hold hands, they can be very difficult opponents.

How was Roger proceeding? He was causing his sister more than a few heartaches. In the morning he played another old family friend, Richard Oppenheimer, who also was destined to partner Joyce to win the Worplesden Foursomes, though that would be two years in the future. Roger finally won on the home green. If he thought that his hard work for the day was finished, he was rudely awakened by a fighting Gordon Simpson. They were the last pair out and a very close game ensued. Joyce's blood must have run cold when Roger did what others have done before and since – he putted off the green into the Roadhole bunker! The evening was well advanced when the intrepid duo returned to the first tee still level; and the crowd had thinned to a handful as they disappeared out into the country once more. At least Joyce did not have to worry about being buffeted by spectators. It was the twenty-first hole before Roger claimed his place in the quarter-finals. He must have slept well that night.

On the morrow, both Jones and Wethered started badly but improved to play immaculate golf. Jones put his tee shot at the first into the burn, and Wethered, with a troublesome putter, started with three fives. He was three down after three holes! Suffice it to say that both played heroically thereafter and both won by four and three, with scores under par.

Roger's opponent in the semi-final was W.L. Hartley of Chislehurst. In the morning, the latter had to go to the nineteenth before seeing off an adhesive opponent, and the effects of his morning exertions became apparent from the start of his afternoon match. By the fifth, he was three down. Nil desperandum.... He came fighting back and it was the seventeenth before Roger was able to seal his place in the final. In the other semi-final, two Americans, Jones and Voight, faced each other. For once Jones's putter would not function, and hole after hole he missed puttable chances. The prophets of doom had written him off when he arrived at the fourteenth two down. So often from such positions he would rally, but on this occasion he had to rely on his opponent to hand him the match. Voight cut his drive out of bounds at the Long Hole, took five at the next, and then drove into the Principal's Nose at the sixteenth. At the Roadhole, Voight lay dead, but Jones's putter at last came to his rescue and he holed a long one for a half. Jones played a glorious pitch at the last to leave himself with an eight-foot putt for a birdie three. He stroked the ball towards the hole and confidently followed to pick it from the cup, but it stopped right on the edge. Voight had a six-footer to keep the match alive, but it was anything but straightforward and required some borrow. After what seemed an eternity, the stroke was made. The ball slid past the hole and Jones was in the final. It had been an almighty struggle. Jones, who suffered from intense nervous exhaustion at such times, was drained. In future years, when his achievement of the 'Impregnable Quadrilateral', as the Grand Slam of golf was called at that time, was recalled, few would ever remember how near it came to never having happened at all.

The final was the match which most people had hoped for when the championship began at the beginning of the week: the captain of the United States Walker Cup team *v.* the captain of the British team. Admiration was such for Bobby Jones and his golf that the usual national bias towards the home man was very muted. The crowd was in the position that it could not lose. Either an Englishman would bring home the bacon or a man worshipped on both sides of the Atlantic would prevail. Joyce Wethered had both of her men playing in the supreme championship at the home of golf, her favourite venue, and she was there to enjoy it. She was a very happy lady. We don't know who she favoured, but it must surely have been the brother who had played with her on her first rounds of golf on those family summer holidays up at Dornoch. To some extent, she was in the same happy position as the crowd; she couldn't lose. If Roger failed, it would be against the man who she most admired in the golfing world.

We won't dwell on the final. It was important to consider the championship, as it helps to describe how Joyce spent her time away from the round of ladies' championship golf. She still played a lot of golf and played with the best, but she did not have to contend with the pressure of being repeatedly expected to win. She was also able to watch and learn, whilst never far from the bosom of the family and close friends. For the record, Bobby Jones beat Roger in a thirty-six-hole final by seven and six. Jones played par golf, the model of consistency. Roger spiced good shots with bad. Several wild hooks from the tee were followed by sublime recovery irons to the heart of the green, but his putting was below average and he paid the penalty.

Bobby Jones was swallowed up by the cheering crowd. Later that year, when he had completed his Grand Slam, he retired from competitive golf, still only twenty-eight, and concentrated more upon his law practice. Six years later, on his way to the 1936 Olympics at Berlin, he joined some friends for a few days at Gleneagles, and being so near, decided that he could not forego the opportunity of one more round at St Andrews. The word went round the old grey toone like wildfire. Quite unsuspect-ing, he made his way to the first tee for this entirely friendly foray, to find a crowd of two thousand people there to welcome him. He later wrote that he had not been playing much golf at the time and his game was very rusty, but for some reason he was inspired that afternoon and played some of the best golf of his life, with a front nine of only thirty-two. When he returned to St Andrews in 1958 with the American Eisenhower team, he had the freedom of the town bestowed upon him, and said in his receiving speech, 'I could take out of my life everything except my experiences at St Andrews and I'd still have a rich full life.'

Although Joyce was not playing in national championships in 1930, it should not be assumed that she had withdrawn from the golfing scene. As has been seen from the men's Amateur championship at St Andrews, she was a keen spectator of events where she had either a family or technical interest. I have found no evidence that she attended ladies' events, partly, no doubt, because she would not wish to be there if she wasn't playing, and partly, dare I say it, because she would have little to learn in that particular theatre.

Also, she was still in demand to open golfing events, such as the construction of a new clubhouse. She often appeared in the golfing magazines of the time, usually dispensing advice on how to play woods or irons or some other skill. Thus, she was very much in the public eye, and continued to be regarded as the top British lady golfer, even though she was not amassing trophies. Today, with the medium of television, and the ability to reproduce events of yesterday, it is relatively easy for the best to remain in the public mind when their careers are in their twilight. The fact that JW could achieve it when newspapers were the main news medium illustrates the huge impact that her golf had made on her fellow countrymen and women.

The articles which she wrote on golfing skills apply as much nowadays as when she wrote them. They are as clear and informative as any produced today. She obviously had wide-ranging technical knowledge, yet was able to convey such knowledge in the simplest of terms. Her ability to teach in articles doubtless arose from the fact that she was by no stretch of imagination a natural golfer in her early years. She had to work at the required skills and thereby she knew in detail why certain movements achieved certain results. Many golfers discover a secret one day and forget it again the next. Joyce obviously retained a knowledge, once she had discovered it, and gradually built a fund of such skills, neatly welded together.

Joyce does not appear to have played in the Surrey matches in 1930, and she was very amiss over the rule of submitting score cards. I suppose the reason was that she was playing mainly friendly matches, rather than any wish to thwart the authorities. The result was that her handicap was +1, whilst there were several ladies on +2 who were obviously inferior players. It prompted a letter from none other than Harry Vardon, criticising the ladies' handicapping system. Another match, which Joyce missed, was the annual Men *v*. Ladies at Stoke Poges, an occasion when she regularly demonstrated that there were not many men who could afford to give her any shots at all, let alone the six bisques which the men traditionally allowed the ladies at that event.

A tournament which Joyce did not miss was the Worplesden Foursomes in October. A main event in the golfing calendar and an occasion of house parties for the well-to-do, who comprised much of amateur golf at that time; it was one of Joyce's favourite events. On this occasion she was partnered by Lord Charles Hope. It was a step too far. She had won the event on four previous occasions, but that would have to suffice for the time being. They negotiated the first three rounds by dint of Joyce's abilities to carry a partner who was, shall we say, less proficient. Not that all of Joyce's shots were beyond reproach. As they neared the end of one close-fought round, their opponents drove their ball into the whins whilst JW drove into the car park. The outcome of this farcical affair was that one couple lost their ball and the other couple could not get to their ball, which rested under a locked vehicle, the owner of which could not be found. I'm sorry to leave you not knowing how the situation was resolved, but that is the limit of my information on the subject.

The exit from the competition of the redoubtable pair in the fourth round was reported thus: 'Miss Wethered, great golfer though she is, was not able to carry Lord Charles any further, as he pulled and sliced into hopeless positions.'

1931 opened with the Americans changing to a larger ball. Its specification required that it should not be less than 1.68in in diameter and not greater than 1.55ozs in weight. The previous specification called for a ball not less than 1.62in in diameter and not greater than 1.62oz in weight. The purposes of the changes were to make the ball easier to hit and that it should lie better in all conditions, and that it should lose a little in length, but give better approach and putting qualities. The days had gone when the USGA took its lead from the R&A, who remained with the old specification for some time thereafter. Incidentally, hot off the press, I have just read that the R&A are to institute a rule dealing with spitting, or, shall I say, the saliva from such an action. It appears that if your ball comes to rest in a deposit of saliva, it can be deemed to be casual water! The rule has become 'necessary' due to the increasing prevalence among professionals for spitting. Tiger Woods and David Duval are among the culprits here. Surely a rule to forbid such ungentlemanly conduct should have been preferred. The answer is 'no', because once in a while anyone is likely to find the need to spit, to rid themselves of a swallowed fly, for example. Therefore, there will be occasion, however gentlemanly everyone becomes, when a ball will land in a saliva deposit. Ah, c'est la vie!

Joyce never spat, of course, and, if she had, it would have been disguised as more of an 'ahem', discreetly, into a pretty little embroidered handkerchief, immediately concealed into her clothing, unnoticed by others.

The R&A are called upon to rule on all manner of queries and unusual circumstances. In this morning's newspaper (at the time of writing in 2003), following the ousting of the Taliban in Afghanistan and the arrival of a peace-keeping force of British paratroops, one (presumably golf-mad) reporter searched for and located the remains of a golf course built by ex-pats on the perimeter of Kabul many years ago. In the middle of the mine-strewn course sat five old, abandoned Russian howitzers. The reporter discovered an old set of clubs in a local shop and also located an Afghan who had acted as professional and caddie when the course was extant. They contrived to play a few holes, but had to refer to St Andrews by satellite telephone to formalise the status of the howitzers. The assistant rules secretary at the R&A ruled that the howitzers would be deemed 'moveable' under rule 24-1 if they could be moved without unreasonable effort. The players heaved on the gun carriages, which would not budge, and they decided that the effort was 'unreasonable'; they therefore dropped the ball within one club length, not nearer to the hole.

A second question referred to the existence of the land-mines – could the balls be moved if they were deemed dangerous? No problem with that one, similar queries had arisen in the past with regard to snakes or a bees' nest, etc. A drop without penalty was prescribed. Apparently, there is a course in Arizona at Glen Canyon where a local rule deals with just that situation – the snakes, not the howitzers. The Duke of Windsor received a free drop from a hippo's footprint in Uganda, another local rule – there is no mention of what happens if the hippo appears in person.

The R&A's rules are all consuming, and I was mildly amused to note that twenty pages are needed to cover all the requirements of the LGU's Handicapping System.

The Royal and Ancient Golfers' Handbook, produced annually, is a mine of information, including a section on 'peculiarities'. When reading the 1998 version, I felt strongly for the poor man who entered the 1952 Scottish Amateur championship, stood on the first tee and proceeded to drive three balls out of bounds in quick succession, and immediately withdrew from the competition. Nightmares can sometimes come true.

At Olton, Warwickshire, a scratch golfer, J.R. Holden, played his ball into thick, long wet rough beside the green. He played an explosion shot and three balls appeared on the green! The famous Ben Sayers was asked by an American what he could play the course in, and replied fours. The American bet him that he couldn't. The bet was accepted and then the American informed him that no threes or fives would be allowed. Stung by the deceit, Sayers proceeded to play every hole in four strokes.

One story from the handbook, which did not impress me unduly, was that in 1920, at Torplin near Edinburgh, William Ingle started his round with 1, 2, 3, 4, 5. I have a friend who started his round 4, 5, 6, 7, 8!

1931 witnessed the first official match between French and British/Irish ladies. Joyce had not been a supporter of such fixtures, but she was still asked to lead the British side, and after the success of the unofficial match against the United States in the previous year, she could see that she was in the minority and backing a losing battle. She stated in her later book that she believed the desire for international matches came first from abroad. 'We seem to have lived up to our reputation – and probably it has been well earned – for being rather self-contained and exclusive'. That was a self-confession; Joyce was certainly a foot-dragger in the introduction of these events.

The French team was comprised of ladies of 'the smart set.' They were keen to give a good account of themselves, but in general were not of the same golfing standard as the ladies from Great Britain and Ireland. Now, had they been playing bridge, there could have been a different result. These were ladies who enjoyed the social side of golf and were most charming and vivacious. Joyce recalled being amused by their captain, Barbara Vagliano, who on the previous day to the match had been deploring the fact that some of her members had been overdoing the practising. She thought that they would wear themselves out. Eventually, she persuaded them to return to their smart hotel and produced two tables so that they could play cards, a much less strenuous occupation.

The match was played at Oxhey and the organisers festooned the clubhouse and surrounds with the flags and emblems of both nationalities. It was October, but the weather was warm and there was no wind, ideal for golf. The French ladies were best turned out in the paddock, looking very chic in their sky-blue jerseys and matching international ties. The British looked more fitted out for action than appearance. The match comprised eighteen holes of foursomes in the morning and singles in the afternoon. Joyce and Mrs Garon led the way for the British, Mme Vagliano and Mme Munier for the French. Each couple was accompanied by a flag-bearer, and a large Union Jack and similar size Tricolour, carried by lady stewards advanced down the first fairway. Those flags must soon have become rather heavy, and Joyce could not help but think to herself that the lack of wind was a blessing to the poor stewards.

There were only three pairs of foursomes and Great Britain and Ireland scooped the pool. Joyce and her partner were particularly severe on the opposition and won by the large margin of seven and six.

In the afternoon, Simone Lacoste joined the fray. She was an old friend of Joyce's and had been hosted at the Wethered household on more than one occasion, especially for 'Worplesden'. She had recently been blessed with a son and was newly back to action, and therefore perhaps somewhat out of practice, but her golfing pedigree was not in doubt, as a previous winner of the British Ladies' Open at Royal County Down in 1927. Joyce spared her no favours, out-drove her by as much as fifty yards, and comfortably beat her by five and four in the top match. The French ladies claimed just half a point, and lost by 8.5 to 0.5. *The Sunday Times* report stated that, 'The mere fact that Miss Joyce Wethered was playing lent a glamour to the occasion.' There were some good British players at that time, but JW was still considered to be out on her own, head and shoulders above the rest. Any opportunity to see her was accepted with glee.

The LGU had done its homework for the event and had formed a new International Hospitality Committee. The players were transported to London and a celebratory dinner was hosted by the LGU. There had been two thousand spectators at Oxhey. I am not aware that they paid for the privilege, but it had already been demonstrated that there should be little difficulty in financing such events in the future.

The ladies were each invited to bring a guest to the dinner (I wish I knew who Joyce took. I believe it would have been Major Hutchison – see later), and a very convivial evening was spent at the Savoy. The ladies' hearts were set aflutter by the appearance of Jean Borotra, who charmingly kissed each lady's hand, danced with the lucky few and then disappeared into the night. It had been a successful event, well organised.

In 1931, Lord Charles Hope had been replaced as partner to Miss Wethered in the Worplesden Foursomes by the Hon. Michael Scott. The pairing was successful and Joyce had won her fifth Worplesden title.

Michael Scott would make headlines two years later, in 1933, when he became the oldest man, at the age of fifty-four, to win the Amateur Open.

On 9 November 1931, the 'Forthcoming Marriages' columns of *The Times*, announced the engagement between Major Cecil K. Hutchison, younger son of Mr and Mrs J.R. Hutchison, and Joyce, only daughter of Mr and Mrs H. Newton Wethered.

The sporting columns of the paper dealt with the subject in rather more detail, and are recaptured here for your delight:

The engagement of Major. C.K. Hutchison and Miss Joyce Wethered is announced on another page. Major Hutchison, who was in the Eton XI, was Keeper of the Field, and was generally regarded as one of the finest of Etonian athletes. As a golfer he has been unsurpassed in style by any Scottish amateur, both in his wooden club strokes and in his play to the green. His match against another Old Etonian, R. Maxwell, in the final round of the Amateur championship of 1909 at Muirfield, has for the quality of the golf displayed never been exceeded. He represented Scotland against England from 1904 uninterruptedly until 1912, and has won many tournaments of importance, including the St George's Vase in 1903 and 1910, both in Scotland and England. Originally in the Coldstream Guards, he joined up with the Royal Scots on the outbreak of war and was made a prisoner of war when serving with his old regiment at the battle of Festubert, being afterwards interned in Switzerland. Since the war he has been interested in the construction of golf courses.

Miss Wethered is admitted by all to have been the greatest of all lady golfers. She won the Ladies' Open championship in 1922, 1924, 1925 and 1929 and was runner-up in 1921. She won the English Ladies' Close Championship in 1920, 1921, 1922, 1923, and 1924. Her method of play is so perfect that she has been deemed by many judges to be 'the best golfer in the world'.

It is amusing that Miss Wethered warranted less than half the space devoted to her less famous fiancé, but I suppose it was a sign of the times (no pun intended).

The announcement seems to have come as something of a surprise. There was no prior indication of it in the social magazines of the time, but the congratulations must have rolled in from around the world. *Fairway and Hazard*, the mouthpiece for the LGU, had to wait until its December edition to offer its congratulations, a fair indication that the golfing world was as much in the dark as everyone else. It shouldn't have come as a surprise. To Joyce it would be a private matter, which had to be revealed to the world. Why it happened is unlikely to have ever been known by other than an intimate few. Cecil Key Hutchison was more of Joyce's father's age than her own; he was born in 1877, some twenty-four years older than Joyce. At the time of their engagement, he was fifty-four. He had attended Eton College, in R.A. Mitchell's House, from 1890 to 1896, and was an excellent all-round athlete and sportsman. He was Keeper of the Field in 1895. In more common parlance, this interprets to his being captain of the college football team. He was a member of the cricket XI, and in his last year he won the School Mile. His father was J.R. Hutchison and their home address was 53 Cadogan Square. After Eton, he was commissioned into the Coldstream Guards. He became Superintendent of Gymnasia in London, from 1904 to 1908, an army appointment for which his athletic and sporting abilities fitted him admirably. In 1909 he was appointed Captain of the Third Battalion of the Royal Scots (Lothian Regiment) Militia. He served in Africa and was back with the Coldstream Guards as a major in the First World War. He was taken prisoner at Festubert.

Cecil was a good friend of Newton Wethered and shared the same interest of golf course architecture. Doubtless, he spent a good deal of time at the family home. He was a soldier of the old school, extremely courteous and good company. Most importantly, he was a good golfer. Perhaps Joyce was looking for a father figure in her relationship. Joyce had always found her salvation from within the family, and Cecil had become very close to that family. The engagement was never fulfilled.

Joyce continued to write her golfing articles, and, in 1931 she contributed three chapters to the publication *The Game of Golf*. In 1932, we find Cecil also engaged upon writing golfing articles. Perhaps Joyce influenced the editors. Indeed, the whole Wethered family seemed to be getting a taste for seeing themselves in print. In *The Times* in November of 1931, Newton Wethered was waxing lyrical on the pros and cons of the golf swing. In 1933 he would expand his involvement to the extent of producing a book entitled *The Perfect Golfer*.

These may have been attempts on his part to earn a little cash, because it was about this time that the effects of the Wall Street Crash descended upon his head. His investments disappeared with alarming rapidity, together with those of many other unfortunates. Tigbourne Court, the family home, was sold, and the Wethereds moved themselves down the road a little to a more modest house in Brook.

In 1932 Joyce seems to have returned to the Surrey fold – golfwise. She was once again the Surrey champion. Later in the year, in October, she had another good Worplesden, with yet another partner. This time it was R.H. Oppenheimer, who joined forces with her and most successfully too. They had their awkward moments, as they must in a tournament of several rounds, but mostly they were clearly in control and eclipsed their finalist opponents by eight and seven.

The golfing highlight of 1932 must, however, be allocated to the first official Curtis Cup Match, between United States and Great Britain and Ireland. The Curtis sisters, who were top American golfers of the early part of the twentieth century, had harboured a desire for many years to sponsor an annual fixture between America and Great Britain and Ireland. This desire had first arisen back in 1905, when they played in the British Ladies' Open at Cromer, and an impromptu match between home players and their American visitors had taken place. Margaret Curtis had won the American Open on three occasions and was still playing in it at the age of sixty-five. The trophy they presented was a simple silver cup, which so embarrassed them by its lack of splendour that they later offered to replace it with something more grandiose and fitting for the important event which the Curtis Cup had become. Not likely, said those who had battled for it over the years. It had acquired a sentimentality value which far outweighed any predilection to grandeur.

Marion Hollins arrived with her team of Americans in May and settled in at the Great Fosters Hotel. They were met off the train at Waterloo station by Joyce, who had been appointed captain of the British team. She looked absolutely charming in a dark suit, close-fitting decorated cloche hat, medium high-heeled shoes and silk stockings, gloves, the inevitable string of pearls, and a luxurious fox-fur round her shoulders. The match was to be played at Wentworth, a more difficult course than the scene of the previous international at Oxhey. There was a general expectation in Britain that the home side would steam to victory. Joyce could never understand how such ideas could have been nurtured. On paper the American team looked pretty formidable, comprised as it was of celebrated players, all of whom had already established a name in top-class competition. The visitors immediately set everyone talking by their obvious commitment to the occasion ahead. They were not only out practising, but were practising 'foursomes', seldom played in America. They tried out all manner of combinations to try to decide upon the correct pairings, and they did not submit their team-sheet for the foursomes, which would precede the singles, until the last possible minute.

In contrast, the Great Britain and Ireland contingent had been asked to arrive at teatime on the day before the match. The lack of professionalism amongst our amateur ladies was all too evident. To be honest, Joyce was not a good choice for captain. The Americans had a non-playing captain who could devote her time to the needs of the position without having to worry about having to play herself. Joyce was not one to impose herself upon colleagues. Even in the team photographs she was often to be found somewhere near the back, rather than taking the central position on the front row, as is traditional for a captain. It probably did not occur to her that the captain had a duty to chivvy the troops into action, to encourage them and offer guidance. To Joyce, being captain simply meant that she was number one player. Her only contribution to the outcome of the match would be achieved by her own performance on the field of play. Perhaps it is unfair to blame Joyce alone. The LGU committee knew the type of person she was and all had gone well the previous year against the French ladies. Her golfing ability was so outstanding that they were simply pleased to have her in the team, and as she was acknowledged to be the best player, then she should be captain. In truth, it was a mistake.

Enid Wilson, who won three consecutive British titles starting in 1931, was one of the British team for the match, and it is interesting to hear what she had to say about it all when she was interviewed for the USLGA many years later, in 1991. She was rather critical.

The LGU were nowhere to be seen. [A slight exaggeration, I think.] *It was the worst day I have ever spent on a golf course, because we didn't know who we were playing in the foursomes until we were on the way to the first tee. We lost all of them. The match was gone beyond redemption. And then, when we got into the club there were no tables set aside or any food for the teams. The spectators had eaten the lot.'*

In fact, the American team had been provided for at their hotel, it was Great Britain and Ireland who were left to find what they could.

When asked what she did, she replied, 'Well, what I did was to go round the dining room and find bits of discarded bread roll and bits of cheese.'

We had been told to arrive at teatime the day before the match, but nobody made any attempt to sort out the details. You couldn't have expected Joyce to organise the thing. We were very proud to have her as our leader, but there was nothing Joyce could do about it, nor was she expected to do anything about it. And so there we were. It was a rout of the disorganised – and deservedly so. On the American side, Marion Hollins did a wonderful job with her team. She had them out playing Scotch Foursomes for days, and her captaincy prevailed. Over the years, I think it is wrong to have a playing captain. You can't look after everything and play at the same time. But for many years people were given charge of our teams who hadn't a notion of what to do.

Enid exonerates Joyce of any blame for the debacle, but in retrospect, I suspect that Joyce felt that she might have done better, if only by ensuring that others had attended to the various necessities of the occasion, particularly with regard to the needs of the team.

In the same interview, Enid was asked about other matters which are of interest in a biography of JW – 'What was Joyce like as an opponent?' 'Well, she was very, very retiring. She never mixed. She was too shy, much too shy. And she'd arrive on the first tee, shake hands with her opponent, demolish the opponent and disappear. And then reappear when the next victim would line up for the slaughter.'

Enid also recalled staying with Joyce and her husband at Knightshayes Court, and commented upon their great interest in art. They had a great collection of paintings and John had taken Enid into the salon and showed her a Watteau painting, and then informed her that he had sold twelve farms to pay for it.

Was Enid afraid of Joyce when she played her? 'I wasn't afraid of her, but I was perhaps afraid of what she might do to me!'

Apart from the social requirements of the position, Joyce's only duty as captain of the Curtis Cup team appears to have been to have selected her pairings for the foursomes, and the order of play of her team. She says that both Marion Hollins and herself were aghast when their respective choices for the foursomes were revealed. What is meant by that, I know not. She stated that Marion Hollins made the better decisions, but I believe that was only because of the subsequent outcome of the matches.

Who better to quote on the day of the match than Henry Longhurst? Although he had heard a figure of five-thousand spectators mentioned, he considered that there were at least half as many again. He had never seen such a crowd on a golf course before, and he had seen a few competitions in his time.

The foursomes started at 10.30, but at 10.00 the crowd behind the first tee was so great that the back of the first green seemed to be the only vantage point. Here I spent a very enjoyable half-hour basking in the sunshine, interrupted only by a large and persistent woman steward who moved everyone on with monotonous regularity. The women stewards seemed almost as numerous as the spectators [evidence that Enid was a little over the top in stating that the LGU were nowhere to be seen], *and waving their flags at all and sundry were obviously having the day of their lives. At about 10.40, the top match arrived, Miss Wethered and Miss Morgan against Mrs Vare and Mrs Hill, and the storm burst. A seething chattering mob of struggling humanity rushed upwards towards the green, but I stuck grimly to my hard-earned position and managed to see the play. America won the first hole of the day in a comfortable five. Miss Wethered cut her second and Miss Morgan went from the rough to a bunker. The mob passed on — most of them via the bunker at the back of the green, pursued by irate stewards. Old gentlemen, photographers, and small girls were, I noticed, the chief offenders. People were still issuing from the clubhouse at the rate of about a hundred a minute.......*

Miss Wethered and partner lost on the last green, and Henry says that their score was well into the eighties! Oh dear! I nearly left that out. Our heroine is undone. It is no good blaming Miss Morgan, Joyce shared the faults and the humiliation. Worse was to come, as Great Britain and Ireland lost all three foursomes. Two were lost on the last green and one at the seventeenth, which suggests three good contests, but the standard in two of the matches was not high, and one can but wonder over the effect of the huge crowds....

For the afternoon, Joyce axed Mrs Watson and Miss Park, and brought in Miss Fishwick and Miss Corlett. Was Joyce getting a taste for this captaincy lark? I doubt it, much more likely that the changes had been decided before the start of play. Got to give all tha gals a go, − what?

Seriously, the morning had not pleased Joyce. She knew that she had let down herself and everyone else. Her opponent for the afternoon singles was none other than her old sparring partner, Glenna Collett-Vare. Watch out Glenna. Signals are at red. Sure enough, Joyce's golf returned to the type of golf which the British had grown to love and adore – immaculate and controlled. When the chips are down, the real champions come to the fore.

Joyce treated Glenna to some of her best golf and Glenna could not respond. Joyce won by six and four. By now, it was raining. Britain had to win five of the six afternoon matches to win the rubber. It was a tall order, but, for a time at least, there seemed hope. Britain led by 3, 2, 3, and 2 in four of the matches and were only one down in the fifth. Unfortunately, the sixth already looked beyond recovery with Elsie Corlett four down to Mrs Cheney.

It got even better when Enid Wilson not only wiped out her one-hole deficit but won the seventeenth to win by two and one and put Britain two up. It couldn't last, however, and although Britain won the singles by three matches to two with one halved, the match was lost by 5.5. to 3.5.

Henry Longhurst wrote:

> It is a long-established precedent, when we are beaten by America at golf, to reiterate that our players are bad putters. Frankly, I have never been inclined to think that our inferiority in this direction is so marked as many people will have it, but yesterday it was true. In nearly every case the American was the better on the green, not only in effect but also in style. They all had a certain similarity of method and a very noticeable follow-through, and in the long run it just saw them home.

I believe I have read the same in 2001. Incidentally, Joyce may not have been the correct choice for captain that day, but when her match was finished, she was back down the course in the pouring rain to encourage the rest of her team.

One newspaper reporting on the match deplored the behaviour of the crowd and included an article on the inadequacies of stewarding for such an event, particularly when admission money has been paid by those desirous of watching proceedings in a modicum of comfort. It declared that there should be an onus on the promoters to ensure that proper and adequate roping off of greens and fairways took place to separate spectators from players, and give the latter the opportunity to properly play their game. It indicated that the match had probably been lost because of these inadequacies, where players were constantly having to ask for room to play their shots. It then purported to quote Miss Wethered as having stated: 'It was all too terrible. I do not understand it. None of us really had a chance.'

A day or two later, a letter from the aforesaid Miss Wethered appeared in *The Times* under the heading 'Ladies' International Golf':

To The Editor of The Times,
Sir, – May I encroach upon your space just to say that certain remarks publicly attributed to me (not in The Times*) with reference to the behaviour of the crowds at Wentworth in Saturday's international match are totally untrue. The crowd, as a strict matter of fact, was ideal and gave every player every chance.*

This habit of publishing alleged interviews and criticisms is, in my opinion, one of the most objectionable features of the time, and in the instance I have mentioned might be highly mischievous in giving a false and ungenerous impression as suggesting that there were other reasons than the correct and obvious one that we were well beaten on the day. I would not refer to what may be after all a small matter, but it might conceivably become necessary to advertise in your 'Agony' column that we are not to be held responsible for our inverted commas.
Yours truly, Joyce Wethered.

Joyce didn't particularly like to be jostled by crowds, but that was infinitely more preferable than having some scoundrel pretending to speak for her. The fact that Joyce wrote to the paper gives some idea of how much the matter irked and annoyed her.

The American match ended Joyce's short international amateur career. Events away from golf were to lead to the loss of her amateur status as she found it desirable, if not absolutely necessary, to put her extraordinary golfing skills to work to earn her a living.

Before we leave 1932, we should devote a few sentences to Worplesden of that year, because Joyce's partner was none other than the golfing correspondent Bernard Darwin. I have been unable to ascertain whether the reports of the matches came from Bernard himself. I don't suppose they could have been as he would have been playing rather than watching, but note some of the comments: 'Miss

Wethered is an irresistible magnet, and I saw her with her back to the wall, with a partner in a patchy and agitated mood.' 'Their opponents seemed certain to be three up at the thirteenth, but here Darwin – and I hasten to say anything good about him – holed a miraculous shot with his mashie round an apparently dead stymie.' 'Miss Wethered has now reached her eighth final. She has played like herself throughout, and there is no more to be said. Her partner was a millstone round her neck on Tuesday, but yesterday he got some hold of himself and his game and played sufficiently well.' 'With a large lead, Darwin became seized with the old terror of holes slipping away and went weakly and meekly into one bunker after another. In a twinkling of an eye five up became two up. However, the criminal steadied himself with a good iron shot, and Miss Wethered rose up to settle the issue with a perfect tee shot to the sixteenth.' 'Miss Wethered and partner won the final by eight and seven over the thirty-six holes. In the morning she played very, very well but not tremendously; in the afternoon there was no standing against her. As to her partner I find it difficult to form an opinion, but I think he did his bit fairly well.' Surely that is Bernard reporting upon himself. In 1937, Bernard, who knew everyone and all the courses, was awarded the CBE for services to golf. Why didn't Joyce receive any such honour?

Mrs Wethered (right) with Lady
Holderness: two mothers of famous
golfing champions.

A budding champion, 1919. Joyce
at seventeen.

Joyce and Roger in the early 1920s.

Joyce and Cecil Leitch – the English Open at Princes, Sandwich, 1922.

British champion – again, and again, and again.

Joyce with Mrs Olaf Hambro – winners of the Autumn Foursomes at Ranelagh.

Joyce and Glenna Collett before their semi-final in the British Ladies' Open at Troon in 1925.

Joyce and Glenna Collett after their semi-final at Troon in 1925. Glenna was destined always to be the loser whenever the two met in a singles match.

The end of another
satisfactory delivery.

Above: The British Open, 1929.

Right: A little anxiety with this one...

Glenna Collett congratulates Joyce in the British Ladies' Open at St Andrews, 1929.

R&A Golf Club, clubhouse and beach, St Andrews.

R&A Golf Club, clubhouse and grand hotel, St Andrews.

FAIRWAY AND HAZARD
THE OFFICIAL ORGAN OF THE LADIES' GOLF UNION

Entered at Stationers' Hall.   Registered at the G.P.O.   Advertisement Offices: 110, Fleet Street, E.C.4.   Telephone: City 8972
Editorial Offices: 24, Chancery Lane, W.C.2.   Telephone: Holborn 0467   Subscription Rates: Six Months, 7/6; Twelve Months, 14/-
Registered as a Magazine for transmission by post in Canada and Newfoundland

THE CAPTAINS MEET.
Miss Joyce Wethered, who is captaining the British team in the Ladies' International Match, greeting Miss Marion Hollins, the American ladies' captain, on the arrival of the American team at Waterloo.

Left: The first official Curtis Cup match, 1932. Joyce, captain of Great Britain and Ireland, greets Marion Hollins, captain of the U.S. team.

Below: The British and Irish Curtis Cup team, 1932. Front row, left to right: Mrs J.B. Watson, Miss Doris Park, Miss Molly Gourlay. Back row, left to right: Miss Enid Wilson, Miss Wanda Morgan, Miss Diana Fishwick, Miss Joyce Wethered, Miss Elsie Corlett.

Above: A putting style.

Below: Joyce's putting grip.

Right: Another Worplesden Foursomes win, with the Hon. Michael Scott, 1931.

Above left: At work: Fortnum & Mason's golf department, 1933.

Above right: Wanamaker's publicity campaign is underway for the American Tour.

Left: Curtis Cup captain, 1932.

Opposite: Advertising Joyce's 1935 American Tour.

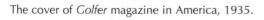

The cover of *Golfer* magazine in America, 1935.

Joyce and Bobby Jones in Georgia: mutual admirers. 1935.

Joyce with Tommy Armour, Cooper and Laffoon in Chicago, American Tour, 1935.

Above: Joyce at a demonstration day with Henry Cotton, Enid Wilson and Simone Lacoste.

Right: Joyce as the subject of her father (H.N. Wethered)'s painting. It is on display at Knightshayes Court. (Courtesy of the National Trust)

Knightshayes Court, Tiverton. (Courtesy of the National Trust)

Joyce, husband John (left), brother Roger and wife at Knightshayes Court. (Courtesy of the National Trust)

The golf room at Knightshayes Court, Tiverton, which is open to the general public by courtesy of the National Trust, houses some of Joyce's golfing trophies and memorabilia.

The gardens at Knightshayes Court, Tiverton, now maintained by the National Trust, but designed and planted by Joyce and her husband Sir John.

8
WORKING FOR A LIVING

Newton Wethered and his family had led a very comfortable life, mostly due to their inheritances from the industry of his father and father-in-law. As is sometimes described, they were of independent means. We do not know the details of their investments, but we do know that the Wall Street Crash of 1929 and thereafter had dire consequences on their income. The Crash started in late October 1929, after unprecedented rises in the American stock market through the preceding year. These rises had occurred for several reasons, one of which was 'trading on the margin', the device whereby stock could be purchased with the need to pay out only a small percentage of the purchase price at the time of acquisition. The Federal Reserve Board and the Federal Bank were the organisations which should have taken action to avoid the abyss, but they failed to take action when it had become apparent earlier in the year that the balloon would burst with a very loud bang. There were many who argued that the Board would be wrong to interfere, and there were those within the Board who stood to lose if a retraction of the market was forced. The principal reason, however, that the Board remained irresolute was that they could not guarantee a method whereby they could prick the balloon and let it deflate slowly as opposed to going down with a bang.

The fall in the market continued with brief minor recoveries through to June 1932. The falls in value of stock were phenomenal. *The Times*

Industrial Index in September 1929 stood at 452; in July 1932 it was fifty-eight. Individual stocks were no better. General Motors dropped from seventy-three to eight; but still worse was the fate of the investment trusts, a new phenomenon which had increased greatly in the year before the Crash. A device called 'leverage' had been promoted, whereby on a rising market most or all of the gain from rising portfolio values was concentrated on the common stock of the investment trust, which as a result rose marvellously. Unfortunately, leverage could work equally forcefully in reverse. Two stocks promoted by Goldman Sachs & Company, an investment banking and brokerage partnership, were Shenandoah Corporation and Blue Ridge Corporation. After flotation in mid-1929, the stock soon reached a high of $36. In 1932, Shenandoah was worth fifty cents and Blue Ridge not much better. The Crash was followed by the Great Depression, which lasted throughout the 1930s. At one time, one in four people in America were out of work.

Much continental money had been sucked into the maelstrom, and Newton Wethered was caught up in this mess. His downfall is usually attributed to the shenanigans of one of the biggest speculators of the time, one Ivar Kreuger. However, Kreuger was only one of several major operators of the time, and sometimes there has been a tendency to use his name to describe the ills of all of the bad men. Kreuger eventually committed suicide in Paris in March 1932. He had seldom been interviewed, and on the one occasion when he was, he ascribed any success which he might have had to three things, '…silence, more silence, and even more silence.' It was certainly true that his dealings were all behind closed doors, and for very good reasons.

At some stage in the 1929-32 period, Newton Wethered found that his resources had substantially evaporated. He was a fairly prolific author, but the titles of his works were hardly likely to raise any significant income and he was by this time in his sixties. The family home was moved from Tigbourne Court, the Lutyens house near Godalming, to Brook, and a more modest house, just a few miles away.

It is obvious that Joyce would feel that whilst she could rely upon her parent's support whilst they were wealthy, the boot was on the other foot when their largesse largely disappeared. She set about finding herself employment, paid employment, for the first time in her life. It was probably a blessing in disguise. It certainly meant that she had to go forth into the big wide world, cast away at least some of her shyness, and come out from behind the family curtain.

Her first venture was to Piccadilly, to manage the Fortnum & Mason golf department. Andrea Duncan, Fortnum's archivist, read out to me extracts from their minutes books. Apparently, at the time, the chairman of the company was Col. Charles Wyld, an ardent golfer and member of the Denham Golf Club. Whether the colonel knew Joyce or the family, I know not, but he would certainly have been very aware of her golfing talents and achievements. The first reference to Joyce in the minutes was on 12 January 1933, when it was agreed that she should be employed on a monthly basis, to promote the sales of sports goods, commencing on 20 February, and that her salary should be £600 per annum.

A minute of 7 February 1933 referred to an unauthorised article in the *Daily Mirror* concerning Miss Wethered's employment. It was decided to issue a statement to the press making it quite clear that Miss Wethered would be acting in an advisory capacity, but this would not include teaching or demonstrating. A minute of 14 February stated that careful consideration should be given to Miss Wethered's probable requirement to work in dignity and comfort. Otherwise matters should proceed on the basis discussed and it should be left to her when she started. Quite obviously, either she was being looked after very carefully by someone (possibly the chairman), or she was considered too good an appointment to lose.

A minute of 21 March 1933 had the general manager reporting to the Board that an approach had been received from a Mr Ellis of A.G. Spalding & Co. making a tentative offer of marketing Miss Wethered's clubs, on a royalty basis. Presumably, this meant that Miss Wethered would receive royalties on clubs manufactured by Spalding's and sold at Fortnum's. There was competition, however, from Kinghorne's, and a minute of 28 March reported that Joyce was still considering alternative proposals made to her by Kinghorne and Spalding. The matter was further reported upon by the chairman in a minute of 9 May. He had been in conversation with the chairman of Kinghorne's, which firm Miss Wethered had selected for marketing her clubs in all parts of the world, except the United States. This was subject to a model being produced which complied with her design. There would be a five-year deal, with five per cent being received on the first two thousand and ten per cent thereafter. Kinghorne would fix the wholesale selling price. I take this to mean that Joyce would receive the five per cent and ten per cent as royalties on the wholesale price and that Fortnum's would set the retail price. Unfortunately, we do not know how many clubs were ultimately sold, but they must have produced a very acceptable income for Joyce. Interestingly, the clubs were matched steel-shafted sets, but Joyce continued to use the old hickory shafted clubs, which she considered gave her a better feel for those important little shots around the green.

The position got even better as the minute of 18 July revealed when the general manager reported that a Mr Harlow, Walter Hagen's publicity agent, had volunteered to act for Miss Wethered in America, in the sale of clubs and film work. The Fortnum's Board was happy with these proposals and that they should be on her terms. What a wonderful employer! The film work is interesting because a film was made of Joyce in action, but to my knowledge she never saw the finished article. As has been written earlier, Hal Rhodes, a Canadian teaching professional, made a cine-film of Joyce in 1935; and apparently she did this without payment, so that it could be used for the benefit of others. If that is correct, I don't know what Mr Harlow thought of the matter – not too much, I suspect. Walter Hagen model clubs were certainly marketed under Joyce's name, because she said so, so presumably Harlow did act for her to some extent.

The next reference to Miss Wethered in Fortnum's minutes came on 12 March 1935, when Wanamaker's letter of 18 February was reported to the Board. It contained proposals for Joyce to tour America playing exhibition matches with top American amateurs and professionals. It was a tour which was scheduled to take place from the end of May to September. The Board approved her leave of absence, and that she would receive full salary during her absence. Fortnum & Mason had a store in New York, so I suppose they could expect to gain from the publicity, especially if she performed well, and as usual few doubted that. Nevertheless, it again demonstrated their admiration for the lady.

Many years later, when Joyce had become a nonagenarian, Fortnum's contacted her to see whether she would take part in some project which they were pursuing. She was not in the best of health by this time, and therefore declined, but not without commenting how much she had enjoyed her days at Fortnum's and that she still harboured many happy memories.

Whilst employed at Fortnum's, she lived at Grosvenor Place. Curiously, her erstwhile fiancé, Major Hutchison, had an address at Grosvenor Square.

She had been writing articles for various magazines for some time, and now her activities came before the consideration of the LGU. Her amateur status was in question, because she was professionally engaged upon golfing business which brought her an income. Had she been on another floor in Fortnum & Mason, dispensing advice on other matters, the problem would not have occurred. The conflict of amateur/professional status was a problem which had been in existence for men for many years, and not only in golf, but also in other sporting activities such as cricket. Lord Hawke, the captain of Yorkshire CCC was quite clear in his own mind, in 1909, what constituted the difference between an amateur and a professional, and he had the added problem that some of the amateurs of the day – the great W.G. Grace, for example – took home more in 'expenses' than the professionals took in wages. Lord Hawke's simple definition of a professional was that he spent all of his time playing cricket and that was his one and only source of income. Conversely, an amateur could take money in the form of 'expenses', providing that was not his main source of income.

I doubt very much whether that definition would have suited the R&A. I do not know their criteria for making a decision and I don't think it is necessary to pursue the matter, but it was likely to rear its head increasingly for a time as more and more women became emancipated and went to work, and yet professional golf for ladies was largely in the future. Edith Wilson, from a working background, suffered the same conflict in 1933, when she paralleled Joyce by going to work at Lilleywhite's, and her amateur status was challenged. The LGU had to refer Joyce's case to the R&A for ratification or decision, as was the normal procedure. Unfortunately, the LGU has been unable to furnish the exact dates of Joyce's dismissal to the wilderness; but the R&A have produced an informative entry for Miss Wethered for the *Dictionary of National Biography*, which tells us that, following a change in the definition of an amateur golfer in 1934, Joyce was ruled ineligible to play as an amateur as from 5 March 1934, if she received any 'consideration' from her employment at Fortnum's. Somewhat academically, her amateur status was reinstated on 23 May 1954. Quite what brought that about, I have been unable to discover. The increasing extent of the problem of amateurism/professionalism is demonstrated by the fact that in the following year the LGU decided that it was necessary to form an Advisory Board to 'assist' players over their status. Any infringement of amateur status would be investigated and with the knowledge of the individual concerned, it would be sent to R&A for decision.

Two examples relating to professionalism, which are of interest, occurred as early as 1878. In the first instance, John Ball III, when only fifteen years old, came fourth in the Open at Prestwick, and on the advice of Jack Morris, he accepted the prize of 10s. His status as an amateur was subsequently challenged, but the R&A found in his favour, presumably because he was young and had been badly advised. John Ball went on to win the Open Amateur Championship on no less than eight occasions. On the other hand, Douglas Rolland, a stonemason, accepted second prize in the 1884 Open, and his amateur status was forfeited.

1934 saw the publication of Joyce's book, entitled *Golfing Memories and Methods*, a sort of golfing autobiography with sections devoted to instruction and golfing psychology. It is a book which is just as relevant today as it was when it was first published. The clarity with which she was able to express herself in writing on often complex subjects confirms that she would have had the technical intelligence to take a golf swing apart and work out and fashion the constituents of a perfect whole.

She seemed to be enjoying her golf again and ready for new challenges. There was without doubt a need in her makeup to test herself every so often to see how she compared with the top players. She had been encouraged on several occasions to visit America. People such as Bobby Jones and Glenna Collett-Vare had made it clear that she would be made very welcome, but for some reason she had never taken up the offers. Her appointment with Fortnum's and move into professionalism by selling her own clubs now produced further overtures for her to visit USA, but this time with an important difference – on a paid basis. She was a working girl now and had to treat herself as a business. The offer she received was one she could hardly refuse. It came via Alexander Findlay, who was golf adviser and wholesale manager to Henry Howe, the manager of the John Wanamaker Men's Store in Philadelphia. Negotiations proceeded through the rest of 1934 into 1935, and apart from the huge financial incentive, Joyce became keener and keener to add this experience to her life. It was evident weeks before the signatures were finally on the dotted lines that she would be going, and in true Wethered fashion she started to prepare. She had never been a great practiser, believing in the idiom, 'if it ain't broke, don't fix it'. She practised when she wished to experiment with an idea, or when a certain aspect of her game had gone off the boil. Once the fault had been corrected – and the big difference between you or I and Joyce Wethered was that she knew how to correct it – she left it alone. She did, however, step up her playing, and played not so much with less freedom, but with more seriousness and thought and with rather more attention to detail and achievement than of late. There was a challenge ahead – which was just what she wanted. By the time the contract of her tour was settled, she was already playing as well as she had ever played.

1935 was a good year for the Wethereds; in January, Roger won the President's Putter, played annually at Rye by Oxbridge folk, often in appalling weather. Roger took the title five times in all, and in the 1935 final he was only one over fours for the round.

In February, however, at the AGM of the LGU, a motion was tabled that women professional golfers should be allowed to participate in all events controlled by the LGU. It was defeated.

In March, JW made what was described as a welcome appearance in the Sunningdale Foursomes, an event which was open to all golfers. JW and J.S.F. Morrison were the victors, beating Pam Barton and Leslie Garnett by three and two in the final.

In April 1935 she was able to test herself out in the annual Stoke Poges' Men *v*. Ladies match. The men that year were required to give their female counterparts nine bisques. Some of the ladies needed the help, but it was laughable and insulting for JW to be receiving nine shots from any man on earth. She confirmed the fact. The luckless Jack McLean was the man who had to play Joyce. He played out of his skin, reached the turn in thirty-four, four better than scratch, and was three down! JW won the match by five and four. Poor Jack McLean won two holes only, and those were where he birdied a long par-four and when he drove the 295 yards tenth green. His comment afterwards was that he did not think that there was any amateur in the country who could concede anything to Joyce Wethered.

Just in case there was any doubt, together with Molly Gourlay, Joyce won her Foursomes match also, by four and three.

It should be pointed out that the men actually won the match by ten points to eight, a point being awarded for a win and half a point for a tied match. This amply demonstrates that the majority of the ladies needed all of their nine bisques and perhaps a few more. There was quite a gulf between men and women's golf. Joyce was simply head and shoulders better than the ladies, and could and did compete on the same level as the men.

Chuck Howe and Alex Findlay's idea to bring Joyce over from England to play exhibition matches in America was a winner. Several previous attempts had been made to secure her services, including an offer from Gene Sarazen, but Joyce had held out until, as one journalist put it, a tour with dignity was on the table. She did not wish to stand hitting balls into the harbour or towards the Empire State Building, nor did she wish to demonstrate her skills prior to a baseball game in the Yankees stadium. Such eye-catching endeavours just were not Joyce. Howe and Findlay were happy to go along with Joyce's wishes. This was no desire to satisfy a whim, they were business men. Based in Philadelphia, Howe was interested in putting on matches in that district to advertise the merchandise which he was selling in his store. But no sooner did others hear about the intended visit than they wanted a piece of the action also. The itinerary grew and grew. Originally, it was intended that the visit would last about nine weeks. In the event, it was stretched to over three months before a halt was called. Alex Findlay had the job of promoting and directing the tour, something he was well qualified for, as he had handled Harry Vardon's tour some years previously. Weeks before Joyce was due to arrive on American soil, the US sporting press was eulogising about the great British golfer. Some of it was no doubt sponsored by Findlay, if he was doing his job properly, but it was much more than that. Hadn't Bobby Jones said that she was the best and most consistent striker of the ball in the world? Bobby was still hero-worshipped; if he said that then it must be true. There is no doubt at all that the golfing populace of America, including the sporting scribes, were anticipating the tour with relish.

The marketing continued and Gene Sarazen, no doubt well paid, put his name to a well-publicised statement, congratulating 'The John Wanamaker Store for its momentous contribution to the advancement of the Royal and Ancient pastime in the United States, by sponsoring the first exhibition tour of Joyce Wethered, which will supply a unique and highly important chapter in the already glittering annals of American golf.'

On 22 May 1935, Joyce boarded the SS *Bremen* for the transatlantic journey. She was accompanied by a Miss Shaw, who would be her companion throughout the tour. Whence came the idea of a chaperon, I know not, but it was a good idea. Joyce would have someone with her whom she knew, someone with whom to discuss, and, importantly, someone who could share the workload of a hectic tour. Miss Shaw would be available for a chat when one was needed, she would provide guidance when it was sought, and she would be able to act as a deterrent to unwanted visitors. It was an excellent idea. Five days later they steamed into New York harbour.

The financial arrangement, widely and publicly reported, was that Joyce would receive $200 for each game and also a percentage, reported to be forty per cent, of the profits. In those days there were almost five dollars to the pound, so we are looking at £40 plus forty per cent of the profits. If those figures are correct, whoever negotiated on behalf of Joyce had not done a bad job. To put it into some sort of perspective, you could get accommodation at a good hotel for about $3.50 (70 pence) per night, and a week at a luxury holiday club would cost about $27.50 (£5.50). Good golf clubs cost about $10 (£2) each. The charge for spectators at the exhibition matches was variously in the region of $1 or $2 and the number of spectators per match averaged something in excess of 1,000, but we do not know the costs of putting on the events, and therefore the profits are an unknown. Several newspaper reports indicated that Joyce could expect to take home a total of $20,000 (£4,000). Some put the figure much higher.

Even as Joyce was cruising towards America, one problem area of the forthcoming matches was being resolved by the USGA. Those taking part were to be a combination of the best amateurs and professionals. Would the amateur status of the former be prejudiced if they took part in matches for which entrance monies would be charged? The USGA issued a bulletin explaining its position, 'Amateurs may play in exhibitions, but only when net proceeds go to an organised charity. Professionals may be paid appropriate amounts and the club can be reimbursed only for actual expenses.' Whether charities benefited greatly from the edict I have been unable to ascertain.

As the *Bremen* steamed up the bay, Joyce and companion were on the foredeck taking photographs of the New York skyline. Reporters and cameramen who had boarded the ship harassed them for quotes and interviews and posed pictures. Joyce revealed that she had been practising for the previous month with the larger American ball, with which she was required to play whilst in the States. When she crossed the Canadian border she would then be required to play with the smaller British ball. She told the reporters that she preferred the smaller ball, particularly as it gives more distance. Playing with the larger ball was just one of the impositions with which she would have to contend whilst playing in America. Apart from the different set-up of the courses, about which we shall hear more later, the climate was going to be very different from that in England. Indeed, it transpired that she was often playing in temperatures around the 100°F mark. Typically Joyce, she never let that be an excuse for anything; she said that she enjoyed warm weather. She was anxious to hear what had happened in the British Amateur Open. The Californian, Lawson Little, had won and she wanted to know the details. Then she was asked whether she considered Little to be a better golfer than Bobby Jones. 'Jones is the greatest golfer who ever lived,' came the reply, without hesitation. She believed it and meant it, but it was a wonderfully diplomatic plus for her to applaud the hero of US golf, as she prepared to set foot on American soil.

At Woodbridge the previous year, she had played her lowest round ever − a sixty-eight − and in 1935 it still stood as the world record for the lowest score by a woman. I believe the record currently is held by Mickey Wright, the great Dallas golfer and stands at sixty-two, further confirmation that the difference between Joyce's playing days in the 1930s and modern golf is about six shots per round. This is something worth remembering when considering the scores.

Joyce modestly informed the reporters that she could usually play a course in England in even fours, but added that she had no experience of American courses, had heard that they were very tight, and therefore she may not score as well.

She was straight into action as soon as she had disembarked, whisked down to the Fresh Meadow Golf Club in Flushing, where she posed for photographs before spending time demonstrating her technique to the gathered audience for almost an hour, by hitting shots, whilst still dressed in her travelling clothes − and shoes! When you write a biography you come to know your subject pretty well, and one of the real gems at Fresh Meadow for me was that when asked to spend time posing for photographs before demonstrating her golf shots, she simply washed her hands. There was no powdering the nose or attending to the hair, etc. Joyce had come to demonstrate her golf. All right, no doubt it had been impressed upon her that she must pay due respect to the public relations aspect of the visit, and she would appreciate that was a necessary part of the tour, but she dressed to please herself. She would always be neat, but she had never been a glamour-puss, and tour or no tour, she didn't intend starting now. In truth, she didn't always make enough of herself; she could be very attractive, as some photographs bear witness, but I suspect that a little bit of obstinacy would mean that she would underplay her physical attributes precisely because she knew that others thought that she should overplay them. Joyce was friendly, affable, and all of the endearing adverbs which people have used in describing her, but most of all she was her own woman, and in the end she would do exactly as she decided. On the tour, she was always smart and well turned-out, as she was always anyway, but some of her outfits looked a little dated, particularly for America. Yet, on other occasions, she matched up admirably to the description of 'English Rose' which was used in the American press, and she exhibited those little pieces of English upper-class finesse, such as the string of pearls or sweet little handkerchief tucked into the waistband of her skirt. There could be no doubting that she was English.

The tour would take Joyce to fifteen different States and three Canadian provinces, travelling thousands of miles in so doing. Many of her journeys from one venue to the next would be of the order of 100 miles, but there would be a thousand-mile return trip from the North-East to Bobby Jones's home state of Georgia, the huge journey from Missouri across America to Los Angeles, and the mighty big hops from Vancouver eastwards across Canada. On average, she would be required to play every other day, so she was unlikely to have much time for sightseeing, except in the course of travelling from destination to destination. In the event, she played fifty-three exhibition matches.

Her hostess for her first few nights at Roslyn, Long Island, was Rosalie Knapp, USGA committee member.

The first match had, of course, to be a cracker. The venue was the Women's National Golf and Tennis Club at Sea Cliff, Long Island. The opposing lady was none other than Joyce's old sparring partner, Glenna Collett-Vare, who had been blessed with two children since they had last met. Glenna had never beaten Joyce in head-to-head play, and presumably hoped to put an end to that particular matter. The organisers had arranged that each match should be a four ball, but also included that all four competitors should putt out so that the respective scores of individuals could be assessed. This was a tremendously wise decision.

Joe Public wanted to see how Joyce compared with both the ladies and the men. Foursome results only would have been open to argument about the merits of partners and how they had affected the result etc.

The two men selected to do battle were arguably the two best-known golfers in America, Bobby Jones and Gene Sarazen. My word, if that foursome didn't bring in the crowds, nothing would. Unfortunately, Jones suffered a bout of appendicitis just before the match could take place and the doctor advised him to withdraw and to take things easy for a few days. His place was taken by Johnny Dawson of Chicago, known as the 'businessman amateur', who was Joyce's partner. Men and ladies played from the same tees, as they would throughout the tour, and all played off scratch. The match was halved, the individual scores being Sarazen seventy-two, Dawson seventy-five, Wethered seventy-eight, and Collett-Vare seventy-five, with one hole missing, which she did not complete.

The press and the knowledgeable crowd of about 2,000 were tremendously impressed by the Wethered. She was disappointed with her score, but as many an observer pointed out, it was only her putting which let her down. She found the greens very slow, compared with those at home, and repeatedly left her approach putts short. If she had putted as well as Sarazen she would have all but equalled his score, was the general opinion. The bunkers she also found different. The sand was much heavier than in England and she even left one bunker shot in the trap. Her golf through the green, however, was a revelation. The watchers were most impressed by her driving and iron play. Her drives were straight down the middle, usually within ten or so yards of Sarazen's, and with one exception the same distance in front of Glenna's. But it was her swing which so enthralled the spectators, professionals included. They adored its simplicity and fluidity, and readily agreed that they had never seen a swing so under control throughout. Joyce had made a conquest.

The golfing scribes were unanimous in their adoration, and it was noticeable how many golf instructors were present to see what they could learn. One said afterwards, 'I wish all of my pupils were here to witness Miss Wethered's economy of effort.'

I will quote just one of the gathered journalists, as an example of what appeared in all of the papers and magazines. George Trevor of *The Sportsman* wrote:

June was an exciting month in golf with two unknowns winning the United States and British Opens, but I do not wish to write about them as in a few years time they will just be two more names in the record book, men who enjoyed their brief day in the sun. Good golfers pass in an endless parade, but when genius shapes a swing in the very glass of fashion and mold of form, you have something which belongs to the golfing ages — something which should be preserved in motion pictures for future generations of would-be golfers.

We stood near the first tee and watched as a slim girl with fair hair, prematurely grey at the temples, stepped up to the starting box. Her natural simplicity, her gracious bearing during the trying ordeal by camera, her unaffected modesty — the hallmark of good breeding — her shy smile, her innate charm, captivated the gallery. A stranger in a strange land, she seemed a bit bewildered and embarrassed by the battery of cameras trained upon her, by the babble of orders from the news photographers, and by all the fuss and fury with which America greets its sports celebrities. Obeying the obvious command, she forced a thin smile.

Finally the hubbub was stilled, the cameramen were shooed away, and the supple girl in blue, who gave the impression of slightness, despite her five feet eleven inches, took her stance and addressed the ball. All eyes were fixed on the slim girl with the typically English face. She had lost any trace of self-consciousness as she settled her feet firmly, fingered the club with the assurance of one who knew what it was all about, and started a swing which for pure grace has never been equalled, no, not even by Bobby Jones himself. The slender girl in blue was in her element at last.

Genius is a disquieting thing. It defies analysis, cannot be translated into words. That graceful fluid swing epitomised the effortlessness of art. Even tyros in the gallery, realised, perhaps subconsciously, that here visualised in the flesh, was a living picture of everything the textbooks and theorists had written about the perfect golf swing.

For once, few spectators followed the ball with their eyes as it sped some 230 yards down the fairway. They were still looking at the girl poised there like a figure on a Grecian urn. They were trying to recapture each move in a swing so deftly modulated, so smoothly blended, that the component parts were lost in contemplating the homogenous whole. The gallery's long drawn out, 'Ah!' was a tribute more spontaneous and flattering than any words. Joyce Wethered had driven her first ball on American soil. What matter if her scores do not always do justice to that flawless swing. Her American audiences are the richer in golf lore from having seen Miss Wethered strike the ball. Theirs is an experience no golfer can forget.

A bit over the top perhaps, but all of the scribes wrote similarly. They were of one accord that the Wethered and her swing were something very special.

Following the Thursday match at Long Island, Joyce's next two engagements did not entail too much travelling. They were on the following Saturday and Sunday. It was already clear to Joyce that the differences between playing in America and playing in Britain were greater than she had thought. The fairways were more lush and narrower, generally with more trees lining them to swallow the errant shot. The greens were slower and time would show that they varied considerably across America, depending upon the types of grass used. The sand in the bunkers was coarser and heavier. She was required to play with the bigger American ball, and although she had practised with it over the preceding month, she much preferred the smaller ball and this could be at the back of her mind if she encountered any loss of form.

A factor which must be taken into account in considering her performance on any particular course she played was that she had never set eye or foot on the course before. She was required to play most of them blind. This meant, of course, that she often had to rely on her caddie for direction. There was a problem here in that she did not have a caddie who travelled all of the courses with her, and therefore each caddie knew Joyce no better than she knew the caddie. After one match, Gene Sarazen's caddie stated that Joyce's caddie, assuming that she was good but a woman, had been handing her the wrong clubs. He hadn't realised that she could hit the ball more like a man than a woman.

All of these problems had to be added to the effects of the hubbub of the crowd, cameramen, reporters, and so on. Of course, she knew when she accepted the assignment that she would have to tolerate this entourage of all sorts, but for one who preferred the peace of a quiet round with a few friends, it could be an added frustration.

So, how did she fare with this multitude of problems? If her scores are anything to go by, not too well at first. That first match had unsettled her in as much as it had revealed these problems, and she realised that she would have to combat them as best she could. Also, it weighed upon her mind, that she was being paid good money to perform well and she had a commitment to the paying customers and her sponsors – something she had never faced before in her life. Yes, life was not a bed of roses at that time. It was not a case of just swanning round America and picking up the money.

Her second match at Winged Foot Golf Club, Mamaroneck, New York, set Joyce and Glenna against Sarazen and Sweetser. The proceeds after expenses were to go to hospitals in the area. The two ladies received six shots each, but all played off the men's tees. The men won by two and one with Sarazen playing to the par of seventy-two. Glenna had an eighty-two and Joyce an eighty-three. She again had awful troubles on the greens. She was most apologetic to the 2,000-plus audience, and it has to be said that some of them were disappointed. The more knowledgeable might applaud the style, but the run-of-the-mill spectators were more interested in the score.

By now she had acquired a sand-iron from Sarazen, and the heavier implement soon became a favourite with Joyce, including playing short fairway pitches to the flag. The next match at Ridgewood, New Jersey, found Joyce with the South African, Sid Brews, as a partner. They won, but it was Brews who was the star and Joyce's eighty-two was one more than her opponent Maureen Orcutt.

At Winchester, Massachusetts, on a course made heavy by overnight rain, Joyce returned her highest score of the whole tour – eighty-five; yet she and Bill Blaney, the State Amateur champion, won by seven and six. Blaney had a seventy-four and their opponents, Francis Ouimet and Jean Bauer had eighty and ninety-one respectively. Joyce was presented after the match with a gold medal bearing the club's coat-of-arms.

By now, Joyce had realised that she must change her putting stroke to suit these troublesome greens, but with match following match she had little opportunity to practise anything, except during the course of play. Worcester provided the welcome breakthrough. Playing with Benny Ayres, they defeated Jesse Guildford and Jean Bauer by five and four. After a hesitant start on the putting green, that section of her game was as excellent as the remainder and she scored an excellent seventy-six, the best score of the four.

The tour now turned southwards to Philadelphia and the famous Merion Golf Club. Far from being aloof, Joyce invited the reporters to attend her on the practise ground as she wished to hit a few practise shots before the match began. 'You can ask me anything', she said, and between hitting shots she answered the many questions whilst apparently retaining her concentration for hitting the ball. 'No, I don't mind the rain, but it is very unpleasant for the spectators,' was her genuine reply to another question. She didn't think that professionalism in women's golf would take off, but she did hope that she would meet and play with Helen Hicks, America's first female professional, during the course of the tour. Philadephia was Glenna Collett-Vare's home town, and she provided part of the opposition but Joyce was getting better on the greens and she and her partner, George Ayres, turned a halfway deficit of two holes into a one-up victory. Joyce, on her first outing round the course and in rain for much of the round, beat ladies' par by three strokes, and set a new course record of seventy-six (but were two putts conceded?). During the whole of the tour she was to set no fewer than thirty-two new records.

The tour swung through Washington, Virginia, Delaware, Pennsylvania, back to Virginia and Baltimore. At the Wilmington Club in Delaware, Joyce experienced her first game, where she was matched with three men. She came out of the comparison exceedingly well, scoring seventy-six in reply to seventy-two, seventy-four, and seventy-five. At Philmont, she was again Glenna's house guest and opponent in the match. Poor Glenna! Joyce seemed to save her best for when she played against her, and had a seventy-three, her lowest score to date. She was now beginning to break records on a frequent basis, but some probably did not stand, as she was conceded tap-in putts. The Philmont Club made Joyce an honorary life member.

The next match was without doubt the most important of the tour, as far as Joyce was concerned. At Bobby Jones's request, a trip south to Atlanta in Georgia, Bobby's home territory, had been included into the schedule. As the following game was to be in Pittsburgh, nearly a thousand miles to the north-west, it was a brave decision to go to Atlanta, but there is no way in the world that Joyce would not have acceded to Bobby's request. Joyce was not the only one making brave decisions. Bobby had to drop out of the first match of the tour due to a recalcitrant appendix. It was still grumbling and Bobby was accompanied by his doctor when he played with Joyce on 18 June on a beautiful sun-kissed day at the East Lake course in Atlanta. Indeed, two days after the match, Bobby, by arrangement, was in hospital having the appendage removed. He had looked forward to playing with Joyce almost as much as she had looked forward to playing with him; and as he said, he wanted all of his friends in Georgia to have the opportunity, at least once in their lives, of seeing Joyce play.

There was great excitement for Joyce and Dorothy Shaw when they hesitantly decided to take up the suggestion that they should fly down to Atlanta. Dorothy in particular could not stop talking about the experience, which they both enjoyed enormously. That evening they dined with Bobby Jones and his biographer, the columnist O.B. Keeler, and marvelled at the Georgia sunset with fireflies flitting in the shrubbery. Joyce had adopted a new putting technique, similar to that acquired by Bobby himself many years previously, and they discussed the merits in earnest conversation. On the morrow she would experience another first, putting on Bermuda grass greens. Ted Ray, the English professional, had likened it to putting on grape-vines.

The match was between Joyce and the Georgia Collegiate champion, Charlie Yates, v. Bobby and a fifteen-year-old golf starlet, Dorothy Kirby. Joyce said afterwards, when congratulated on her fine exhibition, that it was an occasion when she just had to play well, otherwise she would have been very disappointed. The outcome was a tied match, with Bobby scoring seventy-one, Joyce seventy-four, Yates seventy-six, and Dorothy eighty-four. Charlie Yates said afterwards that it was the first time that he had played fourteen holes as a ladies' partner before he had figured in the match! 'She was carrying me around on her back, and all I could do was try not to let my feet drag. I reckon I would have been pretty embarrassed, but I was sort of hypnotised watching her play.' Apparently, in the week before the game, there were a good deal of bets being placed in Atlanta that Joyce, on her first acquaintance with the East Lake course, would not break eighty.

It was around this time that the English girls were introduced to one or two American peculiarities. Iced tea was tried. Dorothy Shaw quite liked it, but Joyce was not too impressed. Cafeterias had already established themselves in America, and they thought them a good idea, particularly if a quick lunch was required.

At twenty to nine the next morning, Joyce was aboard the train to Cincinatti, on the way to Pittsburgh, a distance equal to twice the journey from London to Edinburgh. She declared that the Oakmont course was one of the best but also hardest she had played to date.

She was amazed how fast the greens were compared to all the other courses she had played. She now travelled west round to the south of the Great Lakes, through Ohio, where she had two days rest at Cleveland, Pennsylvania, and Michigan to Chicago. In Cleveland she had booked into her hotel, incognito, to avoid the media following, which hounded her almost continually. She visited the cinema to see a Joan Crawford film and relaxed in the city.

In Chicago, Joyce was scheduled to play three games in four days against some of the best pros in the land, but the big newspaper story was not about them at all. It was rumoured that America's favourite girl, Ruth (the Babe) Didrikson would be in one of the line-ups. It was a rumour which proved to be true. Didrikson, better known, perhaps, as Babe Zaharias, had taken the 1932 Olympics by storm, breaking world records in the eighty-metre hurdles, the high jump, and the javelin, before turning her mind to golf, and with the passage of time she would become a great golfer as well as a great athlete.

The first match was played at the famous Medinah course, which had just been revamped. Joyce's partner was Tommy Armour against Harry Cooper and Ky Laffoon. They lost, after a titanic struggle, by two and one, but Joyce wowed the crowd with some of her best golf to date. She created a new women's record of seventy-seven, whilst the men each had seventy-fives. The following day, a huge crowd of 4,000 people turned out to witness Joyce against Babe Didrikson. With apologies to Horton Smith and Gene Sarazen, that is exactly what they wanted to see. Joyce coolly played her game and the Babe could not match her consistency. She was still raw material, exploding with long drives which went everywhere. Later, the Babe immodestly stated that she could hit a two iron as far as Joyce's woods. Joyce said nothing – she had a seventy-eight against the Babe's eighty-eight. The men both had seventy-ones. One columnist reported on the good work of the marshals, and said that nobody had been hurt, although the Babe had hit five people with her boomerang shots. He said that even the guy raking the bunker, who saw the Babe's ball coming and figured he should duck right when in fact he should have chosen left, was none the worse for the experience.

Minnesota, Ohio again, and Missouri were all traversed, as the tour swung south from the Great Lakes down to Kansas City and then eastwards via Pennsylvania, to Atlantic City, New Jersey and then Buffalo, New York.

The American press must have found interviewing Joyce somewhat difficult. She did not drink or smoke, had no particular favourite foods, was not superstitious and did not have favourite numbers or colours or film stars. She was always very pleasant and even-tempered, but these things did not make for exciting copy.

Babe Didrikson was on show again for the match at Meadowbrook Country Club, near Buffalo, New York. She partnered Gene Sarazen against Joyce and the home pro Elwyn Nagell. The match was decided by points, one for low ball and one for low aggregate. Joyce and partner won by four points. The scores were Wethered seventy-seven (five below course record), Sarazen seventy-two, Nagell seventy-three, and Didrikson eighty-one. The Babe was the very antithesis of Joyce on the course, very noisy, clowning and joking with spectators, and totally extrovert. I doubt whether Joyce would have chosen her to play a friendly four ball normally, but she never complained, of course, and the American spectators loved it. Didrikson added 'colour', or perhaps 'color', to the game, quoth one journalist, and he was right, but it wasn't the normally accepted attitude on a golf course

The dauntless duo crossed into Canada to Toronto, taking a day off to see Niagara Falls en route. They then flew back over Lake Ontario to Rochester, on to Vermont where Joyce had her lowest score of the whole tour, a seventy, which could have been sixty-nine had she sunk a seven footer on the last green. On to New Hampshire she went, to Rhode Island and Connecticut, where she completed her tour of the Eastern States.

Joyce and Dorothy boarded a train for a twenty-four-hour journey westwards to St Louis, a one-day stop before they proceeded to California on the West Coast. How St Louis got missed from the schedule when she was at Kansas City, I do not know. However, this was another opportunity for the folk of Missouri to see the British star. Again, with their new-found fondness for flying, why did they take the train? Perhaps it was one way of getting a well-earned rest. The advance publicity played strongly on Joyce's record to date on the tour; she had broken the record on no less than twenty-five of the thirty-seven courses which she had played. At Algonquin Country Club, where the greens were burned brown after a prolonged dry spell, Joyce was partnered by Roger Lord. They absolutely whacked the local pair of Sara Guth and Dick Bockenkamp, by eight and six. Joyce and Roger both had seventy-fives. At midnight they were on the train again bound for LA, but before that they had attended the theatre to see *Desert Song*. Joyce must have had a constitution like iron.

In California, Joyce was the guest of Marion Hollins, who had captained the first American Curtis Cup team in England in 1932. Joyce had captained the Great Britain and Ireland team. Marion had been a non-playing captain and it was generally agreed that her ability to give all of her attention to her organisational duties and players had contributed greatly to the US victory.

The coast of California provided the venues for several golfing exhibitions, and a little more time for leisure than in the east. The golfing highlight had to be Pebble Beach, and the leisure highlight a visit to MGM studios.

The American part of the tour finished in Seattle, then games followed in Canada at Victoria and Vancouver, before the transcontinental railway journey on the Canadian Pacific railway across the Rockies and Central Plains to Ottawa via Winnipeg. Then there was the comparatively short trip to Montreal for the last game of the tour. The weather had turned nasty. It was definitely time for Joyce to shut-up shop, and take her well-earned cash back to Britain. A cold drizzle failed to repress the size of the crowd, which numbered 2,000.

In approximately three months, La Wethered had travelled 15,000 miles, played fifty-three official matches and several friendlies, broken women's course records on thirty-four occasions (though some of those might be contested due to conceded tap-ins), and averaged 76.9. As indicated previously, to put that into today's context, you would have to deduct about six shots per round. With one exception, her achievements were made playing on courses she had never seen before, let alone played! And of course she had to play with the large ball in all of her matches in America.

Joyce travelled to Boston for a well-earned break with friends, before catching the boat back to England. What did she think about the whole affair? She remembered with affection the blessed water fountains, dotted around the courses, which she visited frequently when the temperature neared three figures. She recalled that there were even super-fountains, with ice packed round the base and delicious cool water emanating from them. The air in Virginia appeared to have a soft, velvety quality about it. The best course was without doubt Pebble Beach – unforgettable. She considered playing in America was more difficult for women, because the fairways were of a coarser grass and the ball did not run as far as in Britain. The fairways were tighter and the greens smaller and more closely guarded, but they were softer and it was easier to stop the ball on them. She returned having learned a great deal. She had given to North America an exhibition which would boost women's golf over there enormously.

Details of her tour, course by course, are given in Appendix 5.

9

KNIGHTSHAYES

Before Joyce departed for America, she had stated quite adamantly that on her return to Britain she would not be playing golf as a professional. She was totally content to go back to her work at Fortnum & Mason, and to play her golf for pleasure. That is exactly what happened, and in her first appearance following the American tour she captained the British ladies to victory against Cambridge University. The ladies received six bisques, and Joyce's own margin of victory was only three and two, so she obviously faced a worthy opponent that day.

1936 continued in much the same way as the years before the American tour, with Joyce enjoying both her work and her golf. She capped the year by winning her seventh Worplesden Foursomes, this time partnered by the Hon. T. Coke.

It appeared that the next year might go the same way, but 1937 was to be perhaps the best year of Joyce's life, even better than 1929 and the St Andrews Championship. Before we embark upon that story, let us just finish with brother Roger. He was a member of at least a dozen clubs, though Woking was perhaps the one with which he was mostly associated. There is a lovely story from Woking Golf Club history, which recalls the appointment in 1948 of a new Secretary, Col. J.C. Cameron Cooke. It was not a passion for golf which made him apply for the post, though he did take up the game on his appointment. His knowledge of the game and its history displayed some significant gaps. One day, Roger Wethered returned to the club of which he was an honorary member. Cooke asked if he could be of assistance in arranging a match. Roger said not, as he was playing with his sister. Cooke fatally continued the conversation with, 'Ah, your sister plays golf too, does she?'

Roger was president of the Woking club for twenty-one years, until his death in 1983. In 1939 he had the honour bestowed upon him to be Captain of the R&A, but due to the outbreak of war, he had seven years to wait and think about having to make that captain's drive-in from the first tee. In the meantime, he served with the Postal and Telegraphic Censorship Office.

One Saturday in 1936, Sir John Heathcoat-Amory, who lived at Knightshayes Court, near Tiverton in Devon, was asked if he could make up a party of golfers at Westward Ho!. He was due to play for the Tiverton Club, but managed to find a substitute, and duly made his way to Westward Ho! To cut a long story short, Joyce was in the same party. Apparently, it was love at first sight, or very soon after, because the promoter of the meeting between the two, one Dickie Gull, collected five pounds when they married, as a result of a wager he made on that first Saturday that he saw them together. Within three months of their meeting, they became engaged, apparently at Brancaster Golf Course in Norfolk, and in 1937 Joyce Wethered became Joyce, Lady Heathcoat-Amory. Not Lady Joyce Heathcoat-Amory, you will note; she would have to have been a Lady by birth for that, not by marriage.

Once more, she found herself in comfortable circumstances. Sir John, or 'Jack' as Joyce called him, had inherited Knightshayes Court and the surrounding estate, together with the family textile factory in Tiverton. In 1816, John Heathcoat had his factory in Loughborough ransacked by Luddites, who thought that his new machines would prevent them from getting work. Heathcoat immediately decided to transfer his whole business south to Tiverton, where he bought an old cotton mill. Many of his workers made the journey with him, walking the two hundred miles to Devon and taking new machines on horse-drawn carts with them. Heathcoat was a good employer and provided decent wages and inexpensive housing for his employees, and schooling for their children. The business thrived and at one time was the largest producer of lace in the world. Heathcoat's grandson had Knightshayes Court, designed by William Burges, built for himself, the construction commencing in 1869. The house stands high above the Exe valley and looks down on Tiverton and the textile factory which paid for it. In 1973, it became a National Trust property.

Sir John, who married Joyce, was the grandson of the man who built the house. Not only did she go to live in the luxurious old Victorian house, but Sir John also had an estate in Scotland at Glenfernate Lodge, Enochdhu, near Blairgowrie in Perthshire. Scotland, Scottish golf courses and salmon fishing! Joyce had certainly found the right man, and Blairgowrie was not too far from her beloved St Andrews, either. The couple used to go to Scotland regularly each summer for several weeks, and, as late as the mid-1960s, Sir John was able to tell friends that Joyce was still going round the Scottish courses scoring in the middle seventies.

Sir John was the third baronet, the baronetcy having been created in 1874 and bestowed upon his grandfather, and he was a great sportsman, captaining the Devon County cricket team and playing golf with a handicap in single figures. He was a good shot and master of Tiverton foxhounds, though he seldom rode to hounds. The story is told of Sir John, his father Sir Ian, and three brothers all riding in the same Tiverton foxhounds point-to-point and all finishing, with one of the brothers winning the race. Sir Ian was the most enthusiastic regarding hunting, indeed he died following a hunting fall. He had topiary sculpted into the box hedges at Knightshayes, depicting the hunting scene with dogs and fox. They still remain to this day.

Sir John was educated at Eton and Christchurch, Oxford; and saw service with the Fourth Devon Regiment in the First World War in India, Mesopotamia, Persia, and the Caucases, being mentioned in dispatches twice and receiving two medals for bravery. He was born in 1894 and was chairman and later president of John Heathcoat and Co. In 1942-43, he was to become the High Sheriff of Devon, and in the Second World War was a major in the Home Guard.

In spite of all his honours and positions (he was president or patron of a host of clubs), Sir John's greatest claim to fame seems to have been his philanthropic attitude to his workforce and the people of Tiverton generally. Together with his father, he had started pension schemes and co-partnership schemes for the Heathcoat employees, long before most employers ever considered such matters. He built a housing estate to provide inexpensive homes for the workforce. It is not unusual for employees to regard their employers with envy and ill-feeling, even when they are good employers, but there appears to have been a genuine mutual respect between Sir John and the people of Heathcoats. He served on the town council for forty-one years, his proudest moment being when he was made a freeman of the borough in 1959, and in his latter days on the council was regarded as and called 'Tiverton's father figure.'

Joyce had found a man who she could love, admire, and respect. He was a great raconteur, and always had time for people. Indeed, the latter virtue proved trying for Joyce at times, when they were gardening together. Sir John would always happily allow himself to be diverted by a visitor wanting to chat, whilst Joyce was anxious to proceed with the task in hand.

Sir John's philanthropy was readily embraced by Joyce, and their good deeds continued throughout their lives. They purchased a William and Mary mansion in St Peter Street, Tiverton, as a rest centre and headquarters for Tiverton's Aged People Association, and annually entertained them. Another gift to the town was the Bolham Street swimming pool; and the site of the old outdoor baths in Leat Street was given to the Red Cross for their new headquarters.

Joyce held several figure-head appointments in her lifetime, including being the first president of the Girls' Golfing Society in the early 1920s, and the first president of the English Ladies' Golf Association in 1951, but she freely admitted that she felt a degree of guilt in not putting more back into golf by getting involved in the administrative side. At Tiverton, she was a stalwart supporter of the Girl Guides movement and was a Divisional Commissioner for twelve years. She then became president of Tiverton Trefoil Guild, which comprises retired Guiders and raises funds for Guiding. She was described as very generous.

Knightshayes Court is described in the National Trust booklet as 'a rare survival of Burges' work. The rich interiors combine mediaeval romanticism with lavish Victorian decoration, and the smoking and billiard rooms, elegant boudoir and drawing room all give an atmospheric insight into grand country house life.'

One of the wedding presents which Joyce received was a newly laid putting green at the front of the house, provided by contributions from the tenants of the estate. I am told that there was a book in which went the names of all those who played on it, but alas, that particular record, which I am certain would have been more than interesting, cannot be found. The artisans' section of Tiverton Golf Club used to be invited to play a competition on the severely contoured putting green, followed by provision of drinks and refreshments.

Sir John was president of the Tiverton Golf Club. Indeed, he was one of the founding members. In 1930, a small committee, including Sir John, investigated a possible course and James Braid surveyed the prospective site, but problems occurred and the venture was abandoned. The only golf to this point had been a pitch and putt course on Amory Park. The worth of having Sir John involved was soon demonstrated. He purchased Bradford Farm and rented out 120 acres of it as a golf course, laid out by James Braid. The original rent was £218 per annum, with an option to buy, and it was opened in 1932, so they soon got their skates on once they had decided they needed a golf course. The course was partly ploughed up to support the war effort, but restored in 1948, and sheep were allowed to graze it to provide income. There were about a dozen shareholders, including Sir John, but as the years went by, shares started to be left to non-golfers and the golfers began to worry that the course might finish up in the wrong hands. Leave it to Sir John. In 1966 he bought up the shares (no, I don't know the details), and set up a trust with the benevolent ground rent £1 per annum for ninety-nine years.

Joyce, of course, soon became involved in the affairs of the golf club and was made lady president. An Artisans section was started in 1938 and it is said that she was very much in favour of such. Sir John provided them with a club hut. It sounds a bit demeaning, doesn't it, but it was like that in those days. Master and servant only mixed at arm's length. From my reading of Sir John, he would have probably had them straight into the main clubhouse, but the artisans section continued right through to the mid-1980s. Of course, there were advantages to the artisans of the arrangement, particularly as regards reduced subscriptions, without which many of them would not have been able to afford to play at all. What amused me was that the best of the artisans, i.e. the best golfers, were allowed to join the club proper! They needed their skills in the matches.

Malcolm Harvey and Harry Britton (who had been an artisan in his early years at the club) entertained me with stories of the Heathcoat-Amory's involvement with the club. If you enter the clubhouse, their high standing at the club is immediately evident. In the entrance foyer is a life-size tile montage of Lady Amory, and in the lounge/dining area, called the 'Joyce Wethered' lounge, are photographs of the couple. The club's Millenium Trophy is a large Ainsley vase with the old clubhouse depicted on one side and a picture of Joyce Wethered in her playing days on the other.

Harry recalled that Joyce was soon commenting upon the course and making one or two suggestions for improvement. The second hole she thought was too easy in that a miss-hit second shot could easily scurry along the ground and end up on the green. She suggested a strategically placed bunker would enhance the hole. Sir John agreed to pay if the new hazard was incorporated, and ever since it has been known as 'Lady Joyce's bunker.'

Sir John apparently hit the ball with a good whack, but not always straight. Harry recalled one amusing incident when Sir John hit a shot and enquired of his caddie, a man named Hughes, where the ball had gone. Hughes, who suffered from a stammer, embarrassingly replied, 'It went, went, went into Lady Amory'.

Sir John's butler often used to caddie for him, and Harry chortled at the memory of him in his formal dark suit and black bowler; a fore-runner of Odd Job, perhaps, of James Bond fame.

Harry said that Lady Amory was very popular with the artisans, and she certainly had their interests at heart right to the end. She was concerned that the financial burden upon them should not be too great. The Tiverton club debated the possibility of a new clubhouse for some time before it eventually came to fruition. Lady Amory donated £25,000 towards it, and it should not be forgotten that this was long after her playing days had finished. Malcolm informed me that, in her will, she left the club a further £5,000.

When Sir John died, Lady Amory became president, and she not only attended the AGMs, in the early years, but presided over the meetings. Malcolm remembered a charming, modest, self-effacing lady.

Brother Roger and the Hon. Michael Scott were regular visitors to the club, and Harry recalled that her brother always insisted that Joyce played from the men's tees. I doubt whether she would have had it otherwise. Two other snippets of information from Harry: he recalls that Joyce advised against planting too many trees in case they obscured the views from the course. Now, that is interesting. From all that has been said about her tremendous powers of concentration, you would have been excused for thinking that she would not have noticed any views. I expect that was only on the more serious occasions. If you have ever wondered what happened to her hickory shafted clubs; I have three alternatives for you. One of the Knightshayes staff told me that clubs were given to a nephew, but Harry Britton told me that he won them! [I'm sure that is correct, and I haven't dreamt it]. Thirdly,

Sir John Palmer, a family friend of the Heathcoat-Amorys, informed me that Lady Amory's irons had been given to his son. So, there you have it. They were either divided up or there was more than one set.

The Heathcoat-Amorys continued to play golf for pleasure, and obviously to a high standard, because in 1948 they were the first man and wife couple in the final of the Worplesden Foursomes. Unfortunately, for once, Joyce failed to pull it off and they lost by five and four to Wanda Morgan and E.F. Storey, who apparently had his triumph muted by being 'hammered' on the Stock Exchange.

It was not very long after Sir John and Joyce were married that another love entered their lives. No, not a child, they were not to be blessed in that direction – gardening, and it was to become perhaps the greatest love of their lives. In 1937, there were thirteen gardeners employed at Knightshayes, mostly working in the old walled garden, which lies several hundred yards to the north of the house. This part of the estate has only recently been opened to National Trust visitors, having been restored so that they may experience it as in former times. It was the walled garden which was the original garden to the Victorians, and where they used to promenade before tea. It was divided into eight sections and had herbaceous borders, which provided cut flowers for the house, whilst the four acres of vegetables for the household were discreetely hidden away. There was a collection of greenhouses and hothouses, providing all manner of fruit and cover for tender plants and vegetables. The terraces to the front and east of the house were planted out with bedding plants and rose gardens.

Lady Amory remembered the day when Sir John saw the light – the light of gardening, that is. She likened it to St Paul's conversion on the road to Damascus. It must have been an occasion. Sir John used to go down into the field in front of the house and hit golf balls back towards the house. One day, as he returned towards the house through the roses, he was taken by their fragrance, found himself a pair of secateurs and set to dead-heading them. He religiously continued to carry out this task for the following two years, and then, at the outbreak of war, he said something to Joyce which would mean future delight for thousands of Knightshayes visitors… 'If we get through this war, let's make a garden together.'

They did get through the war. Sir John became Major Heathcoat-Amory of the Home Guard and spent time helping to train those who would form the second front. The Heathcoat factory converted to assist the war effort producing parachutes and other products with which to beat the Germans. Joyce became an inspector at the factory.

During the war, Knightshayes Court was used as a rest home for US airmen after a tour of duty. It was regularly 'buzzed' by their colleagues going or returning from a mission or on a training flight. One fateful day in June 1943, a pilot took on rather more than he could chew, and failed to rise above the firs at the end of the driveway. Deprived of his wings, he crashed into the hill across the valley. One eye-witness, who lived nearby, said that it was the last time that anyone flew over Knightshayes. The destruction on the ground of a number of trees was fortuitous only in that it prompted the Heathcoat-Amorys into having to restore the devastated area. It was their first move in remodelling and extending their garden.

After the war they started on their gardening with enthusiasm, though it has to be remembered that Sir John was still the chairman of a thriving company of some 2,000 employees, in addition to his numerous commitments with the town council and a myriad of other organisations, not least being chairman of the Tiverton bench.

Many years later, Nicholas de Rothschild of Exbury House in the New Forest, wrote and produced a video of the gardens at Knightshayes, entitled *A Vision of Paradise*, featuring Lady Amory recalling the making of the gardens. She remembered how enthralled she was as they started upon this exciting venture. Sir John was a great collector and once he got going on a project there was nobody keener, so plants arrived in profusion. Joyce, for her part, loved arranging them in the garden areas; not designing mind you, that smacks too much of formality.

Little by little, the garden was extended. Mistakes were made, and Joyce, with a twinge of remorse, remembered that at times they had to be ruthless, and take out plants which had been ill-conceived or wrongly positioned. In 1963 they were joined by a young man from Cornwall, Michael Hickson. He has been there ever since! When he arrived there were three gardeners, all engaged in the walled garden, mainly occupied with fruit and vegetables. Sir John's chauffeur used to mow the lawns around the house, whilst Sir John and Lady Amory worked on the twelve acres which comprised the rest of their garden at that time.

In the video, Lady Amory recalled the time that Michael arrived, only twenty-three, and yet obviously soon to become one of the family –

perhaps the son that she never had. Their relationship was informal, and, away from the ears of the other staff, he was able to refer to her by her Christian name. She said, 'He was fond of the family, and fitted in.' He remembered that it was quite daunting at his tender age to be in charge of three men much his senior in years. With obvious pride, he spoke to me of how Sir John, Lady Amory and he worked as a threesome. All of the major gardening decisions were made by the mutual consent of this triumvirate, and apparently, if there were a dissenting voice, the proposition would be dropped. Sir John rather thought, on occasion, that the other two would outmanoeuvre him. Sir John referred to Joyce as 'the head gardener', and presumably Michael was 'Michael'. Michael's main job in the early days was to make the walled garden self-financing, but this task became increasingly difficult as more and more inexpensive imported produce arrived in the country, and eventually, in the early 1970s, the area was put down to grass and in effect abandoned.

This, at least, had the effect of releasing Michael to concentrate more on the new initiatives. He recalled that they were both very kind to him, and that both were forward-looking, keen and unafraid to experiment, and that they wanted variety. Lady Amory was an avid reader of gardening books and articles, and not infrequently her ideas would be as a result. The Victorians liked their formal cloistered gardens. The Heathcoat-Amorys wanted almost the exact opposite; they wished to open up vistas and integrate their garden with the wider countryside. Sir John had a good memory, soon picked up plant names and quickly developed into a knowledgeable gardener. Joyce was something of a disciple of Dame Sylvia Crowe's ideas on landscaping, and particularly respected her pleadings for gardeners to harmonise and integrate their gardens into the countryside rather than create a vivid splash of colour which was little more than a blot on the wider landscape.

One of the first of several talented gardeners to extend their expertise towards them was Nellie Britton of Ottery St Mary, who specialised in rock plants and plants of the smaller variety. Lady Amory remembered the dear lady's concern when Sir John became interested in rhododendrons and azaleas, thinking that he was about to ditch the little plants which she had brought to their attention. Nothing was further from the truth. They simply liked variety, and that was how the garden developed, a drift of one type of plant here and just through the trees something entirely different. They desired no repetition.

They enjoyed the social side of gardening, such as the talking and sharing ideas with other enthusiasts, and of course they had a lovely large canvas to present for discussion which must have excited some of the more knowledgeable gardeners of the time. Hugh Roper was but one of those who spent weekends at Knightshayes, advising on proposals which were in the pipeline and no doubt throwing in a few ideas which weren't.

Eric Saville made their day when he requested that he be allowed some of their plants for his own gardens, and he soon became a good friend. They had their disappointments, of course, what gardener doesn't, but gradually, year by year, the 'garden in the wood' developed – no, wrong word – evolved, and what a garden it has become. Sir John used to say that 'gardening comprises eleven months hard work and one month of acute disappointment', something of an exaggeration methinks, when applied to Knightshayes. Without doubt, one of their wisest contributions to Knightshayes and gardening in general has been their realisation that a wooded garden needs open spaces, which not only opens up vistas otherwise hidden, but in turn varies the canopy above and the plants beneath.

They preferred the softer colours in their schemes, as opposed to someone like Eric Saville, who favoured bolder hues, but that didn't mean that a splash of colour in the right place couldn't be welcomed. On the video, Lady Amory revealed that green was one of her favourite colours in the garden and she marvelled at the wide range of different greens there are. She couldn't understand that many people could not accept that green foliage of a multitude of shades could give as much to a garden as the flowers themselves. Perhaps the most telling piece of the video as it relates to Lady Amory herself is in the response to a statement often made to her that she must have loved to sit in the garden and contemplate it all. 'I never did sit in the garden' was her reply; 'I was always looking or working. I liked particularly the clearing of a new area and digging it.' As if she had let the side down (i.e. the female of the species) she added shyly, 'Strange isn't it, my liking digging?'

There came a time after Sir John had died when the estate was handed over to the National Trust. Michael Hickson continued in his role of head gardener, the real head gardener, and Joyce was no longer allowed to do the planting. She had just entered her seventies by then, so could have been forgiven for expecting that someone else should shoulder the work, but that wasn't Lady Amory (or Joyce Wethered). She confided that although she was allowed to continue to do the ordering of the plants, she 'quietly' resented that she was not allowed to take part in the planting.

Sir John in 1967 and Lady Amory in 1982, in turn, were accorded the highest honour of the Royal Horticultural Society, the Victoria Medal of Honour. Twelve acres in 1963 had become fifty acres by the time Lady Amory could no longer take part, due to inner ear problems which resulted in dizzy spells, which she light-heartedly attributed to her height and the fact that the blood could not find its way to her most extreme parts. Michael Hickson put her gardening knowledge and abilities into perspective when he commented, 'How many people would dare to stand up before the members of the Royal Horticultural Society and lecture to them as she did.'

In 1983, a further acknowledgement of Lady Amory's achievements at Knightshayes was demonstrated by the invitation for her to contribute a chapter to a book edited by Alvide Lees-Milne and Rosemary Verey, entitled *The Englishwoman's Garden*, published by Chatto &Windus. It is a compilation of chapters contributed by thirty-six ladies around the country, who not only had gardens of note but were accepted to be knowledgeable in their own right. In her foreword to the book, Alvide Lees-Milne wrote:

> *One thing all of the contributors have in common is unerring taste. Each writer has revealed how her garden evolved, and how against mounting odds it is kept going. Anyone who owns anything over half an acre today is finding it increasingly difficult to maintain. All too often the owner is forced to reduce some part by putting it down to grass. Gradually, many lovely gardens are shrinking, and may well end up like the dodo.*

It is to Lady Amory's eternal credit and to the National Trust also that Knightshayes has continued to develop and, incredibly, becomes lovelier every year. Lady Amory's contribution to *The Englishwoman's Garden* has been included as an appendix to this book.

In her later years, the two greatest interests of her life touched upon each other by virtue of the fact that she toured her gardens seated in a golf buggy. Michael Hickson would often accompany her, and she would listen to his plans and respond with her ideas. I would be very surprised if he didn't take heed of them. In response to the question of what excited her, Michael responded, 'an interesting plant or a good golf shot'.

Long after Jack (Sir John) had died, it was suggested by the National Trust that a room at Knightshayes should be devoted to Joyce's golfing days. Whether this was done as a marketing ploy, I know not. I do know that it was an excellent idea to display for the visitors a little of the story of the greatest British lady golfer of the twentieth century. The room devoted to the display is modest in the extreme, measuring only some fifteen feet square. Apparently we have Joyce to 'thank' for this. She considered Knightshayes as the home of the Heathcoat-Amorys, and did not like to impose her life, particularly before she married, into the house except in a most modest manner.

A description of the contents of the room is warranted. Joyce consulted a good friend, Sir John Palmer, on how the display should be arranged, and he in turn solicited the assistance of F.R. Furber, who was pleased to be of assistance, and who directed proceedings. The exhibition was opened by Lady Amory and Peter Alliss. When Peter was mentioned as a possible celebrity, there was some concern as to whether his fee would be prohibitive. What most people had forgotten was that Joyce was of the same period as Peter's father, Percy Alliss. Peter was only too delighted and honoured to be invited, and recalled at the opening ceremony that his father had told him when he was a young boy that if he could ever swing a club like Joyce Wethered, he would never go far wrong. I am told that Peter attended the occasion without payment of a fee, and that he had to rush back to England from the US Masters, but he said that he wouldn't have missed the occasion for the world. You see, even heroes have heroes (or heroines).

The exhibition is arranged around the walls of the room, with a glass wooden-framed display cabinet on a table in the centre. The central display cabinet houses four scrapbooks, of the kind which could be purchased at any booksellers or store in the 1930s. These scrapbooks are filled with newspaper cuttings, depicting Joyce's achievements over the years from 1923 to 1935, the halcyon years. Unfortunately, her 1920-1922 exploits are not recorded. A small red scrapbook deals mainly with 1923 and 1924. A green scrapbook records events from 1925 through to the 1930s, including details of the first Curtis Cup match and loose press cuttings relating to the Worplesden Foursomes. A thin black book deals with 1935 and has cuttings of the American tour of that year, but is largely superseded by a large red scrapbook, bulging with cuttings of the American tour. The scrapbooks are opened in the display cabinet at appropriate pages, usually with illustrations. There are many newspaper photographs in all of the scrapbooks. Also in the display cabinet are books, including *Golf from Two Sides*, written by Joyce and brother Roger in 1923, but not including her book, *Golfing Memories and Methods*, first published in 1934. Again, the books are opened at pages of illustrations. The frontispiece of the Wethered book is a delightful study of brother and sister setting forth on a round of golf. It is also interesting in that it illustrates the golfing dress of the early 1920s.

One wall of the room is dominated by a watercolour of Joyce standing with her open golf brolly. It was painted by her father, and bears testament to his skills as an artist.

A framed citation confirms Joyce's hallowed position in world golf. The citation is worded as follows:

In recognition of her contributions to the game, Joyce Heathcoat-Amory has been selected as one of the 100 Heroes of the First Century of Golf in America. This honour was presented on 20 June 1988 as part of Golf *magazine's celebration of the Centennial of Golf in America. 1888-1988.*

Below the citation is the following description:

Joyce Wethered could be viewed as the female counterpart of Bobby Jones in that just as Jones dominated American golf in the 1920s then retired, Wethered did likewise in Britain. The one difference was that Wethered came out of retirement to win again. Also like Jones, Wethered possessed a classic swing; in fact Jones once said Wethered was the best golfer – male or female – he had ever seen.

Wethered learned the game at seventeen from her brother Roger, a leading British amateur. Entering the 1920 Women's English Championship 'only for fun', she defeated Cecil Leitch, Britain's leading female golfer, in the final. Then, starting in 1920, Wethered won thirty-three straight matches in the championship, taking the title every year from 1920-1924.

In Britain's other important women's event, the British Ladies' Championship, Wethered won three times (beating Leitch in the finals in 1922 and 1925 and losing to her in 1921). Wethered retired in 1925 but returned in 1929, when the championship was played at St Andrews.

Playing before a huge crowd in the final, Wethered faced America's top woman, Glenna Collett-Vare. After a riveting see-saw battle, Wethered won three and one.

Wethered's swing "was the most lovely and correct golf has ever known", wrote the highly respected Herbert Warren Wind. Her tempo was near perfect and her accuracy was often compared to that of Harry Vardon. Long off the tee, Wethered also had a deadly touch on and around the greens.

In 1935, Wethered turned professional for an exhibition series in America, usually playing with Babe Zaharias, Gene Sarazen and Horton Smith. In the much-touted contest of the ladies, Wethered regularly topped Zaharias (who had yet to turn into an all-round player), and set a large number of course records. Wethered, now Lady Heathcoat-Amory, was inducted into the World Golf Hall of Fame in 1975.

For the record, it is incorrect that Joyce played Babe Zaharias a number of times on her American tour; she played her only twice, winning on both occasions. The lady she did play against several times was her old friend and foe, Glenna Collett-Vare. Glenna never did beat Joyce in a head-to-head, her only compensation being that she did win on one occasion in a four-ball match. Also incorrect is the statement that Joyce won the British Ladies' Championship on three occassions – it should say four.

It is interesting that among the 100 so-called heroes, there are just sixteen women. In 1999, the Associated Press of America assembled a panel of six experts to vote on the top ten female golfers of the century. The scoring was such that the first placement per expert received ten votes, the second nine votes, etc. The winner was the great American golfer of the 1960s, Mickey Wright, who had four first placements and a total of fifty-eight votes. Joyce Wethered came fourth with one first placement and thirty-three votes. There are several points here which demonstrate Joyce's high standing in the history of golf. Firstly, this was an American compilation and there would therefore be some likelihood of a leaning towards Americans. This was borne out by the fact that with the exception of Joyce, all of the top ten were Americans. Laura Davies received only two votes, well outside the top ten. Secondly, Joyce was by far the earliest player of the century to gain entrance to the top ten, having played her golf mainly in the 1920s and 1930s. The fact that experts, who can hardly have seen her play, voted for her in 1999 must have been based upon her record and the writings and comments of their predecessors. She had impressed a lot of people and her memory lingered on when most had been forgotten.

When one enters the Knightshayes golf room, there is surprise that it does not contain more silverware. If Joyce was so prolific a winner, where are all of the cups and trophies? There is a glass trophy cabinet, and in it stands one large, impressive silver cup and a number of winner's medals. The medals were awarded when Joyce won her British Opens and Worplesden Foursomes. The latter, I imagine, were retained because they were reminders of the house parties and social activities which went with the Worplesden event as much as the winning of the golf. It is the large silver cup which reveals the reason that there are not more trophies on display.

The truth of the matter is that Joyce had most of her silverware melted down and incorporated into the one large cup. Some people have regarded this as sacrilege, but the large base to the cup lists all of the major events which Joyce won and therefore, although the trophies individually are lost to posterity, there is a record of their achievement. I have been told that Joyce in later life did not want all of these trophies cluttering up the house and therefore devised the simple solution of having them rendered into one trophy. The cup was commissioned by Lady Amory from the silversmith Omar Ramsden to commemorate her many golfing triumphs. The inscriptions around the circumference of the base are as follows:

Ladies' Open Championship: Prince's Sandwich 1922, Portrush 1924, Troon 1925, St Andrews 1929.
English Close Championship: Sheringham 1920, Royal Lytham and St Annes, 1921, Hunstanton 1922, Ganton 1923, Cooden Beach 1924.
Golf Illustrated Golf Vase: 1925
London Foursomes: 1923, 1925, 1927
Worplesden Foursomes: 1922, 1923, 1927, 1928, 1931, 1932, 1933, 1936
Surrey Championships: 1921, 1922, 1924, 1929

There were many other annual events which Joyce won, but, presumably, she regarded those above as the cream of her achievements.

Her good friend Sir John Palmer was anxious to point out to me that the Ramsden Cup was commissioned precisely because Joyce was a modest person and considered that one trophy was sufficient. It was not produced to glorify her achievements.

Another exhibit with which Joyce was extremely proud to be associated is the 'Joyce Wethered Trophy', a bronze sculpture by Anne Richardson, about twelve to eighteen inches high, depicting a golfer of the 1920s, Joyce's heyday. It is the original of trophies awarded annually, and sponsored by the *Daily Telegraph*, to the outstanding female golfer of the year under the age of twenty-five. It is a delightful statuette sponsored in an endeavour to make some small contribution towards encouraging young golfers in their early years. It was inaugurated in 1994, and Lewine Mair, the *Telegraph* correspondent, went to Knightshayes to show the trophy to Lady Amory. At the age of ninety-three, she found her exasperated that she could no longer get out into her beloved garden in the early morning, due to the inner ear problem which rendered her dizzy and unbalanced. It seemed quite unjust that someone who had been celebrated for her wonderful balance in her golfing years should be so afflicted.

On the walls of the golf room are a number of photographs, citations and other memorabilia. One wall has a number of photographs of her brother Roger, recalling his days as captain of the R&A. It will be remembered that he was chosen for this august office before the commencement of the Second World War and had to wait for seven years until that conflict had been resolved before he took up office. One photograph shows Roger with General Eisenhower, the United States Supreme Commander, who was an enthusiastic golfer and appears to have found time for the odd game or two. A framed citation with photographs recalls Joyce's famous 1929 British Open victory over Glenna Collett at St Andrews.

In one corner of the room stands an old golf bag containing hickory shafted irons. They are not labelled and I failed to inspect them to see whether they were the type marketed by Joyce and bearing her name. If my memory does not fail me, they were marked as 'mashie', 'niblick' etc., giving cognisance of a bygone age.

In one of the scrapbooks, I was delighted to discover a copy of a Tiverton Borough Council Sewerage Committee paper. Presumably, Sir John was a member of the committee. On the back of two pages, in his handwriting, he had composed a small piece for an article in which he briefly recounted his wife's career. Towards the end, he wrote that she played little now, preferring gardening, but did play on their Scottish holidays, when she would often score in the mid-seventies. The date of the Committee paper was September 1959! I like to imagine Sir John at the committee meeting, surreptitiously scribbling his notes, whilst the business of the day proceeded. Perhaps it is an illustration of how he was able to cope with his large range of commitments!

Writing of Scotland has reminded me that when Gene Sarazen came over to Scotland for one of the British Opens, he invited Joyce and Jack to join him for nine holes of golf and a chinwag. I won't mention the club involved, but Joyce knew that they were still a bit stuffy at Blairgowrie about the privileges accorded to professionals, and therefore she decided it best not to seek permission to play in advance, but simply to turn up, which is what they did, without mishap. Sarazen was one of her old golfing friends, with whom Joyce exchanged Christmas cards to the end. When they met in Scotland, he advised her to keep supple by swinging two clubs of a morning. Although she played little golf by then, she obviously took note of the tip because she said that she found it good advice. Sarazen was the one on her American tour who introduced Joyce to the sand-wedge, which she found indispensable, having previously played her bunker shots with a niblick, so he was helpful to her on more than one occasion.

Returning to the Golf Room at Knightshayes, I have to say that it is modest in the extreme. This was Joyce's choice; she would have it no other way. It was secondary to the house. Now that she is no longer with us, perhaps the National Trust will consider something slightly grander. After all, they are lucky enough to house the memorabilia of our greatest lady golfer ever! Perhaps one end of the wonderful large billiards room? No, perhaps not.

Sir John Palmer and Lady Palmer were good friends of Joyce and live not far from Knightshayes. They recounted some of their memories: an old builder, for example, who said, very genuinely, that it gave great pleasure to the people of Tiverton to see Sir John drive by in his best Bentley. A very real indication of the respect which the Heathcoat-Amory's enjoyed in the town!

Apparently, in the Worplesden Foursomes one year, Joyce put her partner Cyril Tolley into a bunker, and then started to tell him how to play out. Cyril told her to shut up! Joyce said that it was the only time that she had been spoken to like that.

One year, Sir John Palmer had taken Joyce to St Mellion to watch the Dunlop Masters. She had been introduced to Jack Nicklaus, who had been quite charming towards her. Most Americans knew of her achievements, and at Knightshayes many American visitors to the house knew more of her golfing prowess than the British visitors.

Sir John Palmer was a modest golfer and laid out five holes in his garden. Joyce bade him change them around as they were too easy, and he found to his chagrin that one hole came perilously close to the drawing-room window. It concentrated the mind rather more than he wanted. When Joyce was eighty-five, she walked round his course with him one day, and, at the last hole, she wondered if she could still hit the ball. She borrowed a club and hit a perfect shot. To satisfy herself, she hit a second, also perfect. Those were probably the last two golf shots she played. 'No practise swings', recalled Sir John, in admiration. When asked which he regarded as Joyce's main attributes, Sir John thought carefully and started with 'powers of concentration', applied to whatever she was doing. That didn't come as a surprise after reading of the way she could go round a golf course in a cocoon of concentration. Modesty was the next virtue mentioned. He recalled that, although she was somewhat retiring, this was not due to shyness, and she could be quite outspoken, not in an aggressive manner, but in a matter-of-fact sort of way.

The Palmer's house is adorned with several examples of Joyce's skill as a needlewoman, a skill inherited from her father. She enjoyed poetry and wrote down in a small book any sayings which appealed to her. *Renouncement,* by Michael Albery, was one of her favourite poems. She was interested in politics, leaning towards conservatism, and I was quite surprised to hear that she had a wide knowledge of the world. Perhaps I thought that she so concentrated on golf, or gardening, or whatever might be the immediate matter of concern in her life, that she would not have had time to appreciate the wider world.

Other friends remembered that Joyce had known Virginia Woolf and many others of the 'Bloomsbury' set of artists and writers and intellectuals, who inhabited that particular area of London between the wars. A special friend from that group was Dame Ethel Smyth, who was an outstanding composer, fêted for her operatic works on the continent, but continuously unable to break into the male preserve of serious music composing in this country. Virginia Woolf records in her diary making a visit to Dame Ethel's home and finding there Joyce Wethered and the

Duchess of Sermoneta, wife of the fifteenth Duke, who was a lady-in-waiting to the Queen of Italy, together with Lady Balfour and Dame Edith Lyttleton, widow of the Rt Hon. Alfred Lyttleton.

Dame Ethel was quite a character, who took two years off from her composing to play a leading part in the suffragette movement, and actually composed their marching song, whilst 'banged up' (a phrase she would have liked), in gaol for two years. Ethel's father was a general and she moved in high circles. Her intimate friends included Lady Ponsonby, who was Queen Victoria's right-hand lady, and Mrs Benson, the Bishop of Lambeth's wife. She was that rare 'animal', a lover of both music and sport. She was much older than Joyce Wethered, and had discovered golf in the 1890s, a pastime which she found preferable to hunting, in which she had engaged until that time. In her seventies and still playing golf, when Joyce was still in her early thirties, she was a dedicated friend and admirer of JW's skills. Her diary makes reference to Joyce's birthday and occasions when she was invited to dinner. Indeed, on one such occasion, she recalled Joyce telling of a renowned lady who had been jilted in favour of a shop girl, and sought her revenge by going around shops being beastly to the assistants and making them cry. She had also said that the girls at Fortnum & Mason were poorly paid, but that there were seldom any vacancies as they were always anxious to get a job.

Another of Dame Ethel's accomplishments was writing, and, encouraged by Virginia Woolf, she produced several autobiographical books. In 1933, on the occasion of her seventy-fifth birthday, she was at last accorded the musical acknowledgement which had for so long been denied her, when a festival of her music, including her first and last major operatic works, *The Mass* and *The Prison*, was presented at the Albert Hall with Sir Thomas Beecham, the conductor, and a full turnout of royalty, including the Queen, in attendance.

A short extract from Dame Ethel's book is reproduced as it lists the people in attendance at her festival party, which gives us information concerning possible friends and acquaintants of JW.

After the concert came the improvised 'Mad Tea Party' at an adjacent Lyons, where the guests paid for their own tea and buns, and whence one patroness of music, finding herself for the first time in her life in such a low place, fled a prima vista – in other words did a bunk. O what fun it was, though we of the family, Nina, Nelly, Bob and I, were thinking of three sisters who during their lifetime had faithfully followed my musical fortunes year after year, and of whom two, Alice and Mary, had died only a few months ago. And I am certain that many besides us were thinking of Mary, who had always undertaken my post-concert entertaining, and done it so splendidly. Of course, if she had been alive, Lyons would never have taken place, but it made us laugh to think how she would have loathed it and its suggestion of a new harum-scarum school feast at which the unfortunate children pay for their own victuals. That wonderful collection of friends new and old – Joyce Wethered, Laura Lovat, Thomas Beecham, Hugh Allen, Violet Gordon Woodhouse, Virginia Woolf, Duncan Grant, Vanessa Bell, Maud Warrender, Diana Cooper, Vera Brittain, Winifred Holtby, Ethel Steel of the Royal School, Bath – greatest of headmistresses (seated on an umbrella stand full of umbrellas) and many who are less well known but equally cherished by me – all these might doubtless have been got together elsewhere, but at the price of foregoing a memory the comic value of which Time will, I fancy, be powerless to efface.

Sir John Palmer remembered that JW was extremely kind and generous with the provision of plants if a friend was setting up a garden. She enjoyed walking, before her ailment overtook her, and adored retriever dogs, usually owning one. She was somewhat awkward with children, particularly small children, with whom she found it difficult to communicate.

Her helpers, they wouldn't be servants to Joyce, remembered a gracious tolerant lady, who was always grateful for what was done for her. She never partook of alcohol and had not throughout her life, but she was not a fussy eater and would eat practically anything set before her. She was very fair to the staff and often quite serious, but she could drop down the fences as when she helped a young waitress who became interested in golf. Her housekeeper of eleven years recalled a perfectionist at whatever she pursued. 'Strong-willed', was an adjective which frequently arose. She may have been pleasant and modest and retiring, but the lady was certainly no pushover; there was steel and determination in the makeup.

Other staff remembered:

A proper lady, who knew her own mind. Definite, polite, but in control. Slightly reserved and unassuming, and well liked by all. Genteel and discreet in letting you know when it was time to go. Always interested in what was happening in the gardens, and in the numbers of visitors.

After Sir John died, his younger brother Derek, who became Chancellor of the Exchequer, and was a bachelor, would escort her to functions and parties.

Sir Ian Amory, son of one of Sir John's younger brothers, William, and nephew and next of kin of Joyce, gave permission for me to have access to the golfing memorabilia at Knightshayes. He explained that the Heathcoat-Amory's decided in the late 1960s that they could not privately finance the expansion of the John Heathcoat & Co. textiles business, which was necessary to keep it modern and competitive. They looked for a buyer who would look after the employees properly and in 1969 it was sold to Coats Patons, later to come under the Viyella brand name. In 1984, there was a buyout by the management who were locals, and the business is still going strong. Sir John would have been very pleased, as I am sure was Lady Amory.

Sir John died in 1972, and was survived by Joyce for more than twenty-five years. Her main interest in those years was gardening and Knightshayes Court garden in particular, and she continued to derive tremendous fulfilment from seeing it develop. She was still very interested in golf but for many years had to rely upon television for her watching. She thrilled to see the great players of the modern age and to follow the way in which the game changed. She didn't applaud all of the changes. Slow play was not to her liking. When she watched championship rounds taking five hours, she recalled how Roger had been in trouble with the authorities for taking three! Her eyes grew large when she was told that there had been occasions when the players had been asked to slow down a little to suit a television schedule!

It was strange when one considered her own demeanour when playing, that she seemed to have a liking for the more extroverted of golfers. She liked to watch Nick Faldo, but thought that his continual tinkering with the mechanics of his swing had divested it of some of its beauty. Laura Davies she thought was a tremendous character, and Seve Ballesteros was a favourite for his exciting play. She also had a soft spot for Nick Price, however, and Lewine Mair was sure that was because he was always such a chivalrous and charming competitor, and reminded Joyce of days gone by when the playing meant more than the winning to many of the players.

Joyce was surprised how the players in modern golf use the rules to their advantage and stretch them at times as far as they can. She said that they hardly ever received a free drop in her day, whereas now it happened all the time. She suspected that some of the more famous ones might not return if they did not get their way. I think she said it with her tongue in her cheek. Having watched Seve in the flesh demanding a drop in an antagonistic manner from an official, when he knows full well that he is only trying it on, I can appreciate her bewilderment.

When the National Trust took over the running of Knightshayes, Joyce moved into quarters in one of the wings. She had in her drawing room only a painting of St Andrews and a train puffing by the seventeenth fairway to reveal to guests any indication of her golfing days of yesteryear. Many of her trophies had been given away.

Her other great interest at this time was her religion. She had been a Christian Scientist for many years, though nobody seemed to know how she first came to the faith, and other members of the family were not of like mind. She enjoyed talking about spiritual matters, and would on occasion write to those nearest and dearest to her commenting upon her faith, but she never became over-zealous in trying to convert others. She was a regular reader of the Bible, and as she was a Christian Scientist, presumably their second bible, 'Science and Health'.

Christian Science teaches that there is no such thing as illness; it is a mental delusion. The way to cure it is to help the afflicted person to understand that he is not really sick, but that his pain is imaginary and his imagined disease the result of a false belief. Consequently, Christian scientists do not take drugs or refer to a doctor, they overcome their malady by prayer, and are assisted in this by 'practitioners', who are members of the faith who have received instruction and devote their time to the practice of healing methods.

The members meet for services, which vary significantly from Church of England and other denominations, and Lady Amory used to be a regular attendee at Exeter. Indeed, she was a 'First Reader' at the services, demonstrating that she was by no means a lukewarm member of the faith. Blundell's School is a boys' boarding school in Tiverton, and she would collect several of the boys on Sundays, whose families were Christian Scientists, and convey them in her Jaguar to Exeter to their Sunday school. She and Sir John, who was not a member of the church, were very generous in their financial support of the faith in Exeter. On occasion, when Lady Amory had 'some sickness', she would take residence at a Christian Science nursing home. She received great comfort from her faith.

On 18 November 1997, Lady Amory died peacefully at home at Knightshayes. It was the day after her ninety-sixth birthday. There was a private funeral service, and the following month a memorial service took place at St Peter's church, Tiverton, on 12 December. It was attended by friends and family, representatives of organisations with which she had been associated and golfing representatives from far and wide.

Something tells me, if you were able to ask Lady Amory whether golf or gardening was the love of her life, it would be a very close-run thing, but it would be gardening which would get up by a short head in a photograph finish. The following are two quotes from her contribution to *An Englishwoman's Garden*:

There are gardeners who like to work on the ground with their hands and this was our way.

Gardening has been full of excitement for me. Although the joy and adventures I shared in laying out a garden can never fade, I know at heart I am a plantswoman, and in company with all those who are devoted to horticulture. Knightshayes has been for me a constant source of delight.

Golf gave Joyce an overwhelming interest and, I think, *raison d'etre*, in the earlier half of her life, and she remained tremendously interested when she could no longer actively take part. It also caused her some anxiety and distress. She did not appreciate being a celebrity; she enjoyed a more tranquil lifestyle, and though she appeared calm and imperturbable to the onlooker, she suffered internally as many others do in the stressful moments of high competition.

A less active role has always suited me perfectly. I can enter into the emotions of the game and enjoy them just as I like without having to preserve a state of elaborate calmness as a player over incidents which are in reality causing me acute excitement and probably no little apprehension and alarm.

Gardening provided equal pleasures without the accompanying worries.

Joyce Wethered was one of the greatest golfers, man or woman, of all time, because she made herself understand the game technically, had the ability to put that knowledge into practice and had the strength to conquer and subdue any doubts from within. Sometimes she suffered greatly, but her secret was to control such emotions until after the work was done and the championship won.

Jack White, an Open Champion himself, said, 'The four greatest golfers of my era were Vardon, Wethered, Jones and Duncan – in that order.'

Bobby Jones famously said, 'I have never played with any golfer, man or woman, amateur or professional, who made me feel so utterly outclassed.'

Walter Hagen said, 'She had grace, timing and touch.'

Glenna Collett said, 'She is as near perfection as I ever dreamed of being when I sat in a deep-seated rocker on the front porch in the cool summer evening years ago and dreamed my best dreams.'

Lady Amory, in her later years when she was unable to get to sleep, used to dream of the days when she was Joyce Wethered. She used to retrace her steps around her beloved St Andrews and was annoyed at times when she reached the middle of the course and could not remember which hole came next. 'After all, I should have remembered, shouldn't I!'

APPENDICES

APPENDIX 1

JOYCE WETHERED'S ANCESTORS

A great deal of research into the Cossham history has been carried out by Susan Dean, whose grandmother was a Cossham, and the close association of the Wethereds to Handel Cossham gives us an insight into their lives. The wills of the eighteenth-century Cosshams make for fascinating reading and indicate the comparative poverty of all but the gentry in those times. Charles Cossham, who appears to have been a carpenter and perhaps a builder, died in 1721. His eldest son Joseph received one shilling (he had obviously blotted his copy-book at some time previously). Daughter Ann received the best feather bed and bedstead. Son Charles received all his father's wearing apparel, both linen and woollen, and all his working tools. Special provision was made for George, the baby of the family. He was to be apprenticed to a convenient trade and when his time was finished, given five pounds.

One of the elder Charles' sons, Matthew, had predeceased him, but it is interesting to note that Matthew made his brother Joseph, (he who received one shilling) a trustee of the will, so the two brothers were not at war. It is comforting to know that Joseph was not a complete outcast to the family. Matthew's will makes provision for repayment of a debt of £5 to his sister Sarah. He left his brewing furnace and 'potts' to his son, another Matthew, and his best bed and bedstead to daughter Mary, and his second best to daughter Olive. What intrigues me is, where did the widows of these men sleep from then on?

Handel Cossham's father, Jesse, was a carpenter and builder and his mother ran a grocery business. They were a very industrious family, and they were also staunch Liberals and devout religious non-conformists. Handel, who was born in 1824 at Thornbury, was in the same mould and when only sixteen he was a Sunday school teacher at the Congregational chapel. He took to serious studying of science and geology, and in 1845 he obtained a job as a clerk at Yate collieries. It was at this time that he first became acquainted with the Wethered family.

William Wethered of Pigeon House Farm, Little Marlow, was apparently a farmer, but he and his sons had an interest in the Yate collieries; indeed, they were part owners. The Wethereds soon appreciated Handel Cossham's geological skills and business senses, and a strong friendship developed. This, of course, promoted Handel's position in the company, and the bond was further strengthened when Handel married Elizabeth Wethered, the youngest of the Wethered daughters, in 1848, by special licence at the parish church in Little Marlow. Handel was described on the marriage certificate as being a coal merchant; the title meant rather more than retailing coal, as it does today. His father Jesse was described as a builder.

Susan Dean informs me that Little Marlow church contains several gravestones to the Wethered family, but states that she has not been able to prove any connection with the famous brewing family from nearby Marlow.

Handel and Elizabeth Cossham set up home in Wickwar, north of Bristol, and the closeness of the Cossham/Wethered alliance is demonstrated by the fact that at the time of the 1851 census, Elizabeth's brother Edwin and his wife were at the same address. A little further down Wickwar High Street, in lodgings, lived Henry Wethered, now twenty-five years of age and also described as a coal merchant. Henry was to father the man who would, in turn, father Roger and Joyce Wethered.

The marriage of Handel and Elizabeth was the catalyst for business partnerships between Handel and the Wethered brothers. Firstly, they were part owners of Yate collieries; then the firm of Wethered, Keeling and Cossham came into being, described as 'sole agents for the Farnley Iron Co. Ltd for the sale of their vitrified stoneware, sanitary tubes, chimney pots and terracotta ornaments' from their premises in Nelson Street, Bristol. In 1852, a new company was launched, Wethered, Cossham & Wethered, proprietors of Shortwood and Pucklechurch collieries, with a coal distribution centre at the

Midland Railway's yard in Midland Road, Bristol, and with offices in Baldwin Street, which were previously the offices of the Bristol Coal Mining Co.

The partners prospered quickly, and, in the early 1850s, a major development took place at Parkfield Colliery, which was connected underground to Brandy Bottom Pit, leased from Lord Radnor, and which helped enormously to ventilate and drain the larger colliery. Both pits had sidings adjoining the Birmingham to Bristol line of the Midland Railway with a direct route through to their coal yards in Bristol.

In 1855, Handel's skills and knowledge were recognised when he was made a Fellow of the Geological Society.

Business interests continued to expand with the acquisition of Shackleford, Ford & Co., which built railway wagons. A new company called the Cheltenham and Swansea Railway Waggonworks Co. was formed in 1867. There were suggestions that Handel and the Wethereds had undervalued Shacklefords, allowing them to buy out the company cheaply. They were certainly astute business men, but Handel, as chairman of the new company, was angered by this accusation printed in the *Bristol Times and Mirror* newspaper, and brought an ill-conceived libel action against the paper, which lost him a lot of money.

Speedwell and Deep Pit Collieries were undergoing work to make them the most modern and productive in the country. Then, in 1867, came the formation of yet another company, the Kingswood Coal and Iron Company.

The shafts at Parkfield Colliery were 280 yards deep and the coal was in four seams each between two and three feet in depth. The colliery continued in production until 1936, when East Bristol Collieries Ltd closed it as being uneconomic.

The Kingswood Collieries were up to 400 yards deep and the bulk of the production came from a seam called the Great Vein. The coal was in demand as household coal and was also used in locomotives.

In 1879, the firm was turned into a limited company, and the Wethereds, who were bought out, benefited greatly. The pits continued through their prime years in the 1880s, and then production started to fall. Handel Cossham died in 1890 and the collieries went to new owners. The Kingswood collieries also survived until 1936, by which time the labour force had dropped to 310 men. In 1889, Kingswood and Parkfield collieries had raised 210,000 tons of coal.

APPENDIX 2

MAIN GOLFING ACHIEVEMENTS

Joyce Wethered's principal golfing triumphs included:

British Ladies' Open Champion: Prince's, Sandwich 1922
                                  Portrush 1924
                                  Troon 1925
                                  St Andrews 1929

English Ladies' Closed Champion: Sheringham 1920
                                  Royal Lytham and St Annes 1921
                                  Hunstanton 1922
                                  Ganton 1923
                                  Cooden Beach 1924

London Foursomes Winner: 1923, 1925, 1927

Worplesden Foursomes Winner: 1922, 1923, 1927, 1928, 1931, 1932, 1933, 1936

Golf Illustrated Gold Vase Winner: 1925

Surrey Ladies' Champion: 1921, 1922, 1924, 1929

Appendix 3

Top Ten Female Golfers of the Twentieth Century

In 1999, The Associated Press of America drew up a list of the top ten female golfers of the century, as voted by a six-member panel of experts. Each expert placed their top ten choices in order of merit, giving ten points to the top selection, nine to the second, etc. through to one point for the tenth-place vote.

The results are in the following table. Several facts are noteworthy. Nine of the selections are American, the one exception being Joyce Wethered, who gained thirty-three points. (It was an American selection panel.)

Secondly, Laura Davies, the outstanding British competitor of the late twentieth century, did not make the top ten, and received only two points in comparison to Joyce Wethered's thirty-three points.

Without exception, all of those in the top ten played more recently than Joyce Wethered, and are likely to have benefited from more recent exposure to those doing the judging.

Rank	Golfer	1st	Points
1	Mickey Wright	4	58
2	Babe Zaharias	1	45
3	Kathy Whitworth	0	39
4	Joyce Wethered	1	33
5	Glenna Collett-Vare	0	30
6	Nancy Lopez	0	29
7	Louise Suggs	0	26
8	Patty Berg	0	22
9	JoAnne Carner	0	20
10	Betsy Rawls	0	17

APPENDIX 4

THE FIRST CURTIS CUP
21 MAY 1932

Harriet and Margaret Curtis were notable American golfers, who had dreamed of a regular challenge match between American and British ladies for many years before it finally came to pass. The big day finally dawned on 21 May 1932, and Joyce Wethered was asked to captain the Britain and Ireland team. The result was the same as it has so often been since – a win for America. In the morning Foursomes, the Americans wiped the board, even Joyce and her partner Wanda Morgan being on the losing side. In the afternoon singles, in the number one match, Joyce was once again facing her old adversary, Glenna Collett-Vare. Joyce convincingly won by six and four. (Glenna never did beat her in a championship singles).

The match result was: USA 5.5, Great Britain and Ireland 3.5

INTERNATIONAL MATCH RESULTS

WENTWORTH, MAY 21st, 1932

⚜

GREAT BRITAIN	UNITED STATES
Captain : MISS JOYCE WETHERED.	*Captain :* MISS MARION HOLLINS.

FOURSOMES

	Score			Score
Miss JOYCE WETHERED - - ⎫ Miss WANDA MORGAN - - ⎭	0	*v.*	Mrs. EDWIN H. VARE, Jnr. ⎫ (1 up) Mrs. O. S. HILL - - - ⎭	1
Miss ENID WILSON - - - ⎫ Mrs. J. B. WATSON - - - ⎭	0	*v.*	Miss VIRGINIA VAN WIE ⎫ (2 and 1) Miss HELEN HICKS - - ⎭	1
Miss MOLLY GOURLAY - - ⎫ Miss DORIS PARK - - - ⎭	0	*v.*	Miss MAUREEN ORCUTT ⎫ (1 up) Mrs. LOUIS D. CHENEY ⎭	1
	0			**3**

SINGLES

	Score			Score
Miss JOYCE WETHERED (6 and 4)	1	*v.*	Mrs. EDWIN H. VARE, Jnr. - -	0
Miss ENID WILSON (2 and 1) -	1	*v.*	Miss HELEN HICKS - - -	0
Miss WANDA MORGAN - - -	0	*v.*	Miss VIRGINIA VAN WIE (2 and 1)	1
Miss DIANA FISHWICK (4 and 3) -	1	*v.*	Miss MAUREEN ORCUTT - -	0
Miss MOLLY GOURLAY - - -	½	*v.*	Mrs. O. S. HILL - - - -	½
Miss ELSIE CORLETT - -	0	*v.*	Mrs. LOUIS D. CHENEY (4 and 3) -	1
	3½			**2½**

TOTAL :

United States - 5½

Great Britain - 3½

Supplement to

" FAIRWAY & HAZARD,"

The Golfer's Journal.

Appendix 5

The American Tour

Arguably the two best-known golfers in America, Bobby Jones and Gene Sarazen, were selected to play with Joyce Wethered and Glenna Collett-Vare in the first match at the Women's National Course at Sea Cliff, Long Island, a foursome guaranteed to attract massive media and public interest. However, Jones suffered a bout of appendicitis just before the match could take place and was advised to withdraw from the tournament and to rest for a few days. He was replaced by Johnny Dawson of Chicago, known as the 'businessman amateur', who partnered Joyce Wethered. Men and ladies played from the same tees, as they would do throughout the tour, and all played off scratch. The match was halved, the individual scores being Sarazen seventy-two, Dawson seventy-five, Wethered seventy-eight, and Collett-Vare seventy-five with one hole missing, which she did not complete.

Her second match at Winged Foot Golf Club, Mamaroneck, New York, set Joyce and Glenna against Sarazen and Sweetser. The two ladies received six shots each but all played off the men's tees. The men won by two and one with Sarazen playing to the par of seventy-two. Glenna had an eighty-two and Joyce an eighty-three. Joyce struggled on the unfamiliar greens again, and much of the audience likely felt a little let down, being perhaps more interested in a good score than in appreciating the syle of her swing. Still, there was a large audience, of more than 2,000, and most of the proceeds of the game went to local hospitals, so the game should be construed a success.

Joyce acquired at about this time a sand-iron from Sarazen, and she found the heavier implement a great help and chose it increasingly, particularly for playing short fairway pitches to the flag.

Joyce won her next match, at Ridgewood, New Jersey, where she partnered the South African, Sid Brews. They won, but it was Brews who was the star of this battle. Joyce's eighty-two was one more than her opponent, Maureen Orcutt.

Joyce returned her highest score on the tour at Winchester, Mass., ine difficult conditions on a rain-soddened course. She and Bill Blaney, the state champion, won by seven and six. The scores were, respectively: Wethered eighty-five, Blaney seventy-four, and opponents Francis Ouimet and Jean Bauer had eighty and ninety-one. After the match Joyce received a gold medal bearing the club's coat of arms.

The schedule of Joyce's tour was intense, leaving her little time to rest or to practise and with the added difficulty of playing on unfamiliar and challenging greens. She rallied magnificently, however, as her victory at Worcester proved, in which match she beat Jesse Guildford and Jean Bauer by five and four, with Benny Ayres as her partner. After a slow start, she put together a splendid round to achieve a score of seventy-six, the best score of the match.

The next phase of the tour took them south, to Philadelphia and the Merion golf club. Philadelphia was the home town of Glenna Collett-Vare. Joyce stayed briefly with Collett-Vare as her houseguest, and rather than using this time to relax and gather her reserves, Joyce was characteristically eager to play a friendly round at Pine Valley, where they made up a foursome with Glenna's husband and a friend. Joyce found herself more at home on the greens, and she beat ladies par by three strokes, setting a new course record of seventy-six, despite it being her first outing on the course. It was really amazing that she managed to set thirty-two new records on the tour, when it is taken into consideration that she was playing all of the courses for the first time. In this match at Pine Valley, Joyce partnered George Ayres and they turned a halfway deficit of two holes into a one-up victory.

Sunday had quickly come around to find Joyce in Washington DC, at the Columbia Golf Course, near Baltimore. Rain again spoiled the day somewhat. Despite missing several putts within five feet of the cup, Joyce returned an eighty, which was three strokes more than the ladies' record. Together with F. McCloud, she defeated Roland Mackenzie and Glenna Collett-Vare, by three and one.

Into Virginia travelled Joyce, this time by boat down Chesapeake Bay to Norfolk, on the edge of the Atlantic, where she was once more partnered by Johnny Dawson, who had been stripped of his amateur status earlier in the year because he was involved in the merchandising of golf equipment. Johnny refused to class himself as a professional, but he certainly played like one, and he took the honours on this occasion by scoring a sixty-six, six shots under par, and one below the previous record; but at least he had the opportunity of two practise rounds the day before. Their opponents were the Portsmouth brother and sister, Chandler and Lily Harper. Joyce, on her first sight of the course, shot eighty, as did Miss Harper, with Chandler posting a seventy-four. Joyce and partner, or perhaps on this occasion it should read Johnny and partner, won by three and two. I have to admit that Joyce arrived at Norfolk several hours before the match was due to start and was offered a sight of the course, but she gracefully declined, saying that she would prefer to see a little of the city and Virginia Beach.

The next game was 200 miles north once more, to Wilmington beside the Delaware. On this occasion she was teamed with three men for the first time. This was going to be interesting, could she survive with them? She certainly did, and although she and the redoubtable Johnny lost to the local pair of Leo Diegel and Alex Tait by four and three, there was little to separate the scores of the four players. Tait had seventy-two, Diegel seventy-four, Dawson seventy-five, and Wethered seventy-six. She had competed with the men and stayed with them, in so doing she had trimmed a stroke from the women's record, but she was conceded one or two tap-ins, so the new record may not stand.

Not much travelling was required for the next game, which was held at Glenna's home course at Philmont Country Club. Once more Joyce was a guest of Glenna and no doubt Glenna had high hopes of beating Joyce on her home territory. It was not to be. It was almost as though Joyce purposely saved her best for Glenna. She sliced her first drive to the amazement of many and then played doubly well to make up for it and carded her lowest score to date – seventy-three. It was six strokes better than the previous record set up, by none other than Glenna, several years previously. Again, however, tap-ins were conceded, and therefore the authenticity of the new record was in doubt. There seems no doubt to me; if they weren't holed it could not be an official record, but perhaps they were more tolerant in those days. I was especially pleased to note that Joyce was more casually dressed for this game. Previously, she had played in one of two suits, and although the audience was always comprised of different people, surely a star should be sporting more than two outfits in the course of nine outings. In the evening, the players were presented with medals to mark the occasion and Joyce was made an honorary life member of the club.

The very next day she was driven over 200 miles to Richmond in Virginia to face the Southern Amateur champion Freddie Haas, still only nineteen, and the local veteran celebrity, Bobby Cruikshank. Johnny Dawson was again her partner. They had bitten off more than they could chew on this occasion and were whacked by seven and six. Cruikshank broke the course record with a sixty-seven. Haas had seventy-one, Dawson seventy-four, and Joyce eighty. Joyce suffered from the intense heat and was clearly not feeling at her best, but in spite of this her score was one better than the previous women's best. At Wilmington she had shown that she could hold her own with the men. At Richmond that assertion was turned on its head. It made the remainder of the tour all the more interesting.

Back north to Baltimore went Joyce. Some of the travelling could have been eliminated with a little more attention to the schedule, but I suppose there were good reasons for what was done. The Five Farms Country Club provided the venue, and once more Joyce was teamed with Johnny Dawson. The local opposition was provided by Ralph Beach and Roland Mackenzie of Washington. Five Farms is a long and difficult course. Joyce was not driving well for the first half, but when she got into her stride the spectators marvelled at the 260-yards-plus drives she sent down the middle of the fairway. The men outscored her, Dawson and Beach recording seventy-ones and Mackenzie seventy-four. Joyce had a seventy-eight, which was two under women's par and alleged to have been eight better than the previous record.

Next up was a match that would have meant more to Joyce personally than any other on this tour, for she was to play her hero Bobby Jones, at his invitation, at Atlanta, Georgia, where the star lived. To play this match meant Joyce deviating dramatically from her route, as the next stop on the tour was Pittsburgh, nearly a thousand miles to the north-west. But clearly nothing would prevent Joyce from playing against Jones and acceding to his request, and the game must have been equally as important to him as he was still suffering from his appendix, which ailment caused him to need the constant supervision of a doctor throughout the game. Just two days later Bobby Jones was operated on, but evidently considered the prior discomfort well worth it, for he was as keen to have his friends come and watch the great lady play as to play her himself, despite his worsening condition.

So Joyce and Dorothy Shaw flew to Atlanta, and spent a brief visit there with glorious sunshine. They dined with Jones and his biographer, and Joyce had the opportunity to discuss at length with Bobby the new putting technique to which she was adapting, and to gain from his experience.

They played their match on 18 June at East Lake in Atlanta, Georgia. Joyce partnered the Georgia Collegiate champion, Charlie Yates, and they played against Bobby Jones and Dorothy Kirby, a highly promising young golfer just fifteen years old. The match was a tie, with Bobby scoring seventy-one, Joyce seventy-four, Yates seventy-six, and Dorothy eighty-four. Joyce recollected afterwards the feeling of just having to play well, for in such a match not to play well would have been an awful disappointment. Charlie Yates said afterwards that it was the first time that he had played fourteen holes as a ladies' partner before he had figured in the match! 'She was carrying me around on her back, and all I could do was try not to let my feet drag. I reckon I would have been pretty embarrassed, but I was sort of hypnotised watching her play.'

A rail journey took Joyce to Pittsburgh, via Cincinatti. She checked in at the William Penn hotel and then had a hide-and-seek game with the local reporters, hungry for copy. She eventually granted them a five-minute interview and photograph session. Her destination was the Oakmont Country Club, where she teamed up with the inevitable Johnny Dawson against Emil Loeffle, the Oakmont pro, and Ray Babcock, club champion. Joyce described the course as one of the best she had played and also one of the most difficult, and she enjoyed the round tremendously. She was surprised with the speed of the greens, whereas most others had been slower than in England, Oakmont's were fast. She scored eighty-one (equalling the women's record), Dawson was seventy-five, Babcock seventy-eight, but the hero of the day was Loeffler with seventy-two.

Next stop was Portage Country Club, at Akron, Ohio, south of Lake Erie, where Joyce played with Ed Kirby, a professional from a nearby club against the home professional Al Espinosa and the District Champion, Mary Jane Schiltz. A feature of this game was that the ladies' course record had been set some years previously by Glenna Collett-Vare. It was something to aim at for Joyce, but the course had been lengthened in the meantime and she was not playing from the ladies' tees. In the event, Joyce had a cracking game and equalled the record of seventy-four. She three-putted on the final green from twenty feet, otherwise she would have set a new record. Espinosa and Kirby had seventies, and Schiltz eighty-five.

At the Riverside Country Club, of Cambridge Springs, Pennsylvania, for the first time, Joyce was in a head-to-head battle with a young man, Sam Parks, who had recently shocked the golfing intelligentsia by taking the National Open title in a star-packed field. The first nine was probably the most thrilling of the whole tour to date. They were all square, Joyce having taken thirty-eight, including missing a hole-in-one by two inches, and Parks thirty-nine. Joyce then seemed to tire in the heavy ground and she ended with three putts on the final two holes for an eighty. Sam Parks played the second nine in two under fours for a seventy-three. After the match, the two players gave a school where they demonstrated various types of shot.

For the first time on the tour, Joyce now had a short break, three days without the need to perform. She and Dorothy booked into a Cleveland hotel, incognito, in an attempt to escape the constant attention of the media. They treated themselves to a visit to the cinema as a form of relaxation and saw Joan Crawford in *No more ladies*, which they enjoyed very much. They were also able to see a little of the city. Her two matches near Cleveland were at the Kirtland and Manakiki country clubs. At the first she partnered Phil Perkins, a British Open winner, against Billy Burke and Mary Browne. The course was set up for a drive-and-pitch-match and the two men, who had obviously played this type of course before, registered the impressive scores of sixty-five and sixty-eight. Joyce had a seventy-four. At Manakiki, her partner was Bob Shave, the club pro. This must have been a blessing for her, so often had she been pitched against the home custodian on the tour, and who can play a particular course better than the home professional. Their opponents were Lloyd Gullikson and Mary Browne, once more. Joyce and partner squeaked home by one hole. Joyce had a seventy-nine, Gullikson seventy-five, Browne eighty-four, and Shave failed to finish one hole.

It is noticeable that Joyce, whilst not outclassed by the men, usually takes a few more strokes per round, but without fail she is usually several strokes better than the ladies. At Manakiki, the assistant professional was Luke Ross, who had caddied for Bobby Jones for seven years in his heyday. 'She's a sweeter golfer than Bobby,' said Ross. He also commented upon the fact that she was being over-clubbed by her caddies – by two clubs, at times. She didn't know the course so she had to rely upon them.

In Toledo, Johnny Dawson, who had been Joyce's partner on several occasions, turned opponent. It was another singles match and Dawson gave Wethered four shots, before beating her one up on the eighteenth. For the first time, there was some criticism in the press. Apparently, on several holes one or other conceded, whilst it was felt that they should have played them out. Joyce was accorded an eighty and Dawson seventy-four.

The tour continued westwards around the southern shore of Lake Erie to Detroit, city of fast cars and fast music. Her partner at the Red Run Country Club was none other than Walter Hagen. They were well beaten, four and three, by the local professionals, Mortie Dutra and Al Watrous, who had a joint best score of sixty-seven to the visitors' seventy. The men were several strokes better than Joyce, who found sand-traps on a regular basis and had an eighty on this occasion.

Then came a development that heralded the greatest news coverage so far, and it had nothing to do with the top pros against whom Joyce found herself playing over the four days she was in Michigan, the next place on her tour. The rumour starting to spread was that Ruth (the Babe) Didrickson would be among the line ups; the Babe was a star beloved by Americans, who had won several Olympic gold medals in 1932 before deciding she would like to try her hand at golf. She was to become a great golfer in time, but for now she was new to the sport. The press seized upon the prospect of seeing their darling play against the great Joyce Wethered.

The first of the three matches saw Joyce paired with Tommy Armour at the recently improved Medinah course, where she and Armour played against Harry Cooper and Ky Laffoon. Despite the eventual loss of the match, Joyce played tremendously well, setting yet another women's record, this time of seventy-seven. The men scored seventy-five's.

The following day had the crowds surging to see the great spectacle of Joyce Wethered against Babe Didrickson. Joyce's cool head and concentration again won out, for the Babe was still a new player with little control over her drives, despite all her confident assertions over her own prowess in the sport. Her shots did indeed end up far and wide, even hitting five people during the course of the game, but, as one columnist reported, no one was hurt or came off worse for the experience. Still, the scores spoke the truth; Joyce conquered with seventy-eight, the Babe had eighty-eight, and the men, Gene Sarazen and Horton Smith, scored seventy-one's.

The third match on the environs of Chicago was Wethered/Johnny Dawson v. Tommy Armour/Jim Noonan, at the Ravisloe Country Club. Unfortunately, we do not have the details of this match, other than that Joyce scored a seventy-seven.

Even further west went the tour to Interlachen Country Club at Minneapolis. Joyce was in tremendous form and nipped three strokes off the women's record with a seventy-five from the back tees. Her partner, Johnny Dawson, (he must have made a few dollars on this tour) had seventy-three, and their opponents Willie Kidd and Jock Hendry had seventy-six and seventy-seven respectively. Joyce and partner won by three and two.

Now they turned south into Ohio and Davenport, before proceeding to Kansas City. Joyce returned a seventy-eight at Davenport, which was no less than four strokes under the previous record. She played with Arthur Andrews, seventy-six, against two amateurs, Lucille Robinson, eighty-five and Dr Paul Barton, seventy-five. Joyce and partner won, but we don't have the margin. She must have travelled overnight by train to Kansas City as she arrived at half past seven in the morning. She was a luncheon guest of the Women's Golf Association at Indian Hills, and in the afternoon partnered Al Collins against Bunny Torpey and Bill Wotherspoon, all three being golf professionals. Juniors were allowed entry to the exhibition match for thirty-five cents as an incentive to encourage junior golf, but the total gallery was only 300, so perhaps golf was not high on the agenda of most Missourians. They were probably rounding up cattle. Incidentally, how come that Kansas City is in Missouri and not in Kansas State? The match was halved; Joyce shot seventy-six, three under the women's par, whilst the men had Collins sixty-eight, Torpey, sixty-nine, and Wotherspoon seventy-five. Joyce left on the evening train for the 500-mile journey to Indianapolis.

The Highland Country Club was the venue for the game and 700 spectators were in attendance. Joyce was partnered by the State amateur champion, Johnny McGuire, against the local pro Neal McIntyre and Elizabeth Abbott, a local girl who had made a name for herself in Los Angeles. The locals were the winners by three and two, and perhaps the feature of the match was that Miss Abbott matched Joyce's score of seventy-six, four under women's par. McIntyre had an excellent seventy, but McGuire slipped to seventy-seven.

The question at Columbus, before Joyce arrived, was whether she could outdrive the men. The chairman of the Scioto Club decided to have white lines marked 250 yards from the tees for the benefit of the audience. 1,000 spectators turned out to witness Joyce playing with Charley Lorms against P.O. Hart and Mrs Linton Fallis. Joyce was again in scintillating form and repeated her lowest score of the tour, returning a seventy-three. It was another record. Lorms had seventy-five, Hart seventy-one, and an overwhelmed Fallis ninety-two. Nevertheless, they could do no better than a half. Did she cross the 250 mark? Yes, she did, on more than one occasion.

Two Philadelphians, Jack Kelly and Willard Groeckler, provided the opposition at the next venue which was the Eagles Mere Country Club, where the home pro, Clarence Ehresman, was Joyce's partner. They succumbed to the Philadelphians by two and one. Joyce had a fine seventy-four, Ehrsman seventy-one, Kelly seventy-five and Groeckler seventy-four. With those scores, I can't for the life of me see how they could have lost; Kelly and Groeckler must have had one or two very bad scoring holes. After the match Joyce was surrounded by small autograph hunters and satisfied them graciously. A reporter asked what she thought of Babe Didrikson. Ever the diplomat, Joyce replied, with full honesty, that she thought she must be the most powerful woman in golf – clever!

Incidentally, Joyce must have been a terribly difficult subject for the American press to interview. Her quiet, even temperament and distinct lack of vices – she did not drink, smoke, or succumb to any superstitions and had no strong likes or dislikes apparently about anything – must have left them somewhat at a loss. But she was always very pleasant, despite having a character that would suggest her finding little to enjoy in being out in the spotlight as much as an interview would require.

Back on the Eastern seaboard at Alantic City, Joyce was opposed to Glenna Collett-Vare once more. They had two young teenagers for partners, Clarence Hackney and James Fraser. Lo and behold, it was Joyce's putting which won the day. She had several single putt holes from appreciable distances. Her score was an impressive seventy-eight in difficult conditions. Glenna had eighty-one and Hackney eighty-two. Fraser failed to hole out, and Joyce and partner prevailed by one up.

At the next match Joyce found herself playing against the outgoing Babe Didrickson once again, at Meadowbrook Country Club near Buffalo, New York. Joyce and the home pro Elwynn Nagell played against Gene Sarazen and the Babe, in a match decided by points, one for low ball and one for low aggregate. The scores were: Wethered seventy-seven (five below course record), Sarazen seventy-two, Nagell seventy-three, and Didrikson eighty-one, with Joyce and Elwynn winning by four points. The pitting of Joyce against the Babe was something the American public would have flocked to see, as the two could not have been more opposite; yet for all the extrovert behaviour of Babe Didrickson and its entertaining qualities, it was indisputably Joyce who was the more effective on the golf course.

For the first time, Joyce now crossed the Canadian border, round Lake Ontario, to Toronto. She visited Niagara Falls en route, evidence that the tour was not totally devoted to golf, though there was not much time for sightseeing and other such matters. She booked into the Royal York Hotel on the Thursday evening. The match was not until the Saturday, but there was plenty of official action beforehand. She had the inevitable sessions with the newspapermen, of course; and had the honour of being the guest at a civic reception at City Hall. She was looking forward to the Saturday game because the course was named after her favourite venue, St Andrews.

Her partner was the amateur champion Ross Somerville, and they played two of Canada's best amateurs, Bud Donovan and Ada MacKenzie. The starter and Joyce's caddie for the day wore full Scottish dress, including kilt. Whether he was any good as a caddie, we know not. Bearing in mind that Joyce had never seen the course before, as has been said previously, she depended on her caddies! However, undaunted, she had another marvellous day and thrilled the crowd as she broke yet another record and won the match, Her score was seventy-five, as against Somerville, seventy-six, Donovan, seventy-eight, and MacKenzie, eighty-five.

As the next game was at Rochester, back on the American side of Lake Ontario, and as it was on the following day, Dorothy Shaw suggested that they might fly. Joyce was only too pleased with the suggestion. The Brook Lea Course provided the venue in Rochester, and she paired with Bill Chapin against Jack Tucker and Miss Wattles. She went round in seventy-seven, which broke the previous record by nine strokes. I know that sounds incredible, perhaps Rochester didn't have many lady golfers. Joyce had the distinct impression that the golf was not the major interest at many of the American Country Club courses.

A new State was now entered – Vermont. The day was organised by the Green Mountain Girls' Club Association at Ekwanok Country Club, near Manchester. The match was a singles with Joyce matched against Edmond Driggs. Not at her best, she lost four and three, and shot eighty-two. However, the ladies of the club were delighted with the exhibition and felt certain that it would encourage their members to increase their golfing interest. At Pittsfield in New Hampshire, Joyce was not only back in the winning mode, but had her lowest total of the tour – a seventy. She had a seven-foot putt on the last green for sixty-nine, but it was not to be. It equalled par for the men and broke the women's record, which had been set only the previous week, by eight shots. Her partner Prince Smith and opponent Dan England both had seventy-ones, whilst Deborah Verry had a seventy-six.

The holidaymakers on Rhode Island were the next to witness the triumphant tour at the Point Judith Country Club. It was a ladies' four ball, and Joyce and Helen Waterhouse lost by two and one to Glenna Collett-Vare and Mrs Fred Davis, both old Rhode Islanders. Joyce and Glenna returned seventy-eights, but it has to be remembered that Glenna had played the course many times and knew all of its peculiarities. The ladies wined and dined them for both lunch and dinner.

At Rockledge, near Hartford, Connecticut, Joyce played with Sid Covington against Jean Bauer and Dave Campbell, the local professional. Jean had taken rather a mauling on a couple of occasions earlier in the tour, but had recently beaten Didrikson, and was 'up for it', as they say. Not to be, the Wethered/Covington pair won by two up. Joyce, with seventy-five, had the lowest score of the four, Campbell had seventy-six and the other two had eighties. It was noticeable that Joyce was now often outscoring the males.

The last match on the Eastern seaboard was at Shenecossett Country Club, New London, and Glenna Vare had her last opportunity to outshine Joyce, who was teamed with the long-driving Tommy Tailor. Glenna must have gone home in despair. She didn't play to her normal standard and was again on the losing side. Tailor was lowest scorer with seventy-four, Marston seventy-six, Wethered seventy-nine, and Vare eighty-one.

Joyce and Dorothy settled themselves for the twenty-four-hour train journey west to St Louis, before heading to California on the west coast. It is surprising that they did not go to St Louis previously in the tour when they were nearer at Kansas City, but at least it allowed the people of Missouri to see her once again. She was doing extremely well at this stage in the tour, having broken the record on twenty-five of the thirty-seven courses on which she had played.

Neither did Joyce seem perturbed by extreme conditions; she partnered Roger Lord to play a game in tremendous heat at Algonquin Country Club, but still triumphed over their local opponents, Sara Guth and Dick Bockenkamp, winning by eight and six, each of them with winning scores of seventy-five. After this surely arduous experience, Joyce then found the energy to attend the theatre before boarding the train for L.A. at midnight.

In California, Joyce was the guest of Marion Hollins, who had captained the first American Walker Cup team in England in 1932. Joyce had captained the Great Britain and Ireland team. Marion had been a non-playing captain and it was generally agreed that her ability to give all of her attention to her organisational duties and players had contributed greatly to the US victory.

The first match was at the Pasatiempo Country Club, near Santa Cruz, and the play was three-a-side. Joyce's team was defeated by one hole, and it could be called the men's day. Their scoring was better than Joyce (seventy-seven) could produce, though she was seven strokes better than Marion Hollins, who apparently owned the club. A spectator that afternoon was the world tennis champion Helen Wills Moody, and time was found on the course for the two stars to have a short tête-á-tête. Sequoyah Country Club came next and it is reported that the committee spent a worrying time trying to decide what they should provide for Joyce's tea. Bets were flying concerning the probability of the course record being broken. You could get odds of three to one, and Joyce's score seemed to be the preoccupation of most people. The women's record stood at seventy-five, and when Joyce, with an errant putter, went out in forty, the odds no doubt improved considerably. What did she do? Came back in thirty-four, beating all the pros., and taking the record by one shot. Her best effort was to place her tee shot nine feet from the cup at the 246-yard fourteenth. Wethered and Goggin won by four and three.

At San José, Joyce broke yet another record with a seventy-six and matched the men. The following day she played ten balls at a hole-in-one competition for charity. She had recorded only two holes-in-one in competition in her life, so that was not one of her speciality tricks. Nevertheless, the congregated throng were very impressed with the consistency with which she placed nine of the ten balls around the hole. At San Francisco Country Club the next day she fired a seventy-eight, and then on to Pebble Beach, which she had hungrily anticipated. Here she was paired with Willie Goggin against the Puget brothers, professionals on the course. The bets had been that she wouldn't break eighty at either San Francisco or Pebble Beach. She proved them wrong at the former, but had to settle for eighty-two at the latter. She so wished that she could have had another tilt at that one. It was the first time that she had been outside women's par (by one), but she was playing from the men's tees. The brothers won by two and one, scoring seventy-five and seventy-six to Coggin's seventy-eight.

Her next two matches were at Del Monte Country Club and Montecito Country Club, Santa Barbara. Unfortunately, I have only Joyce's scores, which were seventy-three and seventy-four, respectively, and do not have the names of the other players or their scores.

There was a gap of a whole week before the next 'official' exhibition match, so what did Joyce do? She played golf, of course. On 27 August, Joyce got her wish to play Pebble Beach once more. In a hurriedly arranged game, she played with Marion Hollins, Ty Cobb, one of baseball's greats, and C.P. Erdman. She managed to equal the women's par of eighty-one. I'll bet she would have liked a week playing that course. She played a further friendly game with Marion Hollins, who was proving to be an excellent hostess. A visit to the Metro-Goldwyn-Mayer studios was arranged. History has it that she did not get any of the stars' autographs because she was too busy signing her own. The game at the Wilshire Country Club, not too far from Hollywood, was awaited excitedly by the ultra-rich of the area, and some high profile names were imported to play. Joyce was paired with the 1934 Open champion, Olin Dutra, against two top professionals, Willie Hunter and Charley 'Beau' Guest. It was amusing to read the account of the match in one newspaper, where it was described as unexciting because the players were too accurate with their shots, seldom getting themselves into places which required miracle recoveries. Joyce had an excellent round until the last two holes, when the wheels came off and she had two sixes – most un-Joyce-like. It took her total up to seventy-nine, as opposed to Dutra, seventy-three, Hunter, seventy-six, and Guest, seventy-one.

For her last match in the United States, Joyce travelled north to Seattle. It was a course which boasted more than its fair share of trees, and Joyce left her driver in the bag and opted for the middle of the fairway with her brassie or spoon. It is only fair to say that the crowd were slightly disappointed with her distance off the tees. It was as far as they had seen a woman hit the ball, but by now fantastic stories were circulating of superhuman powers. Joyce equalled the women's record of seventy-eight, which had been set the previous year by one of her opponents, Mrs Ford. The other players were Forest Watson and Lee Steil, who incidentally hit the ball a country mile. Joyce was on the winning side once more, securing a five-and-four victory.

And so, farewell to America, and hello to Canada. She sailed across to Victoria from Vancouver. The large crowd of 1,200 saw Joyce score a seventy-five over a difficult course. Her partner, Joe Pryke, had a bad day and the pair lost by two holes to Phil Taylor and Marjorie Todd. Back on the mainland, the venue was the picturesque Jericho Golf Club, where Joyce scored seventy-three, four shots under women's par, one over men's par. In a rather different format from previous games, Joyce was teamed with Ada McKenzie against two men, Davie Black and Alec Duthie. It sounds like there was a lot of Scottish ancestry there! The two ladies were given three holes start and the match ended all square.

Golf now took a back seat for a while, as Joyce embarked on the Canadian Pacific Railways journey eastwards, across the fabulous sights of the Rockies, and over the Plains to Winnipeg, for a brief stop and one exhibition, before continuing onwards to Ottawa. In Winnipeg, at the St Charles Golf club, she had a seventy-four. At Ottawa, we can refer to full information. The game was played at the Rivermead Golf Club and the beautiful weather of the rest of the tour seemed to be coming to an end. A pleasant morning gave way to a cold afternoon, but the rousing play of Joyce and her companions kept the spectators warm. She was partnered by Frank Corrigan *v.* Mrs Fraser and Jack Littler. The points scoring system of one for lowest score and one for aggregate was used, and Joyce and partner romped away to win by fifteen points. Joyce had a seventy-three, the lowest of the four, with Corrigan, seventy-four, Littler, seventy-five, and Fraser, eighty-three.

There was then a comparatively short trip to Montreal for the last game of the tour. The weather had turned nasty. It was definitely time for Joyce to shut up shop, and take her well-earned cash back to Britain. A cold drizzle failed to repress the size of the crowd, which numbered 2,000, one of the highest attendances on the tour. Joyce, seventy-five, and partner Eddie Innes, seventy-five, outscored their opponents Mrs Fraser, eighty-five, and Gordon Taylor, eighty-one, to win by three and two.

In approximately three months, Joyce Wethered had travelled 15,000 miles, played fifty-three official matches and several friendlies, broken women's course records on thirty-four occasions (though some of those might be contested due to conceded tap-ins), and averaged 76.9. As indicated previously, to put that into today's context, you would have to deduct about six shots per round. With one exception, she achieved that playing on courses she had never seen before! And, of course, she had to play with the large ball in all of her matches in the United States.

The American Tour, 1935

Date	Venue	Players	Opponents	Result	Scores	Attendance
30-05-1935	Women's National Course Glen Head, Long Island	Joyce Wethered Johnny Dawson	Glenna Vare Gene Sarazen	Halved	Wethered 78 Dawson 75 Vare – Sarazen 72	2000
01-06-1935	Winged Foot Golf Club Mamarmeck, New York	Joyce Wethered Glenna Vare	Gene Sarazen Jesse Sweetser	Lost 2 and 1	Wethered 83 Vare 82 Sarazen 72 Sweetser –	2000
02-06-1935	Ridgewood Golf Club Ridgewood, New Jersey	Joyce Wethered Sid Brews	Craig Wood Maureen Orcutt	Won 1 up	Wethered 82 Drews 72 Orcutt 81 Wood 76	
05-06-1935	Winchester Golf Club Winchester, Mass.	Joyce Wethered Bill Blaney	Francis Ouimet Jean Bauer	Won 7 and 6	Wethered 85 Blaney 74 Ouimet 80 Bauer 91	2000
06-06-1935	Worcester Golf Club Worcester, Mass.	Joyce Wethered Benjamin Ayres	Jesse Guildford Jean Bauer	Won 5 and 4	Wethered 76 Ayres 81 Guildford 76 Bauer 87	
08-06-1935	Merion Golf Club Philadelphia, Pennsy.	Joyce Wethered George Sayres	Max Marston Glenna Vare	Won 1 up	Wethered 76 Sayres 81 Marston 77 Vare 84	500

Date	Venue	Players	Opponents	Result	Scores	Attendance
09-06-1935	Columbia Golf Club Washington D.C.	Joyce Wethered Fred McCloud	Roland Mackenzie Glenna Vare	Won 3 and 1	Wethered 80 McCloud 75 Mackenzie 75 Vare 83	1200
11-06-1935	Norfolk Golf Club Norfolk, Virginia	Joyce Wethered Johnny Dawson	Chandler Harper Lily Harper	Won 3 and 2	Wethered 80 Dawson 66 Harper 76 Harper 80	1500
13-06-1935	Wilmington Country Club Delaware	Joyce Wethered Johnny Dawson	Leo Diegel Alex Tait	Lost 4 and 3	Wethered 76 Dawson 75 Diegel 74 Tait 72	
14-06-1935	Philmont Country Club Pennsylvania	Joyce Wethered Leo Diegel	Ed Dudley Glenna Vare	Won 2 up	Wethered 73 Diegel 68 Dudley 72 Vare 78	1500
15-06-1935	Richmond Country Club Richmond, Virginia	Joyce Wethered Johnny Dawson	Bobby Cruickshank Freddy Haas	Lost 7 and 6	Wethered 81 Dawson 74 Cruickshank 67 Haas 71	
16-06-1935	Five Farms Country Club Baltimore, Maryland	Joyce Wethered Johnny Dawson	Ralph Beach Roland Mackenzie	Halved	Wethered 78 Dawson 71 Beach 71 Mackenzie 74	1000
18-06-1935	East Lake Country Club Atlanta, Georgia	Joyce Wethered Charlie Yates	Bobby Jones Dorothy Kirby	Halved	Wethered 74 Yates 76 Jones 71 Kirb 84	

Date	Venue	Players	Opponents	Result	Scores	Attendance
20-06-1935	Oakmont Country Club Pittsburgh, Pennsylvania	Joyce Wethered Johnny Dawson	Ray Babcock Emil Loeffle	Lost 3 and 2	Wethered 81 Dawson 75 Babcock 78 Loeffle 72	500
23-06-1935	Portage Country Club Akron, Ohio	Joyce Wethered Ed Kirby	Al Espinosa Mary Schiltz	Halved	Not known	600
25-06-1935	Riverside Country Club Cambridge Springs, Pennsyl.	Joyce Wethered	Sam Parks	Lost 4 and 2	Wethered 80 Parks 73	700
29-06-1935	Kirtland Country Club Cleveland, Ohio	Joyce Wethered Phil Perkins	Billy Burke Mary Browne	Won 4 and 3	Wethered 74 Perkins 65 Burke 68 Browne –	500
30-06-1935	Manakiki Country Club Cleveland, Ohio	Joyce Wethered Bob Shave	Lloyd Gullicksen Mary Browne	Won 1 up	Wethered 79 Shave – Gullickson 75 Browne 84	700
02-07-1935	Inverness Country Club Toledo, Ohio	Joyce Wethered	Johnny Dawson	Lost	Wethered 80 Dawson 74	–
04-07-1935	Red Run Country Club Detroit, Michigan	Joyce Wethered Walter Hagen	Al Watrous Mortie Distra	Lost 4 and 3	Wethered 80 Hagen 72 Watrous 72 Distra 70	1200
06-07-1935	Medinah Country Club Chicago, Illinois	Joyce Wethered Tommy Armour	Harry Cooper Ky Laffoon	Lost 2 and 1	Wethered 77 Armour 75 Cooper 75 Laffoon 75	1000

Date	Venue	Players	Opponents	Result	Scores	Attendance
07-07-1935	Oak Park Country Club Chicago, Illinois	Joyce Wethered Horton Smith	Gene Sarazen Babe Didrikson	Won 8 and 7	Wethered 78 Smith 71 Sarazen 71 Didrikson 88	4000
09-07-1935	Raverloe Country Club Chicago, Illinois	Joyce Wethered Johnny Dawson	Tommy Armour Jim Noonan	n/a	Wethered 77	
11-07-1935	Interlaken Country Club Minneapolis, Minnesota	Joyce Wethered Johnny Dawson	Willie Kidd Jock Hendry	Won 3 and 2	Wethered 75 Dawson 73 Kidd 76 Hendry 77	500
14-07-1935	Davenport Country Club Davenport, Ohio	Joyce Wethered Arthur Andrews	Paul Barton Lucile Robinson	Won	Wethered 78 Andrews 76 Barton 75 Robinson 85	500
15-07-1935	Indian Hills Country Club Kansas City, Missouri	Joyce Wethered Al Collins	Bill Wotherspoon Bunny Torpey	Halved	Wethered 76 Collins 68 Wotherspoon 75 Torpey 69	300
16-07-1935	Highland Country Club Indianapolis, Indiana	Joyce Wethered Johnny McGuire	Neal McIntyre Elizabeth Abbott	Lost 3 and 2	Wethered 76 McGuire 77 McIntyre 70 Abbott 76	
17-07-1935	Sicoto Country Club Columbus, Ohio	Joyce Wethered Charlie Lorms	P.O. Hart Linton Fallis	Halved	Wethered 73 Lorms 75 Hart 71 Fallis 92	1000

Date	Venue	Players	Opponents	Result	Scores	Attendance
19-07-1935	Eagles Mere Country Club	Joyce Wethered Clarence Ehresman	Jack Kelly Willard Groeckler	Lost 2 and 1	Wethered 74 Ehresman 71 Kelly 75 Groeckler 74	
21-07-1935	Atlantic City Country Club Northfield, New Jersey	Joyce Wethered Clarence Hackney	James Fraser Glenna Vare	Won 1 up	Wethered 78 Hackney 82 Fraser – Vare 81	
24-07-1935	Meadowbrook Country Club Buffalo, New York	Joyce Wethered Elwynn Nagell	Gene Sarazen Babe Didrikson	Won 4 points	Wethered 77 Nagell 73 Sarazen 72 Didrikson 81	2500
27-07-1935	St Andrews Golf Club Toronto, Ontario	Joyce Wethered Ross Somerville	Bud Donovan Ada MacKenzie	Won 10 points	Wethered 75 Somerville 76 Donovan 78 MacKenzie 85	2000
28-07-1935	Brook-Lea Country Club Rochester, New York	Joyce Wethered Bill Chapin	Jack Tucker Peggy Wattles	Won 5 points	Wethered 77 Chapin 78 Tucker 77 Wattles 87	500
30-07-1935	Ekwanok Country Club Manchester, Vermont	Joyce Wethered	Edmond Driggs	Lost 4 and 3	Wethered 82	
31-07-1935	Pittsfield Country Club Pittsfield, New Hampshire	Joyce Wethered Prince Smith	Dan England Deborah Verry	Won 1 up	Wethered 70 Smith 71 England71 Verry 76	

Date	Venue	Players	Opponents	Result	Scores	Attendance
01–08–1935	Point Judith Country Club Narragansett, Rhode Island	Joyce Wethered Helen Waterhouse	Glenna Vare Mrs. F. Dawes	Lost 2 and 1	Wethered 78 Waterhouse – Vare 78 Dawes –	300
02–08–1935	Rockledge Country Club West Hartford, Connecticut	Joyce Wethered Sid Covington	Dave Campbell Jean Bauer	Won 2 up	Wethered 75 Covington 80 Campbell 76 Bauer 80	300
04–08–1935	Shenecosset Country Club New London, Connecticut	Joyce Wethered Tommy Tailor	Max Marston Glenna Vare	Won 2 up	Wethered – Tailor – Marston – Vare –	500
06–08–1935	Algonquin Country Club St Louis, Missouri	Joyce Wethered Roger Lord	Dick Bockencamp Sara Guth	Won 8 and 6	Wethered 75 Lord 75 Bockencamp 78 Guth 83	500
10–08–1935	Pasatiempo Country Club Los Angeles, California	Joyce Wethered Stuart Hawley	Marion Hollins Willie Goggin	Lost 1 down	Wethered 77 Hawley 73 Pieper 69	
		Ernie Pieper	Benny Coltrin		Hollins 84 Goggin 68 Coltrin 70	
11–08–1935	Sequoyah Country Club Los Angeles, California	Joyce Wethered Willie Goggin	Benny Coltrin Various	Won 4 and 3	Wethered 74 Goggin 71 Coltrin 72 Various 74	1000

Date	Venue	Players	Opponents	Result	Scores	Attendance
15–08–1935	San José Country Club, San José, California	Joyce Wethered, Eddie Duino	Willie Goggin, Arthur Brooks	Not available	Wethered 76, Duino 78, Goggin 75, Brooks 74	
17–08–1935	San Francisco Country Club, San Francisco	Joyce Wethered, Frank Dolp	Stuart Hawley, Jack Finger	Not available	Wethered 78, Dolp n/a, Hawley n/a, Finger n/a	
18–08–1935	Pebble Beach Golf Club, Del Monte, California	Joyce Wethered, Willie Goggin	Campbell Puget, Henry Puget	Lost 2 and 1	Wethered 82, Goggin 78, Puget 76, Puget 75	
24-08-1935	Del Monte Club, Del Monte, California	n/a	n/a	n/a	Wethered 73	
25–08–1935	Montecito Country Club, Santa Barbara, California	n/a	n/a	n/a	Wethered 74	
01–09–1935	Wilshire Country Club, Los Angeles, California	Joyce Wethered, Olin Dutra	Willie Hunter, Charley Guest	Lost 3 and 2	Wethered 79, Dutra 73, Hunter 76, Guest 71	1500
04–09–1935	Seattle Golf Club, Seattle, Washington	Joyce Wethered, Forest Watson	Lee Steil, Mrs. C. Ford	Won 5 and 4	Wethered 78, Watson n/a, Steil n/a, Ford n/a	700
07–09–1935	Oak Bay Golf Club, Victoria, British Col.	Joyce Wethered, Joe Pryke	Phil Taylor, Marjorie Todd	Lost 2 down	Wethered 75, Pryke n/a, Taylor n/a, Todd n/a	1200

Date	Venue	Players	Opponents	Result	Scores	Attendance
08-09-1935	Jericho Golf Club Vancouver, British Columbia	Joyce Wethered Ada MacKenzie	Dave Black Alec Duthie	Halved	Wethered 73 Black n/a Mac Kenzie n/a Duthie n/a	1200
14-09-1935	Rivermead Golf Club Ottawa	Joyce Wethered Frank Corrigan	Jack Littler Mrs Fraser	Won 15 points	Wethered 73 Corrigan 74 Littler 75 Fraser 83	700
15-09-1935	Marlborough Golf Club Montreal	Joyce Wethered Eddie Innes	Gordon Taylor Mrs Fraser	Won 3 and 2	Wethered 75 Innes 75 Taylor 81 Fraser 85	2000

APPENDIX 6

GOLFING LESSONS BY JOYCE WETHERED

Perhaps the most impressive aspect of Joyce Wethered's golfing achievements lies in the fact that she was by no means a natural golfer as a child. She had to work at the game and develop her skills. This meant that, as she matured, she understood the mechanics of all the golfing shots. She not only could efficiently execute them, but knew exactly how she was achieving her aims. Many top golfers can put into effect what a good coach instructs them to do, but left to their own devices they would struggle. Their knowledge of the mechanics is limited. JW had golfing intelligence. Moreover, she could put this intelligence into words and writing, for the benefits of others. In 1934 she published what is in effect a golfing autobiography, *Golfing Memories and Methods*, which is as clear an instruction book on golf as I have seen, and prior to that, in the spring of 1930, she wrote two short articles for the magazine *Fairway and Hazard*, which was the LGU's mouthpiece at the time, which are reproduced below. They are lessons on how to play woods and irons.

Iron Shots

IMPORTANCE OF CONTROL.

By JOYCE WETHERED.

WITH iron play especially it is necessary to play with a purpose, to make up one's mind what exactly is to be done and the kind of shot best calculated to effect its object. The problem is more difficult than that of wooden-club play, where direction is practically the only thing to think of, except the desire to get as far in that direction as possible.

The controlled iron shot, which we are considering, is played at a definite mark. The question of exact distance has to be calculated and the shot ruled on a line instead of, as in a drive, down a comparatively wide pathway. Also, maximum strength is rarely required; and as greater exactness is necessary, the freedom of the swing employed with wooden clubs must be curtailed.

There is actually no reason whatever why precisely the same swing used with a wooden club may not be used with an iron club also in approaching; only, if it is, the result will be that you will get somewhere near, but not near enough, to your object of aim to be entirely satisfactory. T h e method must be tightened up to ensure absolute accuracy. The ball has to be made to travel along a definite line and to pull up quickly. There may be plenty of other iron shots in the bag, but this is the normal shot from which one rarely departs in playing with the rubber-cored ball. In fact, one plays it wherever possible in order to maintain one consistent method throughout and avoid the losses which generally accompany any unnecessary striving after variety or novelty.

Action of Hands and Knees.

The main difference which distinguishes iron play from wooden-club practice is that the hands and the knees come into greater prominence. These are the real guiding forces. A wooden-club shot is essentially a clean hit in a certain direction; the iron shot is a hit that must grip the ball more closely. The club head must, as it were, cling to the ball as long as it can, and the hands and knees are the chief factors in the stroke which make this possible.

The stance may be a little more open, if preferred. Stand in whatever position makes you feel the line to the hole most naturally, so that the ball shall be hit down that line. You must take great pains how you sole your club. If a perfectly straight shot is required, see that your blade is at right angles to the hole. Where a pull or a slice is wanted, then it may be necessary to lay off the blade. But for the moment we are confining ourselves to the simple direct shot.

I believe strongly in the shut face—that is, in making no definite turning movement of the wrists in going back. Let the club face go back square to the ball and let it turn only gradually until at the top of the swing the toe of the club faces the hole. The point to watch is that the wrists do not turn in such a way that the toe of the club is pointing behind you to the left of the hole. See that the left wrist is well under the right at the top of the swing. I am not recommending an exaggerated shut face at the top of the swing, only that there must be the least possible disturbance of wrist control by bending or turning—in fact, a movement in which the back swing is all in one piece.

Keep the Club-head Straight.

To make this successful, the club head must follow straight through after the ball is struck—without either letting the toe turn in, or the hands drag the club head across the ball, or the heel go through before the toe of the club. If these errors are guarded against the shot will be a straight one ; the ball will be truly hit and remain under control when it pitches.

Finish of Iron Shot

The chief things on which to concentrate are the path of the club-head, the cutting of a straight divot, and the true angle of the blade at the moment of striking. The method covers the whole range of iron clubs from a driving iron to a mashie niblick. It may not be as simple to do as it sounds ; but it must be remembered that to acquire the best methods needs time and practice, although force of habit makes them the easiest in the long run.

Weight Transference.

The part that balance plays in the iron shot is similar to that advocated for wooden-club shots—only considerably modified. I do not believe in having the feet too far apart: a sway must be avoided at all costs. But I do believe in shifting the weight from one foot to the other—no shot can be made effective without weight transference. In order, then, to reduce the movement, feel that the weight is shifted by the knees and not by the hips, as with wooden clubs. The feeling of movemen must be lower : the knees are going to lead the pivot. In the back swing let the weight be on the right foot (as if you were standing on it from the knee only), but take care that the upper part of the body does not change its central position. As the stroke is being made let the weight change to the left foot. Let the right knee come into the shot, with the feeling that it is directing it. This is only possible if the weight is taken firmly on to the left foot, which leaves the right knee free to swing forward.

Do not let this knee movement lead to ducking, which is a deadly sin. On the other hand, remember that all will be well if the shoulders are kept at the correct level as well as central, and if the transference of weight is carried out with decision.

Wooden Club Play

BALANCE THE SECRET OF POWER

VERY often instruction in golf begins at the wrong end. Instead of being told what are the great things to aim at and incited to work out the problem, the player is generally first taught a particular way of standing or an approved method of holding the club. These are of course important matters, but they are adaptable. Questions, on the other hand, affecting the path of the clubhead are fixed and must be mastered if the best and most consistent results are to be obtained.

The two great objectives in wooden club play are that the ball must be struck absolutely plainly (that is, without spin), and that a maximum length is gained (that is, the employment of all the power available). Put briefly, the solution of these two problems lies in the true swinging of the club, as opposed to hitting; and secondly, in bringing the body muscles into play in order to get the necessary strength. Bodywork must invariably come second to the swing. In fact, they can be regarded as two separate functions.

There is no disguising the truth that the art of striking the ball absolutely truly with wooden clubs, without imparting spin, is an exceedingly difficult habit to acquire. It cannot come naturally. No greater mistake can be made than to imagine that the natural swing is the ideal swing. For one thing, it is invariably uneven and unformed. The perfect arc of the clubhead has to be formed, to be consciously cultivated. It will never arrive by the light of nature in spite of the fact that when one sees it, it appears the simplest of all. Curiously enough, the further any player gets in perfecting a swing, the simpler the method will look, the reason being that a swing when properly developed is actually the simplest, although it may be the result of a rather complex evolution.

Swing and Rhythm.

Balance lies at the root of the application of power. To apply our maximum strength needs the co-operation of the body with the arms. Our object must therefore be to get the body into the position which helps and controls the swing of the arms. We cannot swing our arms in a rhythmical manner unless the shoulders and the hips are both assisting smoothly without pulling or jerking. A wrong position is fatal for the delivery of the swing. I have come to the conclusion that, from the point of view of hitting the ball really perfectly, the greatest fault of all is to get the body too far forward in the back swing. If you are too far forward, you must get back in order to allow the clubhead to get through; and that involuntary backward movement is going to interfere sadly with the rhythm. The perfect wooden club shot is a swing pure and simple. That is the whole point of these remarks.

I am taking it for granted that the player is able to stand perfectly still and swing a club with the arms only (without exerting any strength), so that the arc described by the clubhead has no kinks in it at any point and is perfect in shape, the arms being neither crumpled up nor stiffened.

The next step is for the player to take up an easy stance square to the line of play. The first movement is that of the clubhead moved by the hands and wrists, all in one. Almost simultaneously, but just afterwards (I believe this to be a very important point) let the weight go on to the right foot. I should describe it as a move-

ment of weight from the hips downwards, the shoulders remaining as far as possible where they were. If you allow the hips to get well back, they are in a splendid position from which to be released as the club comes down. Remember that if you move your shoulders appreciably out of position, either backwards or forwards (naturally they must pivot) you are altering the perfect shape of the arc by shifting the centre—and the less that is done the better.

Body Action.

In order to apply your full strength to the shot, reliance must be made on the action of the hips. The left heel should be allowed quite a free movement in the back swing. Then with the weight well back on your right foot the body is correctly poised and the hips are held in a position which retards them from coming in too soon. As the clubhead comes down through the ball the hips are set free, released like a spring. This sends the clubhead swinging on through the ball to a complete finish. Everything, right knee and all, is working in the one direction.

This perhaps sounds like a terrific sway, and it might easily lead to one. But it will never happen if the shoulders are controlled, pivoting freely with the right shoulder following well after the ball. Keep them, so to speak, in the centre of the balance of the swing, neither lifting nor ducking. Have the feeling that they are being kept level, although in reality they are pivotting in the same place, within the same area.

I have laid considerable emphasis on this question of body action during a drive, but it should not mislead people into thinking that the body plays the most important part in the swing. As a matter of fact, it plays the subordinate part. To swing the arms freely and rhythmically requires correct co-operation; but to bring in the body movements *without* a free swing will only lead to a horrible lurching blow—all body and no arms. It is for the primary reason of encouraging a free, wide and unchecked swing that I have tried to describe the essentials of the body balance; how it is necessary that bodywork must not be allowed to clog the swing, but used rather to give it life and crispness.

Learn to Hit Through.

For a beginner I would recommend concentration on the arc of the swing being large and regular. When it is found that the swing does not move evenly right through, that it gets checked or hung up at some point or other—generally half way through the finish—then it is advisable to examine carefully the body movements to see where the action is interfering. Put in a little less power if necessary. It may mean that you actually gain more.

To more experienced players I would suggest that they should never rest satisfied with an uncertain balance either during or after the playing of a shot. Heaviness is imperfect balance. If you are in doubt, try a swing with feet touching one another until you master its difficulties. This will at any rate teach you to swing the club and to hit through the ball rather than at it. Get that perfect and you can then with your ordinary stance concentrate on adding your power by bringing in the hip movement smoothly, yet with fire and energy. Feel that the balance and control are above and that the power comes from below.

JOYCE WETHERED.

Appendix 7

The Englishwoman's Garden

In 1983, *The Englishwoman's Garden*, edited by Alvide Lees-Milne and Rosemary Verey, was published by Chatto & Windus. Each chapter is a contribution from a lady with a noteworthy garden, usually describing its evolvement and specific features associated with it. Lady Amory contributed a chapter on Knightshayes to this fascinating book, and her words are reproduced as this appendix. My original idea for including the chapter was to try to compare the skills and philosophies which she applied to gardening with those she applied to her golf. Having decided that this would be too contrived, the appendix has been retained so that the reader can read in Lady Amory's own words of the pleasure which her gardening hobby afforded her.

[The following is an extract from *The Englishwoman's Garden*.]

Knightshayes Court, Tiverton, Devonshire.

Lady Heathcoat Amory's Garden

When my husband and I married in 1937, we inherited a large Victorian house, with a fine view over a park framed by forest trees, and the rolling Devon hills beyond. The setting of the house was fortunate, situated four-hundred feet above sea-level, surrounded by wild woodland – beech, birch, chestnut, lime and oak, and a magnificent stand of Douglas firs overlooking the back drive. Regrettably, many of the fine old trees have now died, either from elm disease or as a consequence of the 1976 drought which was disastrous for the beech and birch trees.

It had certainly never crossed our minds that mature trees could vanish almost overnight, and we had not made a regular practice of planting up young forest trees. Quite rightly, tree planting is now recognised as a duty for the sake of future generations and it is a comfort to know that visitors will one day enjoy the fruits of the consecutive planting which is being carried out by the National Trust, who took over the property when my husband died in 1972.

In 1937 the scope of the garden was confined to a few formal terraces, some bedding out, a tortuously clipped yew topiary and a small paved area with rose beds. The rest was given over to a bowling green and a large expanse of lawn. In short, we were the owners of a typical Victorian garden. The potential for change was enormous, and in my initial burst of enthusiasm I rushed headlong into it, making a new rose garden (which, unknowingly, I sited in the wrong position) and dotting around a few shrubs. Then the war came and our energies were directed elsewhere.

In 1946 we began to plan the garden in earnest, and fortunately we were able to call upon the advice of a splendid old lady, Miss Nellie Britton, who ran a rock-garden nursery near Tiverton. She made us aware of the detail in the smallest plants, and we became conscious for the first time of the perfection of the tiniest petal. I can remember her concern when Jack became excited by magnolias and rhododendrons as she felt he might neglect rock plants forever. But, right from the start, we admired the biggest and the smallest of blooms, and this diversity helped us to create a garden based on plants of any size or kind that appealed to us. Knightshayes has never been a specialist garden containing a comprehensive collection of a few species, but rather a nursery for the plants we fell in love with. We began near the house, loosening the appearance of the stiff formal terraces with small shrubs, roses, and plants. In the paved garden we replaced the roses with low carpeting plants, whose grey and delicate colours spread over the flagstones. High yew topiary hedges surrounded this, as well as the adjacent bowling green, which was subsequently sacrificed to make way for a statue, stone beeches and a weeping pear, which was induced to hang over the pool, and pruned regularly every year, to keep its form light and thin. The atmosphere is peaceful and still, in sharp contrast to the busy alpine border and other distractions outside.

It is difficult to remember changes in their right order. But it is not difficult to remember the friends who over the years have helped us with suggestions, comments and generous gifts of plants. To mention only two, Graham Thomas and Lanning Roper visited us many times, and to our delight accepted us as fellow gardeners.

Sir Eric Savill, who is such an inspiring and encouraging enthusiast, was a tremendous support when we decided to break new ground and extend the garden into the wood beyond the terraces, and 'the garden in the wood' became the most enthralling adventure of all. After the war Jack soon became a keen collector of plants. I was particularly interested in placing and arranging these in the context of the big trees we had left standing, having cut down many hundreds of the smaller ones.

Having removed the boundary fence line out of sight, we brought into the garden, each year, a piece of woodland approximately the size of a tennis court. Later, when with the help of more modern machinery we were clearing bigger slices among the remaining trees, the realisation came that with terraces, lawns and borders, twenty-five acres was more than enough to cope with. But temptation always dwelt just beyond the fence which was pushed back many times.

In 1963 we were joined by Michael Hickson as a very young head gardener, full of enthusiasm, and at the same time talented and efficient. His help and devotion to the garden, which has been so appreciated by us, has led to one scheme after another and also, we are sure, to the enhanced enjoyment of thousands of visitors.

The garden certainly did not grow from a drawing board. Ideas came, and proved their worth by trial and error. You cannot really foresee how a garden will develop or what it will look like over a period of about thirty years. I think we realised fairly soon that a garden does not stand still. It either improves or regresses. A certain ruthlessness is necessary, particularly, when combating the common error of overcrowding. One is either pulling out or putting in plants, as well as altering the sizes and shapes of borders and glades.

More than once I have been asked whether books have helped in making the garden. Certainly one, written many years ago by Miss Sylvia Crowe, had a great influence. She pointed out how often our beautiful English countryside is spoilt by gardens blazing in colour, which intrude on a natural backdrop of fields and distances. My rose garden had to face this criticism. A lovely vista from the terrace in front of the house stretches away on a slight slope through the park. In the lower foreground of this is a broad grass terrace retaining narrow paving and beds in the Victorian style. And this was the site I selected for my first attempt at a rose garden. I was later shaken by the realisation that the view had been interrupted and the eye distracted. In trying to tone down the disparity, the red roses were changed to cream and soft magenta ones, in imitation of the colour of our wild flowers. However, the effect still jarred, and the problem was not resolved until the rose beds had been flattened and grassed over. The remaining rose beds at either end of the terrace were converted into two flat patchwork circles of scented thyme, each with a stone ornament. Only one original feature was retained, a low fountain of lead dolphins with a single spout to give that enchanting musical sound of splashing water. The transformation was complete and ever since then flowering colours at Knightshayes have been kept on the cool side.

The main object of all our efforts was to introduce new vistas, never if possible to repeat former plantings, and to give unexpected pleasure at the turning of corners. For, instance, one surprise which has been effective is to find, on entering a secluded and shady glade ostensibly planted out with a few unusual shrubs, a spring carpet of yellow, pink and white dogtooth violets on a backcloth of green moss. Elsewhere, beneath very high Douglas firs, the ground is covered with varying shades of blue and green prostrate conifers intermingled with autumn and winter cyclamen.

In other places, low peat walls have been built to enclose and provide safe areas for small plants, so that they do not become lost and overshadowed by larger shrubs. It has been our aim to create a continuous and unexpected combination of flowers and foliage throughout the spring, summer and autumn. A garden need never have an off season, particularly if the beauty and contrasts of evergreen foliage are understood and not forgotten. A rule we have always kept, which is I think a good one, is that if a group of plants is continually passed, or bypassed without being looked at, then this area is obviously dull and must be altered to attract attention.

The last enterprise my husband and I undertook together was to make a willow garden in a neglected fold in the ground to the west of the main drive, where a slope leads to our only small piece of spring water. We uprooted a forest of *Rhododendron ponticum* from this shallow valley, but were careful to retain the clumps of old fashioned Ghent azaleas. We then introduced a variety of willows, arresting with their coloured stems, as well as catkins and summer foliage.

Since I am describing the making of the garden I have purposely avoided introducing nomenclature and listing plants. To mention only a few would be misleading, as the garden is packed with many varieties. At the same time we have always been concerned with leaving open areas of grass in the wood. This, as plantsmen will realise, requires a great deal of self-discipline! Yet a garden can often become too profuse to digest unless there are intervals in it wherein the mind can relax.

The designing and tending of a garden becomes, as all true gardeners know, the obsession of a lifetime; but the form it takes, and how one enjoys it, can differ greatly. There are those gardeners who like to work on the ground with their hands, and this was our way. For years, until Michael joined us, Jack and I planted, propagated and tended everything that two pairs of hands could manage, with help only for the rougher work. Jack enormously enjoyed telling non-gardeners that gardening was, 'Eleven months of hard labour, and one month of acute disappointment'. But he did not really mean it!

It seems to me that the prime objective of a gardener is to show off plants, and certainly this was our sole reason for making a garden. Plants can create peace and contentment, and the opening of a flower and the ripening of a berry can stir the emotions to the full. I think that the thrill of gardening lies in the absorbing interest that the growth and change in the lives of plants holds for us. There are days in early spring when the ground seems almost to be moving, with green tips forcing themselves up to the light, and one can only stand back and watch with wonder the innate vitality of plants, in which one has no part other than in the creation of a worthy home for them. I cannot express the joy we felt, years ago, when for the first time one of our plants was accepted by a very well-known plantsman, whose garden was widely and affectionately known as a 'jungle of gems'.

Other memories spring to mind. The bite of anticipation as we embarked on one of our many projects, the haunting scent of bonfires, or the crash of felled trees in the wood. To some this seemed wantonly destructive, but it was necessary, as it gave light and space to the remain-ing trees which then grew into vigorous and outstanding specimens.

Gardening has been full of excitement for me. Although the joy and adventures I shared in laying out a garden can never fade, I know at heart I am a plantswoman, and in company with all those who are devoted to horticulture, Knightshayes has been for me a constant source of delight. I hope it will continue to give pleasure to those who come to see a rare or unusual plant, or simply to enjoy the surroundings.

APPENDIX 8

CHRISTIAN SCIENCE

Christian Science is a cult started by Mary Baker Eddy in America. She was born into a strict Calvinist family in 1821 and was always a rather sickly person. She was married three times. In 1861, she had her 'revelation', when she claims that after a fall on the ice her doctors gave her up for lost. The healing truth dawned upon her senses, much as 'take up thy bed and walk' in the Bible, and she realised that everything was in the state of the mind. She determined to devote herself to the healing aspect of religion, and later she wrote *Science and Health*, the Christian Science second Bible. It is Mrs Eddy's interpretation of the Bible.

The rules by which the church is governed are in the *Church Manual*, written by Mrs Eddy. No sermon is given at Christian Science services. A Second Reader reads from the scriptures, and the First Reader reads from *Science and Health*. There are hymns and periods for quiet devotion. Baptism and Communion are not practiced, except in a spiritual sense. At a certain point in a service, all will kneel in silent communion.

There are 'Lecturers' and each church is expected to invite such at least once a year. The closest equivalent to ordained pastors of the Protestant church are called 'Practitioners', who have received instruction in Christian Science and devote their time to the practice of methods of healing by prayer.

Christian Science teaches that there is no such thing as illness. It is a mental delusion. The cure of sickness is not by medicine, but by helping the afflicted person to understand that he is not really sick, that his pain is imaginary, and his imagined disease is the result of false belief.

Christian Science states that there is no 'matter', everything is spiritual. There was no 'Creation'. All that truly exists is God.

(Taken from A.A. Hockema's *The Four Major Cults*)

APPENDIX 9

PUBLICATIONS
OF HERBERT NEWTON
WETHERED

From Giotto to John: The Development of Painting (1920)

Mediaeval Craftsmanship and the Modern Amateur — More Particularly with Reference to Metalworking and Enamelling (1923)

The Architectural Side of Golf (1929). Written with Tom Simpson

The Perfect Golfer (1931)

A Short History of Gardens (1933)

The Mind of the Ancient World: A Consideration of Pliny's Natural History (1937)

On The Art of Thackeray (1938)

The Four Paths of Pilgrimage (1947)

The Curious Art of Autobiography: From Benvenuto Cellini to Rudyard Kipling (1956)

Selected Essays of E.V. Lucas (publication year unknown)

BIBLIOGRAPHY

Concannon, Dale – *Golf, The Early Days: Royal amd Ancient Game from its Origins to 1939*
London, Salamander Books, 1995.

Mair, Lewine – *One Hundred Years of Women's Golf*
Edinburgh, Mainstream Pub. Co., 1992.

Morrison, Ian – *Golf Facts*
Quarto Pub., 1993.

Menzies, Gordon – *The World of Golf*
London, BBC, 1982.

Wethered, Joyce – *Golfing Memories and Methods*
Hutchinson & Co. London, 1934.

Wethered, Roger and Joyce – *Golf from Two Sides*
Longmans, 1925.

Green, Robert – *The Illustrated Encyclopaedia of Golf*
Harper Collins, 1994.

Wind, Herbert Warren – *Following Through*
London: Macmillan, 1986.

Steel, Donald – *The Guiness Book of Golf Facts and Feats*
1980.

Penick, Harvey – *Little Red Golf Book*
Harper Collins, 1993.

Collett, Glenna – *Ladies in the Rough*
A. Knopf, London, 1929.

Darwin, Bernard – *Golf Between Two Wars*
Classics of Golf, 1988

The Times newspaper
Fairway and Hazard magazine
Golf Illustrated magazine
The Illustrated & Dramatic News magazine
Various American newspapers

Index